SAN FRANCISCO MURALS

San Francisco Murals

COMMUNITY CREATES ITS MUSE
1914–1994

Timothy W. Drescher

For Jo and Sarah and Meagan, with love

ISBN 1-880654-06-7

Library of Congress Catalog Card No. 94-66695

Cover Mural: Haight-Ashbury Muralists. *OUR HISTORY IS NO MYSTERY*, 1977. Detail from a destroyed mural. #151

Printed and bound in Hong Kong by Everbest Printing Company Ltd.

Contents

Preface

"If these walls could talk, the stories they could tell."

I am reminded of this saying because here in San Francisco the walls *do* talk. And as Tim Drescher so poignantly reveals in *San Francisco Murals*, their stories represent a kind of painted history of our dreams, our struggles and our aspirations.

Tim's book is a welcome addition to the literature of San Francisco, both for its historical accounts and cultural insights, as well as the gorgeous color reproductions of more than fifty murals.

I'm sure that residents and visitors alike will use *San Francisco Murals* as the basis for their own tours and explorations of these unique artistic treasures.

Art Agnos
Former Mayor,
City of San Francisco

San Francisco Murals reflects the cross-cultural diversity that paints the ethnic landscape of our city. A chronicler of changing times and cultural forces, Timothy Drescher explores every nook and cranny, neighborhood and alley, in a photographic essay of San Francisco's murals in all of their colorful contrasts.

Frank Jordan
Mayor,
City of San Francisco

Introduction

This book surveys San Francisco's murals from three painted for the 1914–15 Panama-Pacific International Exposition (PPIE) to today's community walls. The list covers murals completed through 1990, and includes selected destroyed murals which are marked with an asterisk. The text emphasizes contemporary community murals because there is already a substantial body of material published on earlier works (see "Selected Bibliography") and because community murals deserve attention in their own right. In fact, my belief that the community murals and muralists deserve an accurate documentation is my reason for writing this book. I've included selected commercial murals, and a few school murals, too. Children's murals deserve much more attention than they receive here, but this is not the place for such a major undertaking. In particular, Ruth Asawa, "one of the godparents of the community mural movement," and the Alvarado Arts School Program deserve attention. I hope the examples included here will encourage others to pursue their proper documentation.

San Francisco supports the highest per capita mural output in the world. Some 445 have been painted in a city whose population is only about 700,000 (compare Los Angeles, where some 2,000 murals have been painted in a city whose population is 3,000,000). East Bay murals (Berkeley, Oakland, and other cities across San Francisco Bay) should also be noticed. They are a part of the same milieu, and often have been painted by the same artists who have worked in San Francisco. They deserve the same attention, so even though the focus of this book is San Francisco, I have included a listing of East Bay murals with a brief introduction.

The text considers the main community mural areas of the city: the Mission District, the Haight-Ashbury, and Hunter's Point-Bayview, the Western Addition, and the Fillmore (the main areas in which the city's black population lives). When an artist from one of these areas has also done significant work in another area (muralists in San Francisco tend to be fluid in this regard and they also work on each other's projects), it is discussed as it comes up instead of imposing a strict geographical order on the text. Consult the index for complete listings by artist, group and title.

The ordering of murals in the list is basically geographical, with considerations for accessibility. For example, since it is often difficult to cross Market Street, murals to its north and south are put into separate sections. If a fanatic wanted to begin with number 14 and try to see all the murals, I believe that the order given is an efficient way to proceed. In this case, I would also recommend making the tour at 5 a.m. on a Sunday. Otherwise you will be caught in traffic for the first five hours.

Selecting photographs was difficult. Being limited to so few when so many murals deserve full color presentations and close-ups is, however, necessary for obvious reasons. I've tried to have the color plates indicate the diversity of murals in the city, emphasizing community works because others have been covered elsewhere. I've also tried to indicate the range of styles, themes, geographical areas, and artists. I've also included a number of significant destroyed murals, since they cannot be viewed anywhere anymore (see "The Lost Murals of San Francisco").

My own interest in community murals began in 1971 in Chicago, where I first documented them. In the seventies Margo Bors and I studied several Mission District murals, and in 1980 Ruth Gordon helped with a list of East Bay murals of the 1970s. The present mural list is based on my earlier work, *A Checklist of San Francisco Murals 1914–1986*, compiled with Victoria Scarlett and published by the Library at San Francisco State University. Nicole Emanuel's patient, thorough work helped me in compiling that material. There are numerous revisions of the data on the pre 1969 murals contained in *A Survey of Art Work in the City and County of San Francisco* published in 1975 by the San Francisco Art Commission, edited by Joan Ellison, with additions by Joyce Konigsberg. I have made further revisions of the *Checklist* in 1990. Errors and omissions are of course my responsibility, and corrections are appreciated. The murals and their artists deserve accuracy.

Many people have helped gather the material for this book. The muralists were unanimously generous in providing basic information about their works, and patient with my rechecking. Maria Pinedo and Rene Yanez of the Galeria de la Raza have been always helpful since my arrival in the city in 1974 and, more recently, so has Humberto Cintron. At a series of meetings held at Precita Eyes Workshop, Susan Cervantes, Ron Wheeler, Margo Bors, Tony Parrinello and Gary Graham all offered valuable suggestions on this book. Susan's careful checking has made a special contribution to the accuracy and thoroughness of the San Francisco list.

John Pitman Weber, Carol Kenna, Eva Cockcroft, Shifra Goldman, Enrique Chagoya, Jim Prigoff, and Jo Drescher all read an early draft of the text and their comments were invaluable in improving it. Their taking time from already packed schedules to help me indicates their generosity in addition to their expertise. Rodger Birt helped with early slides of the first Western Addition murals. Jim Prigoff shared his entire collection of San Francisco slides with me in order to make the choice of the best photographs possible. His mural knowledge, photographic skills and friendship have meant a lot to this project and to me.

Shelley Kushner entered an early draft into the computer for me, and has been available day and night to answer my questions about computers. Stacey Callahan entered both mural lists and designed the program for them and the basic indexing. Her support, enthusiasm and expertise have been essential to the success of the entire project.

The use of mural photographs by James Prigoff, James Dong, Susan Cérvantes, Ray Patlan, Fran Valesco, Jean Constant Gindreau, Wilfredo Castano, James Pontiflet and Susan Greene is gratefully acknowledged. Permission from the San Francisco Recreation and Parks Department to use a photograph of Maxine Albro's *California* (#46) and from the San Francisco Art Institute to use a photograph of Diego Rivera's *The Making of a Fresco Showing the Building of a City* (#20) is also gratefully acknowledged.

I want to express my gratitude also to John and Molly Harris of Pogo Press, whose belief in the project and whose editing and publishing skills and deter-

mined effort have made it happen. In addition, their knowledge and appreciation of community murals has made this a better book.

The maps which will act as a guide to San Francisco mural seekers were prepared by Travel Graphics International. We thank Stuart G. Sellars for allowing us to use them.

My family has been enthusiastic and supportive throughout the task. Sarah and Meagan have been spotting murals since they could talk, and have grown to enjoy last-minute searches for obscure murals I heard existed. Jo's support has been unfailing in every way, and her encouragement has been matched only by her rigorous editing and perceptive advice.

Timothy W. Drescher
Berkeley, California
August 10, 1990

Introduction to Expanded Edition

Absolutely essential in preparing accurate lists of community artworks is the cooperation of the artists themselves. In this case, several people have been more than generous with their time and knowledge to help make this expanded edition as accurate as possible. They are Jim Prigoff, whose encyclopedic knowledge of spray can/graffiti artists provided an outline of the art form and roster of its practitioners; Susan Kelk Cervantes, who not only put me in touch with new muralists, but even made text suggestions; Ray Patlan and Eduardo Pineda, as always prolific and supportive; Betsie Miller-Kusz, beginning what looks to be a long and strong tenure as Director of the Mural Resource Center; and Josh Sarantitis, whose enthusiasm and knowledge both represent the "new" muralists.

As ever, Jo helped with the text, Sarah with early morning mural hunts, and Meagan with photo critique. Eurydice Thomas created new maps and demonstrated to me a whole new technology besides. John and Molly Harris are finally beginning to realize that mural lists are never complete, and they have generated an ongoing process, not merely the publishing of a book.

Timothy W. Drescher
Berkeley, California
May 5, 1994

Murals: From Cave to Contemporary

Murals have been painted in many ways for many reasons under varying conditions—social, political, economic, aesthetic—for tens of thousands of years. Today, all previous styles and media are available (including fresco, abstraction, mosaic, etc.), but most murals are narratives painted onto walls. Some new possibilities, unknown in previous mural epochs, are also practised, such as extensive collaboration by artists with a mural's audience in its design and execution. Today's community murals are exciting partly because they embody this monumental art tradition, and partly because their world is our world; we can empathize with the paintings we see. I hope this book encourages readers to go see the murals themselves, hear the sounds around them, smell the nearby bakeries and restaurants, and talk to locals so that the entire mural, including its community, comes alive.

THE MURAL TRADITION

One thing today's murals have in common with paleolithic French and Spanish cave paintings is their role in the community. The murals were painted by members of the group which lived with them daily. The role of the cave painting in their societies is unknown, although theories from the hopeful to the plausible have been advanced since their discovery at the beginning of the twentieth century. Some appear to be part of daily community life while others are located in remote sanctuaries deep in their caves. Access to these was probably limited to special occasions. Besides being the product of their community, these murals share another characteristic with today's walls. They have an impact on the people who view them because, however removed they may seem from our lives, they also capture something in common with us, and we are often moved by that feeling of similar experience.

Of post-paleolithic murals it seems that the closer the civilization moved toward modern times, the less the murals retained of community immediacy. Aboriginal peoples in Australia, America and Africa painted murals on the rock walls of caves apparently as fully in-tegrated parts of their daily lives, but in other parts of the world murals became associated with elite interests, decorating the tombs of Chinese emperors, Egyptian pharaohs, and Mayan kings. In several locations temples with painted murals or carved reliefs were open to the "public," such as those at Teotihuacan or Babylon, or Angkor Wat. These works were significant to their populations. Although hardly community-based, they are an important source of information about their cultures and history. Egyptian murals, for example, depict significant commerce between central Africa and the mighty kingdoms of the Nile at Karnak and Thebes. These images support Diop's contention that the early Egyptian civilization was a black culture.[1]

European murals, which are the more direct antecedents of today's urban expressions, divide roughly into religious and secular. The earliest walls were religious paintings in churches: mosaics for the wealthier orders, egg tempera and fresco when mosaic was too expensive. They depicted biblical scenes to the satisfaction of the church fathers and the awe and instruction of the illiterate churchgoers, a didactic function used to great effect in the twentieth century by Diego Rivera. Fresco is a process of applying colored paint pigment to wet plaster. When the plaster dries, the painting becomes a part of the wall itself. It requires skill and confidence, because it cannot be painted over or erased. By the end of the Middle Ages the development of painting techniques included greater use of modeling, making Christian scenes increasingly realistic. Throughout this period, European murals were Christian and the church was almost the sole patron of muralists.

With the coming of the Renaissance, patronage and thematic content shifted, although the religious murals have never died out. Because of the significance of Catholicism, church murals were public art. As Europe moved from religious-dominated feudalism to commodity-dominated capitalism, the favored media of expression kept pace. Techniques of perspective were developed, and oil painting came to dominate plastic expression because it best allowed the newly accumulated secular possessions to be exhibited for what they were: tangible, portable commodities.[2] Oil paint displays the textural richness of the possessions of the wealthy along with their myths and portraits. Earlier murals were not commodities (you could hardly buy or sell a church ceiling, let alone move it to your palace), but with the development of secular wealth, patrons were merchant, rather than religious or hereditary, princes, and their taste demanded subject matter inappropriate for church walls. So from the Renaissance until today, both strains of the mural tradition that split in the late fifteenth century have continued in parallel traditions, one private and secular, the other public and religious. From that time on, not only were churches painted with appropriately devout imagery (by Michelangelo, for example), but murals were painted in dining rooms and living rooms of private palaces and every other portion of the baroque estate. Murals "went public" again in the nineteenth century, decorating public buildings in Europe and the United States. For the community muralists of today, however, a more influential line stems from Mexican murals.

MEXICAN MURALS

There is a direct line from European, specifically Italian, Christian frescoes to the contemporary mural movement in the United States. That line runs through one of the Tres Grandes of the Mexican Mural Renaissance. Diego Rivera, after studying in France and Spain but prior to returning home to Mexico in 1922, toured Italy and viewed first hand many Italian frescoes which taught him a great deal about the use of architectural space in monumental painting. When he returned to his native Mexico, Rivera began painting murals at the behest of the education minister, Jose Vasconcellos, to educate the largely illiterate population, and recover indigenous history (much as contemporary community muralists often try to emphasize ethnic cultural traditions in their imagery). He began applying the compositional lessons he had observed in Italy along with those of his cubist studies in France to the walls of government buildings. Rivera was also influenced by indigenous pre-conquest figurines and, especially, by the codices, which recorded ancient Mesoamerican societies in vivid pictures.

Rivera was soon joined by Jose Clemente Orozco and David Alfaro Siqueiros. Together they were Los Tres Grandes, the Three Great Ones of Mexican muralism, and their works are a major inspiration for today's muralists, particularly in their commitment of their artistic skills to the struggles of indigenous peasants and workers.

It should be noted that there have been many other important Mexican muralists, among them Pablo O'Higgins, Juan O'Gorman, Jose Camarena, and Rufino Tamayo. Jean Charlot brought a significant knowledge of fresco techniques to the Mexican muralists in the 1920s. Many community muralists in the United States have studied in Mexico, either formally or on their own, observing the works of this great tradition. In recent years, the work of Arnold Belkin and others has begun to be known in the United States, and U.S. work has also begun to influence mural painting in Mexico. The main source of Mexican influence for contemporary muralists in San Francisco has been the Tres Grandes.

All three of the Great Ones were politically active and leftist. Siqueiros and Rivera were members of the Mexican Communist party, although Rivera, with strong Trotskyite leanings, was often in official disfavor. When a reactionary administration gained power in the 1930s, all three came to the United States to paint, Orozco in the east and at Pomona College in southern California, Siqueiros in Los Angeles and New York, and Rivera in New York, Detroit and San Francisco, where he painted four frescoes. So the link between the Tres Grandes and San Francisco is direct, and the sources of influence are visible not only in Rivera's works, but in the New Deal murals executed during and after his visits here, and in the contemporary murals as well.

Diego Rivera significantly influenced San Francisco muralists. The New Deal artists watched him paint in person, and sometimes worked as his assistants. Subsequent muralists learned about his murals and those of other Mexican masters by visiting the walls themselves or through reproductions in books. Technical and stylistic aspects were thus passed on to later generations. Above all, the Tres Grandes demonstrated that public art and political commitment were bound together.

Rivera painted a mural at the Art Institute of San Francisco in 1931 (#20). In 1934, muralists painting the interior of Coit Tower were influenced by Rivera's piece just a few blocks away.[3] His other murals were a small fresco painted at the Atherton home of Mrs. Sigmund Stern, now in the downstairs lobby of Stern Hall on the University of California's Berkeley campus (#EB 85), a mural painted on the main stairwell outside the members' dining room of the Pacific Stock Exchange (#79), and a large fresco painted on Treasure Island for the 1939–40 World's Fair, now relocated in

Diego Rivera's enormous engineer-worker in his fresco for the San Francisco Art Institute (20) served as inspiration for Chuy Campusano in the Bank of America mural, *Homage to Siqueiros*. Rivera's monumental engineer becomes Campusano's "The New Chicano" which was also painted as if concealed by scaffolding in this mural-in-progress mural. (294)

the foyer of the Little Theater of the City College of San Francisco (#197).

Rivera's influence is also clear in some community murals, such as Chuy Campusano's *Homage to Siqueiros* (#294), in which he revises Rivera's Art Institute image of the construction of a worker into the construction of a model Latino. Rivera's vision of California's wealth coming from natural resources and labor is also found in the Coit Tower murals and in a number of community murals showing Latino migrant farm laborers.

NEW DEAL MURALS

While Coit Tower was not, strictly speaking, a WPA (Works Progress Administration) mural project, its sponsor, the PWAP (Public Works of Art Project), was the forerunner of the WPA program that sponsored thousands of murals nationwide from 1934 until 1946, and which became the model for the CETA program of art sponsorship in the 1970s (see "Funding"). New Deal murals have been covered in several excellent publications (see "Bibliography"). WPA murals in San Francisco span the entire period of the New Deal from 1934 through the final WPA mural, the panels at Rincon Annex post office (now Rincon Center) painted by Anton Refregier from 1946–48 (#221). During these years murals were painted in public buildings such as post offices, government buildings, the court house, museums and school libraries throughout the city. These murals were public art, executed for official buildings, not generated by the community in the way that today's murals are.

Today's community muralists saw the WPA murals on the walls of their schools, or when they mailed letters at post offices, or when they visited Coit Tower. This mural presence also included the ubiquitous Italian restaurant Venetian gondola paintings, and murals in meat markets and movie theaters, suggesting to them that murals could be a viable means of public artistic expression. When the mass political activities of the 1960s focused artistic energies on social issues, a model for one form of expression was already in place.

The north side of the *I.L.W.U. Mural-sculpture* by the muralists known as M.E.T.A.L can be seen here. (220)

Sometimes the connection was made directly between community murals and their New Deal forerunners. Some muralists who had worked on Coit Tower also worked with younger artists. Emmy Lou Packard, a well known printmaker who had worked with Diego Rivera, served as an advisor on Chuy Campusano's "Bank of America" mural (#294). Several muralists became friends with Coit Tower painters Edith Hamlin and Bernard Zakheim. The style and to some extent the content of the *I.L.W.U. Mural-sculpture* (#220) were selected as a gesture of admiration for Anton Refregier, whose Rincon Center murals are diagonally across Mission Street from the 1986 work. Lucienne Bloch and Stephen Dimitroff, both of whom worked with Rivera, continue to give fresco workshops.

After over fifty years New Deal murals, despite their locations indoors, show signs of damage. Any water leaking into a building eventually damages a fresco so that both its pigment and plaster are apt to fall from the wall. Before attempting to restore the Coit Tower murals, the city had to have workers clean the building and rebuild the roof. In 1990 conservators Anne Rosenthal, Constance Silver, Jim Bernstein and Gregory Thomas completed restoration of the first floor murals. Those murals found upstairs in Coit Tower remain to be treated. Rosenthal and Thomas also restored the Labaudt mural in the Beach Chalet in 1988. The Beach Chalet mural (#182) and those in the Mother's House at the San Francisco Zoo (#186–#189) suffered from dampness and water damage which causes the paint to flake and mosaics to loosen.

Although the original federal groups which sponsored the New Deal murals in the 1930s no longer exist, mural restoration funds have been given to the city by the NEA, the California office of Historical Preservation, and the National Paint and Coating Association, a trade group.

CONTEMPORARY COMMUNITY MURALS

The major political issues of the late 1960s—Civil Rights, the women's movement, education, and above all the Vietnam War—caused millions of people in the United States to become politically active. Many visual artists committed themselves to the social practice of their skills, making posters, silkscreens, book illustrations, leaflets, dances, performances, happenings, music and. . . murals for the general public. These media traditionally have been the means of expression for poor and working class people, and especially people of color who were disenfranchised from access to mass media.

The communities to which these people turned usually meant "neighborhood," but also often included union halls, schools, women's centers, workplaces, etc. "Community" here has a social, not merely a geographical definition. It refers to any group of like-minded people. Including "community" in "community murals" makes these artworks different from any others, and that is why it helps to make a distinction between "community art" and the more general term "public art." Public art is art done for a general, undefined population (although some sort of middle class standard is probably assumed). It is for the most part commissioned by official bodies, governments, corporations and the like. Community art is created by or with a group of people who will interact with the finished artwork. Its standard of satisfaction is determined by its acceptance to the community from which it springs, not by any outside audience. Community arts can include performance arts, film, theater, dance, posters, etc., but the key factor is the work's creation with or by a group of people. The "with" includes projects done by an individual or group in consultation with a community, but in which the community does not actually paint (or dance, or act, or whatever).

Local people sometimes like artworks done "for" them, but their involvement with the work is then very different from one on which they have worked themselves. In both cases the artwork lends prestige to its location, but in community-based arts, its status as art (and relative survival) is dependent on public acceptance, not the reputation of the artist.[4]

Community murals may be painted by groups of individuals (see "Process"), but they are always closely related to those who live or work near them.[5] The relationship of community artworks to their communities is dynamic, intimate, extended and reciprocal. In a real sense, the immediate "support group" of a mural project, its "community," determines the work's meaning. Consciously or not, the image-makers articulate their communities' wishes. If representatives of hotel owners, world's fair organizers, a YWCA, a government bureaucracy, a union, school or neighborhood produce a mural, then that mural will articulate their ideas. Some of these uses are not what we normally mean by "community," and there are exceptions, of course, but the general rule holds. Of all members of a community, the most important is the artist or group. So it is probably more accurate to say that mural art is always an intersection of social and artistic contexts (influences), with some participants playing more important roles than others, depending on specific circumstances. But (especially with murals), the "community" is always a crucial aspect of the work's process and effect: hence the subtitle of this book.

Out of the Closet was the title given to a series of four panels painted inside the Women's Building by muralists Johanna Poethig, Selma Brown, Claire Josephson, K. Bucklew, Ariella Seidenberg, and Deborah Greene. (270)

Flags, relevant faces and books are placed around the doors and windows of *The Socialist Bookstore* mural by Susan Greene and Pedro Oliveri. Photograph by Susan Greene. (307)

Today's community murals represent the coming together of social (historical) and artistic traditions. While this is true of the artwork of any period, it seems more obvious in this case because a) the history is ours; we've lived it or are living it, and b) the murals usually take that experience as their subject, one way or another. Also, we find the often collective, interactive process more compatible than previous generations did.

The earliest community murals in the United States were painted in the mid 1960s in Colorado and California, and in Chicago and New York. Chicago became the focus of the early movement because of the vitality of its mural images, the skill of its artists, and the publicity their work received in national media. All these early works were community expressions generated by political activism.

The earliest corresponding murals in the Bay Area were executed at Grove Street Community College in Oakland in 1968–69 by a group of artist-activists (#EB101). At about the same time artists began painting murals in San Francisco across the Bay. In no time at all (historically speaking), the movement had come to "everybody's favorite city," expressing on its walls the aspirations, problems and hopes of its multiethnic population.

Because of its ethnic diversity, small geographical area (San Francisco is only 49 square miles), the proximity of Mexican and New Deal models, and most of all its concentration of skilled, creative and prolific artists, San Francisco soon became one of the leading mural centers in the world.

Process

There are many ways of painting community murals. At the heart of each one resides the relationship between artist(s) and the social community which will be the audience for the finished painting. The simplest process is when an individual artist paints a mural alone. This kind of work becomes a community mural only if the artist lives or works in the community, or has "done his/her homework" with the community.

The most complicated process is when a group forms within the community or contacts a group of artists to work with them in creating a mural. In this case, the meetings, discussions, sketches and arguments can continue for prolonged periods of time; more than a year or two is not uncommon.

But a community mural process can consist of any variation in between these examples: a group contacting a community group, a community group contacting an individual or separate artists or an established mu-

ral group (from within or outside of the community), and so on. The basic characteristic in all cases is the extensive participation with the people who live/work with the mural. Typically, an artist or group has a particular wall in mind, and usually a subject, too. They then speak with people around the site, and in many cases these "locals" will be instrumental in suggesting ideas for or modifications of the original proposals. By the mid 1980s, however, in order to comply with increasingly demanding civic funding requirements, artists were focusing more on satisfying "downtown" bureaucratic requirements than on working with communities.

The basic question for a muralist to ask the community is "What is important to you?" People know what matters to them, and they are not reticent about telling you. Artists, trained in visual expression, then can give form to the things mentioned by the folks with whom they talk. Sometimes, the question asked is, "What would you like to see?" This sounds good, but too often elicits visual cliches from untrained people, cliches such as an advertising image or a record album cover. Once suggested, such images take hold rapidly because they provide something "pre-approved" and already widely accepted. Such images produce weak murals.

Whatever the details, community-interactive processes lead to artist(s) working out tentative design ideas, presenting them to locals or appointed groups, and listening to suggestions (sometimes in the form of, "Gee, I'd like to see a. . . in the picture," sometimes in the form of "Can't you remove that. . . ?" and sometimes in the form of, "This is terrible. Who do you think you are?"). Design meetings can be heated, but they are an inescapable part of a community interactive process, and of a perhaps unique opportunity for community involvement by artistically untrained members, all of which contributes to the role of the mural in the (social) community from which it stems.

Once agreed upon, the design is ready to be painted. If the site is an outdoor wall, it must first be prepared, which is not terribly exciting, at least after the initial thrill of climbing up on scaffolding and seeing the neighborhood from a new angle. Walls must be sanded, scrubbed, cleaned, sealed and primed before they can be painted. Poor surface preparation leads to an early death of the mural. Almost anyone can help in this work. It mostly takes a desire to help get the mural painted correctly, and a lot of elbow grease.

There are three methods of transferring the design onto the wall. In a few cases the artist simply draws on the wall. More often, the design sketch has been drawn to scale (1″ to 1′ is common, although any scale is possible), and with a surveyor's snap line one foot squares are drawn onto the wall so that each square foot on the wall corresponds to a square inch of the sketch. Then, after triple checking to be sure the squares are right, nearly anyone can transfer an inch of sketch onto a foot of wall without too much trouble. A trained artist can come along later and make changes for consistency, etc.

The third method of design transfer is to use either an opaque projector or slide projector to project the sketch onto the wall. Then the lines are just traced. This is certainly the quickest method for a large wall, but it is best done at night, and sometimes the space available in front of the wall is not sufficient to allow the image to be fully projected onto the wall. Muralists have had some nasty run-ins with traffic while backing up to get the right distance between projector and wall.

Once the sketch is up, the painting begins. Again, nearly anyone can put basic paint on the surface of a

Two student assistants are shown at work on *The Fire Next Time I*. (423)

A parade celebrated the completion of the murals of Balmy Alley in 1984. The musicians are shown walking past a portion of the mural *Culture Contains the Seed of Resistance* by Miranda Bergman and O'Brien Thiele. (347)

Two children at play are painted on the wall of the Baptist church overlooking the Chinese playground in this untitled mural by James Dong. The girl's swing casts the shadow of a phoenix. Photograph by James Prigoff. (69)

wall. It only requires following the lines of the design and asking for help when it gets confusing. Trained artists can mix the colors and finish it all off, giving the final modelling, shading and stylistic contributions necessary for a unified image. In several cases, a decision was made that "participation" on a mural meant that everyone would paint some final portion of the wall, or their design suggestions would be included, regardless of coherence. This often results in an image which looks like it has been painted by several different people of different levels of ability. We should try to keep in mind in such cases that the social element of participation is at least as important to the group as the "professionalism" of the final image.

What this adds up to, no matter what particular process is involved, is an amazing amount of work on the part of the muralists. The actual painting of the mural, which can itself take a year or more, takes place only after endless weeks or months of exhausting, ine-

fficient, time-consuming meetings and planning sessions. Ideally, efficiency in painting is not a consideration for people working with necessarily complex groups of people, but pressures of families, other jobs, other projects frequently place enormous burdens on the muralists. Certainly it's all part of the game, but it helps to understand the sheer quantity of work that goes into creating a community mural.

We should not forget the final event in the process, the dedication ceremony. "Ceremony" is too formal a word here, because the dedication is usually more of a party, the moment on a sunny afternoon when the street in front of the mural is closed off and local residents and admirers from all over the city join to enjoy local bands, dancing, and donations of food—both homemade and from nearby restaurants. The dedication is the celebration of the entire community in honor of its new addition, and the mural's role in that community continues afterwards.

Aesthetics

One person's "subtle" is another's "blatant," to be sure. So we must be clear about our purpose in assessing community murals. If the goal is to try to grasp the work in its many simultaneous relationships with its community, then we must take that community into consideration. The goal of this book is to help the reader understand enough about murals to help him or her do exactly that. Some observations may help. In addition to learning (or asking) about the immediate community surrounding a mural, it often helps to be aware of influences so that you can get an idea of "where the artist is coming from." In San Francisco murals, influences include ethnic location and background of artists, other artists, folk arts, the Tres Grandes, other murals, "fine" arts, photographs, posters, underground comix, and current political issues.

It also helps to understand that community murals are unique in certain ways, when compared to other art forms. First, because they are often so large, community murals have the potential for unique manipulations of scale (both the relationship of the sizes of things within the painting and also between the painting and its audience.) Because of the large size of murals, these opportunities are not usually available to easel paintings. Second, murals can utilize the architectural environment, which includes not only the architecture of the buildings on which they are painted, but the entire visual area seen by a mural's audience. When executed well, a two dimensional painted surface becomes three dimensional and the entire mass of the building on which it is painted contributes to the effect of the painting. Third, a community mural can involve a public process. The images painted "on the streets" are different from the individual artistic expressions of easel artists working alone.

Finally, there is a group of "contexts" which can be utilized in a mural's design. Every mural can be said to exist in several "places," such as architectural (noted above), geographical, historical, and social. A few murals grasp this thoroughly, and become truly astonishing expressions of all these elements.

Windows were thrust forward with vigor by a figure in this detail from the destroyed *International Hotel Mural* by James Dong. (73)

Josie Grant's mural, *Ode to Rousseau*, expands the landscape setting of the Page Street Minipark through its clever use of sky, clouds, and castles in the air. Photograph by Jean Constant Gindreau. (142)

1. See Cheikh Anta Diop. *The African Origin of Civilization: Myth or Reality*. Westport: Lawrence Hill & Co., 1974. This material helps explain the numerous images of Tutankhamen, Egyptian pyramids, etc., in black community murals.
2. John Berger. *Ways of Seeing*. New York: The Viking Press. 1972.
3. See Masha Zakheim Jewett. *Coit Tower: San Francisco, Its History and Art*. San Francisco: Volcano Press, 1983. This definitive study is authoritative and readable, with excellent photographs.
4. I am indebted to John Pitman Weber for this observation. He suggests a multiple distinction based on the different intentions of community artists, audiences, and funders versus those of "fine" artists, audiences, and funders. For example, fine art objects are selected by "experts," while community arts are developed with local audiences. On the whole, some distinctions are useful, but precise denotations are always debatable.
5. In this case, the traditional art theoretical disjunction between Subject (artist) and Object (the painted) crumbles to dust.

San Francisco Murals

THE MISSION DISTRICT

Why are there so many murals in the Mission District? The answer lies in San Francisco demographics and history. The earliest Europeans to visit San Francisco (then unnamed, of course) founded Mission Dolores, which gave its name to today's Mission District. While Latinos always lived in the area, it was not until 1934 that the area began to shift from primarily Irish to primarily Latino in ethnic population. Chicanos had lived on Rincon Hill, but were evicted when the western base of the Bay Bridge was placed there. They moved up Mission Street into the core of the Mission District. A change in immigration laws in the 1950s brought thousands more from Latin America, and although most of the Latino residents are from Central American countries, many people are from Mexico. They brought their tradition of monumental public art, and in particular the history of the Mexican revolutionary muralists. Murals had always been a part of the Mexican community in meat markets, saloons, and restaurants, so when the contemporary mural movement began, the District was ready, with centuries of tradition already in place.

An early significant Mission District community mural was painted in 1973 by a group of artists in the Jamestown CYO center at 23rd Street and Fairview (#309). It is important because it was early, and because it was a group effort; several artists working together created not only a mural but a precedent for subsequent projects. The artists were Patricia Rodriguez, Ruben Guzman, Chuy Campusano, Consuelo Mendez, Tom Rios, Jerome Pasias and Elizabeth Raz. Jamestown was a proclamation that community murals were not the same as individualistic easel paintings, and that the subject matter was, as the artists were, part of the community itself. Jamestown's murals were political, to be sure, because they depicted the human ravages of the Vietnam war, police harassment of local youth, and the notion that drugs corrupt not only a human body, but the body politic of native people, La Raza, as a whole. It was also a celebration of Latino youth and roots.

Jamestown was an interior group of murals, lining both sides of the second floor corridor of the building. The following year, 1974, a number of other murals "went public" in a big way, being painted outside or in more accessible locations.

As part of its heritage from the 1960s, San Francisco became a center of underground comix. This inheritance found its way onto the walls of the city in the Mission District. Early in 1973, along with Ruben Guzman and others, Robert Crumb, the most famous and influential underground comix artist, executed his only mural, on the Mission Rebels in Action building on South Van Ness Avenue (#275). In 1972, Spain Rodriguez (best known for his underground hero, Trashman) and others painted a comix-like panel of local scenes on the Horizons Unlimited storefront on Folsom Street (#304), and Michael Rios painted the *MCO* mural on the side of the Mission Coalition Organization at 22nd and Folsom Streets (#305). Rios' scenes were enacted by rats-as-humans, "Because that's how we're treated here," Rios explained. While painting a scene showing police as pigs, Rios was arrested for an outstanding parking ticket, and beaten up, he says. Upon his release, he returned and finished the scene as he had begun it. All these muralists continued to draw and paint, but Spain alone among them has retained his comix style.

In June of 1974, Jesus "Chuy" Campusano and his coworkers dedicated the "B of A" mural, *Homage to Siqueiros* (#294) in the Bank of America branch office at 22nd Street and Mission. Although it is an interior mural, it can be seen from the sidewalk through the bank's windows. At the dedication reception in the bank, while the bank officials handed out glossy brochures about the mural, the muralists handed out dittoed statements attacking the bank's policies and quoting Diego Rivera in defense of their having painted the mural in such a "bourgeois" location. The mural offers a series of scenes of the Mission District, ending above the corner teller's window with a vision of illuminating hope for the future. A few feet to the left, the mural had shown a serpent-like BART writhing out of downtown into the predominantly Latino Mission District, and to the left of that, a campesino handing an open book across a fallen crucifix. In the book are printed the words, "Our sweat and our blood have fallen on this land to make other men rich." Interestingly, the Bank's brochure included a photograph of this detail with the pages blank. It is likely that the bank's photographer took the photograph before the lettering had been added, and before the mural was completed or installed (it was painted on panels in an unused bank building, then mounted on the wall above the tellers' windows). Cynics, recognizing the profits the bank makes from the local population, suggest that the mural was probably listed under "insurance" by the bank's accountants, not under artworks. However the bank thinks of its mural, it inspired one of the assistants, Michael Rios, to begin painting the *Minipark* at 24th Street near Bryant that same summer.

Campusano also continued to paint murals, the most spectacular of which is the 1986 *Lilli Ann Mural* (#258) at 17th and Harrison Streets. Its brightly colored geometrical abstractions suggesting fabric swatches cover a huge south-facing wall in an industrial area. The mural is a reminder of Tomas Belsky's earlier piece at Potrero and 24th Street, *My Tis of Thee* (#381), but Campusano's is notable for its size, its brighter, acrylic, colors, and for its suggestion that, since it was painted in 1986, it might mark a new direction for Mission District murals.

Another early Mission muralist was Carlos Loarca, who worked on one of the earliest murals in Balmy Alley in 1973, taught classes at the Mission Cultural Center, and in 1978 with students painted *Homage to Woman* (#407) inside the Cultural Center on the second floor. In 1982 he joined with Manuel Villamor and Betsie Miller-Kusz in painting the immense exterior of the building. Their mural portrays Native American Mexicans (#405) in a stylized manner extending around the northeast corner of the building. Villamor's borders are executed in a contrasting style which is much more hard-edged and tightly controlled. The combination suggests the variety of cultures indigenous to Mexico, and that in turn suggests the variety of events and activities available inside the Cultural Center.

The original idea for the *Minipark* murals was Ralph Maradiaga's. Maradiaga was one of the three co-directors of the Galeria de la Raza, half a block away. He was a man filled with joy, artistic vision, and a tremendous dedication to helping his community. Rios took over the idea, and in 1974 observed that Latino children came from wonderfully rich cultural traditions which they were not studying in school. He

remembers being punished for speaking Spanish in grammar school, and never learning about his family's traditional culture, so he set about painting the three walls surrounding the *Minipark* with images from Latino cultural traditions (#357). He, Richard Montez and Tony Machado, who worked on several mural projects with Rios, began on the east front wall by painting Quetzalcoatl, the feathered serpent, chiseled from rock with children frolicking over him amid tropical plants and bubbling waterfalls. Toward the rear of the *Minipark*, two other murals were painted, and on the rear wall they painted a vision of a Latino future filled by learning and a strong sense of community (#365).

Rios' concept was given form on the west walls by the Mujeres Muralistas, who painted *Fantasy World for Children* (#363), but was also joined by an anomalous semi-surrealistic mural (#364) painted by Domingo Rivera which became a focus of ongoing controversy because its theme did not fit in with the other murals in the *Minipark*.

Over the years, Rios returned to repaint and maintain the first panel, while others replaced faded murals with newer visions. Murals were painted by Jerry Concha, Miranda Bergman, Olivia Montez and Emmanuel Montoya, all in keeping with the theme of the *Minipark* and all more or less administered by the Galeria de la Raza located just half a block away. The Galeria, along with local merchants and other community representatives, successfully pressured OCD (the Mayor's Office of Community Development) for funds to enable Miranda Bergman to refurbish the murals in 1990.

Two problems arose in the course of these changes through 1990. The first, in about 1980, concerned the city's Parks and Recreation Department which wanted to plant a New Zealand willow tree in front of the rear wall. At a meeting between the Department and members of the Minipark's community, the shift in cultural make-up of San Francisco was played out in crystal-clear terms. The newer residents, mostly Latino, wanted to paint murals for the benefit of the *Minipark*'s users, and they did not like the tree's location in front of one of "their" murals. The old-line, mostly Irish, civil servants of the Parks and Recreation Department responded by denigrating "murals" as just paint and chemicals, "but a tree is a living, growing thing, and a beautiful thing for everybody." No one disagreed with this, or wanted to harm the tree, but there was a strong feeling that murals were expressions of living, breathing people who used the Minipark. . . and so it went. In the end, nothing was done about the tree, which within a year or two burst into maturity covering most of the rear right wall and providing a large shady area for park users. When the rear image was repainted by Emmanuel Montoya in 1983, the wall was simply painted a bright, friendly yellow, with designs along only the bottom, under the tree's branches, and at the end of the left-hand wall. The Parks and Recreation Department removed the drinking fountain in the *Minipark*, and refused to pick up the overflowing trash containers more often than once a week, so the struggle for *Minipark* maintenance continued, led by the determined efforts of Rene Yanez and the Galeria de la Raza.

The other problem occurred in 1980 when Domingo Rivera's abstract mural, which everybody seemed to think inappropriate in content, was badly in need of repair. Finally, Rivera gave permission for it to be painted over and it was replaced by Rios. He painted giant *ABC* blocks (#365) surrounded by people of all ages, and images of education and learning and achievement, all of which were appropriate to the young clientele of the Minipark and the original conception of its murals. The problem of whether anyone ever has the right to paint over someone else's mural without permission, even if it has become an eyesore, was averted by Rivera's giving permission. In the case of the nearby Garfield Park (#388) mural which he also painted, and which was in terrible condition for several years, the Art Commission refused to allow repainting

because it lacked written permission to destroy or replace it. For several years its disgraceful state continued as a reminder of an impasse between community needs, artistic intransigence and governmental bureaucracy. It was finally painted out in 1988.

The *Minipark* has been inspirational, both in San Francisco and beyond. I have spoken with visitors from Europe, Australia and Mexico, all of whom had heard about the Minipark and wanted to see it for themselves. Within the city, it has been a reference point for other projects, such as Balmy Alley in 1984. Rios' contributions to the murals of San Francisco include an anti-Vietnam War mural (now destroyed), a mural for the Bicentennial Show at the San Francisco Museum of Modern Art, the *BART* (Bay Area Rapid Transit) mural (#312), and the Santana mural, *Inspire to Aspire*, of 1987 (#301).

BART had been pictured as a snake in the Bank of America mural just a block from the corner subway entrance at 24th and Mission Streets, and at first glance one might think that Rios' *BART* mural (#312), painted with Montez and Machado, repeats the depiction of the mass transit subway as a viper threatening the low property values of the Mission District. The question arises in terms of the mural's imagery: does it show BART riding on the backs of the people or does it show that the people support BART? The answer de-

Three apartment buildings form the canvas for *Inspire to Aspire: A Tribute to Carlos Santana* by Michael Rios, Carlos Gonzalez and Johnny Mayorga. The mural honors a local resident who is flanked in the mural by images evoking the community's Mexican and pre-Columbian heritage. Photograph by James Prigoff. (301)

An early flower and plant mural by Patricia Rodriguez and Graciela Carrillo covered this garage in Balmy Alley. (345)

In 1972 Patricia Rodriguez and Graciela Carrillo painted their first mural on a garage across the alley from Rodriguez' apartment. Then, joining with other women artists they knew, they embarked on a major mural project, *Latinoamerica* (#402), painted on the side of the Mission Model Cities program headquarters building. They called their group Mujeres Muralistas, "Women Muralists." *Latinoamerica* was painted by eight women (four artists, four assistants), and the difference in their native cultures is evident in the mural's images. San Francisco's barrio differs from Latin American areas in other cities by virtue of its predominantly Central American population. Its images and traditions are different from the Puerto Rican influence in New York City, or the Mexican and Chicano domination in Los Angeles, for example. The mural has a Bolivian dancer and a Peruvian pan pipe player along with images from Venezuela and, of course, a significant presence of Chicano culture and Mission District mixtures, too. The work, as with many community murals, takes on a didactic function, educating its audience about the diversity of Latino influences in the Mission District. For passersby already aware of the references, a specific image can be a warm reminder of childhood in a distant homeland.

The significance of the Mujeres Muralistas cannot be overemphasized. Muralists, and most especially women, were struck by the fact that a group of Latinas was painting bold, striking murals, and working without men. The group was known and admired throughout the country, and in particular in Latino neighborhoods. The Mujeres painted in various configurations, but the key members were Patricia Rodriguez, Graciela Carrillo, Consuelo Mendez. Others included Miriam Olivas, Xochitl Nevel-Guerrero, Irene Perez, Ester Hernandez and Susan Cervantes. In addition to their joint work, they have painted murals in several locations. Carrillo painted *Humanidad* (#260) at the Mission Neighborhood Health Center in 1976, and a small mural on a bakery two years later. Perez has painted several murals in the East Bay and in Fresno. Hernandez has painted in the East Bay, and did a striking piece at the SFAI mural show in 1986.

Patricia Rodriguez has painted more than a dozen murals. In addition to her work with the Mujeres, she has worked on *Women's Contribution* (#272) on the exterior of the Women's Building in 1982, and *People We Knew, The Beauty of Life, and Dreams and Fantasies* (#306) at the Mission Mental Health Center in 1983.

In 1974, the same year that *Latinoamerica* was

pends on your analysis of BART's role in the community. After a couple of years of informal poll-taking on the site, when I asked Rios which it was he laughed and replied, "I think BART does both. It has raised rents around here and that hurts a lot of people, but it also provides good transportation to downtown. I guess I was ambivalent when I painted it." In either case, the mural is an example of the excellent use of environmental space by a well-designed image. The BART train in the mural begins at the left and curves across the long, narrow length of its wall until it executes a single, lovely swoop at the far right, taking the viewer's eye across the mural and then down, off the wall and

The Bolivian devil dancer was part of the South American section of the destroyed mural *Latinoamerica* painted by the Mujeres Muralistas. (402)

painted, Graciela Carrillo and Consuelo Mendez undertook to paint the fence in the parking lot adjacent to Paco's Tacos, a taco stand at 24th Street and South Van Ness Avenue. The commission to the Mujeres came from the owner, a local realtor who, the muralists said, wanted to establish his taco stand's identification with the Latino population before a McDonald's was built two blocks away. The mural, *Para el Mercado* (#313), showed the gathering, harvesting and transporting of food to market in traditional American settings. The two muralists were busy that summer and lacked the time to get together to fully integrate their design, so they decided that each would paint one half

of the fence. Carrillo asked Susan Kelk Cervantes to help work on an overall color scheme which unites the two portions otherwise clearly drawn by different hands. The taco stand was destroyed by a construction project in July of 1990, but Cervantes has rescued at least part of the fence on which it was painted. The Mujeres continued to paint after 1974, and produced *Fantasy World for Children* (#363) at the *Minipark* and other projects before disbanding at the end of the decade.

Susan Cervantes had worked with young children painting a mural at the corner of Balmy Alley and 24th Street (#345). After the Paco's Tacos fence she initiat-

23

Ray Patlan's mural, *Venceremos*, occupies the main stairway wall at the New California College of Law. Dramatically placed figures, flags, and a distorted bridge overcome the problems presented by the mural's location. (106)

ed a project at the Precita Valley Community Center, *A Day in the Life of Precita Valley* (#400), and went on to paint the monumental diptych, *Family Life* and *The Spirit of Mankind* (#397) on the south side of the Leonard R. Flynn School (formerly LeConte School) at Harrison and Precita Streets, facing Precita Park. Both designs are based on a spiral, with the right side of the diptych, *The Spirit of Mankind*, developing East Indian motifs and the left side, *Family Life*, portraying neighborhood residents, the people who use the park and for whom it has become, as depicted in the mural, a center of neighborhood social life.

In 1977 Cervantes founded Precita Eyes Muralists. It is one of the oldest ongoing mural workshops in the city. She had been a CETA muralist and Precita Eyes Muralists was founded as a portable mural workshop with people who had worked together on previous projects. The goals of the workshop include trying to educate the community about the mural process, and to encourage participation, to sponsor mural walk-

ing tours, and so forth. Regular classes are conducted in the group's storefront studio on the south side of Precita Park. Participating artists include Margo Bors, Tony Parrinello, Denise Mehan, Judy Jamerson and many others. Members have painted twelve murals, including the perfectly appropriate sea-scene on the south front of the Garfield Park swimming pool (#390) which combines images of ocean life, phases of the moon, Jacques Cousteau's ship Calypso, and assorted mythological symbols (a typical element in Precita Eyes' work). Perhaps most typical of their work is the group of six portable murals at the Las Americas school at 20th and Harrison Streets. The murals were painted in the workshop and erected later, after the site was found. These murals, *Reflections*, *Celestial Cycles*, *The Unicorn's Dream*, *Every Child Is Born To Be A Flower*, *Suaro's Dream*, *Masks of God/Soul of Man*, were painted from 1977 through 1982 (#282-#287). Their life-affirming spirit transforms the otherwise conventional stucco walls of the bungalow-style school.

24

Through her work as the central figure in the Precita Eyes Workshop, her unrelenting advocacy of murals to city officials, her organization of mural tours and lecture series, and most recently her murals with Juana Alicia, Cervantes has proven herself to be one of the central figures in San Francisco muralism.

Judy Jamerson, who worked with Precita Eyes, painted two murals at Mission High School in 1981. One showed students with a lamp of knowledge, which, unfortunately, was not popular among local youth (#265). The other, adjacent to it, was a relatively simple silhouette mural showing youth, cars and general high school-type activities (#266). Painted in dark blue and bright orange-yellow, it has remained untouched for a decade. Jamerson also was a major participant in the *Family Life* and *The Spirit of Mankind* murals in Precita Park.

In the late 1970s Ray Patlan moved to the Bay Area from Chicago, where he had been a participant in the early days of the community mural movement. Patlan came with exceptionally powerful artistic skills and years of mural painting experience, having studied and painted in Mexico, Vietnam and Chicago. Besides painting important murals in the East Bay, he was mentor and inspiration to innumerable local artists. In fact, his influence extends beyond the relatively small number of murals he has painted himself.

Each of Patlan's murals has something worthy of close study, from the Orozco-influenced cartoon-like characters in the monochrome *Prime Time/No Time* (#104) at the New College of California School of Law, to the manipulation of a complex stairwell space in *Venceremos* (#106) at the same location, to the innovative design of *Y Tu Y Yo Y Que* (#367), where the mural is composed of snapshots of local residents which are replaced periodically by images of new residents and activities. Working with students at San Francisco State University, and giving them major control over the images, he directed three murals on campus, including the large complex *Communiversidad* (#193). In 1982 Patlan worked with local youth at a Mission District playground called Folsom Park. A city official drove by and criticized the project for exposing young women to the roughness of the playground, but in fact Patlan's achievement was that this was the first time local girls had ever been allowed to use the facility. He was a member of the M.E.T.A.L. group that painted the *I.L.W.U. Mural-sculpture* (#220) in 1986. He worked with Eduardo Pineda at the Flynn School in 1989 and in 1990 in Healdsburg where they painted a mural dealing with the role of Latino laborers in the history of the California wine industry.

Ray Patlan and Carlos Gonzales transform their mural *Y Tu Y Yo Y Que* by changing the photographs of neighborhood people in the angled sections of the mural. Photograph by James Prigoff. (367)

A garage door provided the space for Juana Alicia's now destroyed mural *We Hear You Guatemala* in Balmy Alley. Photograph by Wilfredo Castano. (337)

Perhaps the most influential of Patlan's mural projects is Balmy Alley. The project was his idea, as was *"PLACA"*, the name of the loose group that formed to paint the murals. A "placa" is a graffito tag symbolizing the writer, noting his presence, claiming an identity; an image calling for a response. The group named PLACA sought to do that on a larger scale by painting as many murals as possible in Balmy Alley (officially Balmy Street) in the Mission District. Balmy runs from 24th to 25th Streets between Harrison and Treat

Streets. The alley was historically significant in the local mural movement as the location of both an early children's mural and of the Rodriguez-Carrillo garage mural painted before they founded the Mujeres Muralistas. A half dozen others had been painted in the mid seventies, too. In 1983, after several months of discussion and planning and drawing, $2,000 was donated by the Zellerbach Family Fund. Nearly three dozen people created 27 murals in the alley during the summer of 1984. Their efforts generated a spectacular block-long outdoor art gallery which has received notice in foreign countries and throughout the United States. The dual themes were opposition to U.S. involvement in Central America and celebration of Central America's indigenous cultures. In the summer of 1990, the murals were restored and several new ones added. (PLACA inspired a similar project in New York's lower east side (Loisaida) two years later called *La Lucha Continua*.) A walk through the alley gives the viewer the chance to see the most murals "per step" of any place in the world.

Ray Patlan is the Executive Director of Creativity Explored, an art therapy workshop where trained artists, some of them local muralists, work with developmentally disabled clients. In 1986 Susan Greene directed a mural project with them in which four muralists painted portraits of the clients, while the clients designed and painted the overall mural. It is located at 20th and Folsom Streets, and is titled *New Visions by Disabled Artists* (#281).

From her arrival in 1983 through 1990, Juana Alicia's mural output was tremendous. Working alone, with partners, groups, or collections of community residents, she painted over a dozen murals in San Francisco, Sonoma County to the north, and in Nicaragua. At the same time, like several other muralists, she led workshops, worked as an artist-in-residence at La Raza Graphics Center and in schools, and taught courses at local colleges. She worked with a large group of local residents and three other muralists (Raul Martinez, Susan Cervantes, and Emmanuel Montoya) on *Balance of Power* (#276) in 1985 at the Mission Swimming Pool. Two years later, in 1987, working with Cervantes and Martinez, she painted *New World Tree* (#277), which is a variation on the tree of life theme in keeping with its swimming pool location, and is extraordinarily well integrated with its architectural environment. The design works with the building on which it is painted, and thus enlists the entire mass of the structure on behalf of the image. Painted tree limbs repeat roof angles, the mural image centers on the main door at the center of the building, and foliage in the painting merges with landscape plantings next to the building. In this, *New World Tree* raises San Francisco murals to a new technical level.

Painting alone, in 1985 Alicia created *Las Lechugueras/The Women Lettuce Workers* (#368) dealing with the exploitation of women workers in California's lettuce fields. An interesting comparison can be made between this mural and a panel in Coit Tower painted in 1934 by Maxine Albro (#46). Albro's image depicts New Deal workers, perhaps dustbowl

refugees, picking oranges and glad to be working. It is idyllic, even if quasi-industrial. Alicia's image, much greater in scale and outdoors, boldly declares the problems of subsequent migrant agricultural workers, such as being sprayed with toxic pesticides, spied on by company bosses, and controlled by company-run machines. It is a curious contradiction that a mural treating such harsh themes is so beautifully painted, but, then, viewed in this way many murals articulate the tension between creativity and destruction/exploitation. The destruction of many murals exemplifies this most clearly (see "Lost Murals of San Francisco").

In 1985 a joint committee of local residents and San Francisco Mime Troupe members selected Alicia to paint the history of the Mime Troupe, the neighborhood, and of the Troupe's building, which had been the studio of a Mission District recording company (#290). The resulting mural shows the Mime Troupe's location in the community, with scenes from several of its plays and a surrounding audience. Visually, as in life, neither the audience nor the image is passive, with "layers" of the design interacting in a dynamic fashion. Three years later, troubled by the horrendous human costs of ongoing war in Central America, she painted *Alto al fuego/Ceasefire* (#295) at the bus stop adjacent to Cafe Nidal on Mission Street. It shows a young boy simply holding out his hands against an onslaught of guns, with a lush mountainscape in the background.

In the fall of 1990, Alicia and Susan Cervantes completed a major work at Hawthorne School (#302)

Chilean-style mural painting was seen in this now destroyed mural on the *Casa Sandino*. The mural was one of several painted in the Bay Area by the members of the Brigade Orlando Letelier. (315)

on Folsom Street. The mural has complex images painted on the entranceway and two other supporting buttresses, all against a bright blue repainting of the school building itself. In panels across the long structure are painted letters from Roman, Chinese, Arabic and American Sign Language alphabets, and an image of an object that begins with the letter for the panel. The conception of the whole mural, and its excellently executed integration with the building's architectural configuration, makes it a spectacular addition to San Francisco's murals.

Alicia says that much of her inspiration comes from a belief in education. She sees a big part of her work as passing along various traditions to the youth of her audience, "especially third world people," who thus are given a chance to have an impact on the public environment through their presence in her murals. It is remarkable that, after a decade and a half, the vision of this muralist is so close to the vision of earlier muralists such as Michael Rios, who expressed almost the identical view when he began painting the *Minipark* in 1974.

Larger than lifesize images of children from the doorway to Hawthorne Elementary School where the *El Lenguaje Mudo del Alma* mural by Juana Alicia and Susan Cervantes begins. (302)

HAIGHT-ASHBURY

The Haight-Ashbury is the San Francisco neighborhood most prominently associated with the 1967 Summer of Love, with hippies, psychedelic drugs, free sex and a "no-hassle" lifestyle. It borders on Golden Gate Park, and Haight Street runs parallel to it two blocks away for over a mile. Artists were among the freespirited youths who crowded into the area in the late 1960s, and, as one later put it, "Since we'd been painting the insides of our apartments in all kinds of psychedelic designs it wasn't much of a leap to begin painting outdoors."

The earliest community mural in San Francisco was begun by Joana Zegri in 1967. It was never formally titled, but was called *Evolution Rainbow* (#160) because as the colors of its rainbow design progressed from dark to light, details within each color depicted the evolution of animals from early protozoa through dinosaurs up to modern species. Other murals were painted inside businesses shortly afterwards by Gary Graham and others and have now been destroyed, but Zegri's, in a troubled lifespan typical of community paintings, has withstood two serious challenges.

The first pause came when the artist, in the middle of painting the mural, took time off to give birth to her first child. After several months she completed the mural, and even restored it in 1981 with stronger paints. In 1982, the business on the wall of which the mural was painted changed hands, and the new owner had the mural painted out. This is an example of a common problem with community murals: the art is public, but the wall is private, and without special arrangements, the wall's owner is also owner of the mural (see below, "Legalities"). In this instance, the destruction catalyzed community forces in a way that indicates the role such murals play in forming social communities (or at least in focusing them). Protests, petitions, complaints by the store's customers, letter writing campaigns, and meetings late into the night followed. It is difficult to ascertain exactly, but the popular belief "on the street" is that someone called the store's insurance company and suggested that the store's window was not a good risk. When the insurance company cancelled its coverage, the store owner contacted Zegri and asked her to repaint the mural, thereby regaining insurance and community respect simultaneously.

The most prominent murals in the Haight-Ashbury were painted by a group called Haight-Ashbury Muralists, which in the spirit of the times sought a new way to organize itself into a unified artistic group. Members were Miranda Bergman, Jane Norling, Arch Wil-

liams, Jo Tucker, and Thomas Kunz. They painted a group of significant murals in the area, all of which depicted a belief in the struggles of poor and working people to better their lives and the need for new cultural organizations as part of that struggle. In *Rainbow People* (#156), a multi-racial, multi-generational, sexually mixed group of people was shown cutting off the greedy tentacles of a monopoly corporate octopus which had as its head the combined faces of President Ford and Vice President Rockefeller. The head had originally been Richard Nixon's, but after Watergate's scandal drove him from office, his successors' faces were substituted. Behind the tentacled terror a peace

Evolution Rainbow, painted by Joana Zegri, with its figure-filled bands of color was San Francisco's first community mural. (160)

Signs of protest carried by 1960s marchers were seen in this detail from the destroyed mural *Our History is No Mystery* by the Haight-Ashbury Muralists. (151)

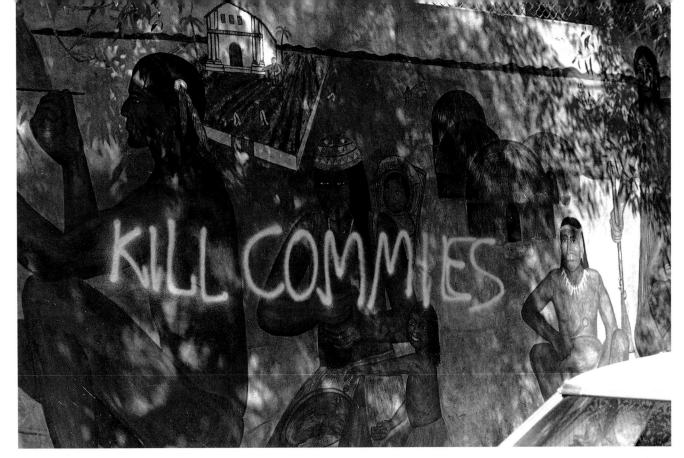

"Kill Commies" was the spraycan message written across the native Californian section of *Our History is No Mystery*, the very long mural painted by the Haight-Ashbury Muralists. (151)

Figures around a campfire are watched by faces emerging from a window in *Each Come Together in Perceiving of Yourself* by Selma Brown and Ruby Newman. (158)

demonstration marched down Haight Street. The original mural was painted to commemorate such an anti-war march in 1972, but the paints were not strong enough to withstand the weather, and the surface was not prepared properly by the neophyte muralists. They repainted the mural in 1974 with several changes. To the right was depicted a countercultural scene of farming and musicmaking, out of which grows a rainbow. Two of the people working in the garden have necklaces with gay/lesbian symbols, and when the mural was attacked, these were one target. The other was the overall idea of the mural, or of murals in general. In foot-high letters, "Fuck people's art," was written across the center of the mural. The mural was restored and eventually was relocated indoors at the Haight-Ashbury Natural Foods Store across the street from its original location.

The largest work done by the Haight-Ashbury Muralists was *Our History Is No Mystery* (#151), which stretched down a low retaining wall at the John Adams School on Hayes Street until it was some seven feet

30

high at the corner of Masonic, where it turned and continued for another two hundred feet along the wall. It "read" from right to left, and showed a school history lesson about the working class in San Francisco. After beginning with Native Americans, the mural shows the gold rush, racist treatment of Chinese, the earthquake and fire of 1906, struggles for education for all citizens, a funeral in the Depression (with some famous muralists and some friends of the muralists helping carry the coffin), the internment of Japanese-American citizens during World War II, a generic march representing the 1960s demonstrations for peace, jobs, civil rights, etc., a section (symbolic of the ravages of urban renewal) depicting the struggle to save Chinatown's International Hotel and its mural from demolition, and finally, at the corner, a scene showing men and women of several races working together to create a society based on a vision of peace and productivity. On the Hayes Street side is a schematic hand pointing at the earth which bends around the corner itself.

One might think that people would appreciate this mural, whose theme and images were taken from a questionnaire circulated at the site by the muralists, and in fact it received a warm reception for years. But shortly before its completion in 1976, it was attacked by a single individual who, as he later explained in a letter, was distraught at losing his girlfriend, and had been drinking the night he defaced the mural. This attack was met with an outpouring of support for the mural by local people, dozens of whom helped restore the mural by cleaning it with special solvents. But in the 1980s, the mural was attacked again, more thoroughly. As is usual in such defacements, the primary targets were people of color, whose faces were covered with spray paint, but in this case the defacement went further, covering large portions of the wall, and adding graffiti saying "Kill Commies," and the like. It has been speculated that the same hand was involved in defacements of both Haight-Ashbury Muralist works because of their themes. Such a right-wing bigot may have been the same person who rollerpainted over the Native Americans in Eugene Curley's 1976 pastoral mural (#161) at Haight and Carl Streets.

The nation's bicentennial came in the middle of a tremendous surge of mural activity in San Francisco, and it made $10,000 available to the neighborhood for "beautification." Although some merchants wanted to use the money to paint fire hydrants, the money was split between three mural projects: *Our History Is No Mystery*, the Paltenghi Youth Center mural painted by Charles Lobdell (#163), and the Park branch library

Faces occupy the corner of *Educate to Liberate* just as they did in its predecessor, *Our History is No Mystery*. The mural on a retaining wall of varying heights was painted by Miranda Bergman and others. (152)

mural, *Each Come Together in Perceiving of Yourself* (#158) painted by Selma Brown and Ruby Newman. The latter is a strong example of how considered use of architectural space can make or break a mural's effectiveness. The mural's focus is at the bottom of a vertical space, where (appropriately for the Haight subculture and its idealization of Native Americans) a group gathers around a campfire. Two stories above is a recessed window well. The muralists made this a strength of their mural by designing their image to take advantage of the otherwise awkward architectural configuration. They reasoned that they were talking about myth in the mural, so they used the recess as the location of a personified sun figure benevolently looking down upon the vision of togetherness below.

Both women have continued painting, and Brown has created a strong image of the history of metalwork in *Masters of Metal* (#421), located at a tool and die works. She also painted a large, stylized historical portrait of Ben Franklin (#118) at the Ben Franklin School in the Western Addition.

By the late 1980s *Our History Is No Mystery* had been cleaned a couple of times, but continued to be attacked and was in bad shape. The muralists, in response to many local residents who liked the mural, decided that the best course to follow was painting a new mural in the space, and after three years of effort, raised enough money to allow the painting of *Educate to Liberate* (#152) in 1988. While the new mural lacks the historical specificity of the earlier mural, it is still current in its depiction of the multiplicity of cultures of

31

A detail taken from Jane Norling's destroyed mural, *Sistersongs of Liberation*, has been used very successfully in this poster printed for International Women's Day. (236)

INTERNATIONAL WOMEN'S DAY
Día Internacional de la Mujer يوم المرأة العالمي
PHỤ NỮ QUỐC TẾ   SIKU YA WANAWAKE WAMATAIFA

working people in the area shown opposed to inimical forces which would exploit them. The latter are painted in monochrome greys and blacks, while above them are the brightly colored cultures of the people who attend the Vocational School on whose wall the mural is painted.

Educate to Liberate was a special regathering of the Haight-Ashbury Muralists, since they had not painted together in over a decade. Still, they had all been active in the mural movement. Miranda Bergman painted in Chinatown, Nicaragua, Palestine-the West Bank, Balmy Alley, the *I.L.W.U. Mural-sculpture*, with Wallspeak! in Oakland, and elsewhere. She is one of the central figures in Bay Area muralism.

Jane Norling had a baby and works as a graphic designer, but found time to paint *Educate to Liberate* and a strong mural in Balmy Alley. Her earlier *Sistersongs of Liberation* (#236) was a brilliant utilization of its cramped indoor space and has since been made into a popular poster celebrating International Women's Day. The mural has since been moved to San Francisco. Jo Tucker continued painting murals, including a mural at CASARC (the Child and Adolescent Sexual Abuse Resource Center) at San Francisco General Hospital (#370). Arch Williams painted in Balmy Alley and executed a number of other murals, such as *Tools for Peace* (#409), the Bernal branch library (#411), and at the Francisco Middle School (#33). Collectively and individually, the group's murals remain a significant presence in the Bay Area.

A word needs to be said about mural defacements (although see below, "The Lost Murals of San Francisco"). The vast majority of community murals are designed and painted with the support of people who live/work with the image on a daily basis, and they approve of its presence in their lives enthusiastically. These murals are not defaced in any way. In fact, they are typically defended against every attack, from graffiti to destruction by urban renewal. Occasionally, especially in areas where graffiti tags are common, murals are "hit," but this is indiscriminate and not directed at the mural in particular; any surface will do. Most people raised with formal training in art history disapprove of this, but in a survey I conducted of California Latino muralists a few years back, every single muralist in the state said that the graffitists had as much right to put their tags on the walls as the muralists did to paint their murals on them. Most of us probably agree that the murals look better without the additions (although some are designed to incorporate graffiti), but it is a fact of life muralists accept. The general idea is that if you do the proper legwork before painting, if you work with the youth of the area, then they will not graffiti the mural. If a mural has been up for eight or ten years, however, the youth at that time have no particular connection with the wall, and it may receive less respect than previously. The sort of attacks that have been directed at the community murals in the Haight are rare, and apparently are the work of a very small number of troubled individuals. They attack images of women and people of color, and seem generally to resent depiction of any sort of cooperative or culturally affirmative scenes, which they label "communist."

HUNTER'S POINT-BAYVIEW, THE WESTERN ADDITION, THE FILLMORE

These areas comprise the main locations of San Francisco's black population. The Western Addition and the Fillmore are directly west of the extent of the 1906 fire. This made them the primary location for the construction of much-needed housing immediately following the conflagration, but in the haste to provide housing and make profits, substandard buildings were built which soon became tenements and were made available to black people settling in the city. Immediately prior to World War II the U.S. Navy decided to build a major shipyard at Hunter's Point, and this in turn brought the major black migration to the city to work there during the war. What was built as temporary workers' housing at that time remained to house the black community until finally replaced by newer housing projects in the late 1970s and 1980s.

Among the earliest black community muralists in San Francisco were Caleb Williams and Horace Washington, whose 1973 work in the Western Addition housing projects depicted indigenous African scenes and cultures (#129). Both have continued to paint in the city, working together in the Bicentennial Show. Washington works primarily as a sculptor of large masks, but was a member of the *I.L.W.U. Mural-sculpture* (#220) team in 1986, and in 1984 created a History of Black Americans (#428) which was installed in Hunter's Point. This mural is a series of glazed tiles comprising stylized portraits of famous black Americans. Also early in the community mural movement such artists as Camille Breeze and Bob Gayton painted in the Western Addition, but most of their works are destroyed, as is the delightful *Sgt. Henderson Park* mural painted by Sondra Chirlton in 1973. On the walls facing a vacant lot at Divisadero and Eddy Streets, she painted a landscape. At the left was Sgt. Henderson whose army jacket was clearly labelled with his name. He was the person who took care of the lot when it was converted into a minipark by residents. In the 1980s, a large housing project was built at the site, obliterating the mural (#116).

An influential black muralist has been Dewey Crumpler, both because of the scale of his works and the fact that they have been painted in several parts of the city, each involving a different set of conditions and interrelations with local community members.

In the late 1960s, Crumpler first learned about the work of the Tres Grandes. By the early seventies, he had visited Mexico to see for himself how Siqueiros, Rivera and especially Orozco, handled architectural space in their works. When the saga of the George Washington High School murals finally reached the point of allowing painting to begin, Crumpler was ready, having painted other murals in the meantime. The students at the school had for years passed by Victor Arnautoff's 1935 entry hall frescoes depicting the revolutionary war and slave society of the late eighteenth century. They felt an uneasiness about the depictions. It wasn't that they were historically inaccurate, but that black and Asian and Latino students felt the need for more positive depictions of their cultures. They respected the progressive elements in Arnautoff's murals, such as the figure of George Washington pointing westward to the future across the continent and directing explorers, mountain men, and pioneers toward it (#176). Arnautoff included the body of a slain Native American over which the "developers" had to step on their journey, along with a Native American conversing with explorers in a pipe ceremony. The

Ceramic tiles were used for Horace Washington's series of six portrait panels of black leaders and entertainers on the wall of the Martin Luther King Jr. Swimming Pool. Washington was assisted by Seitu Din and Kate Singleton. (428)

Dewey Crumpler designed a very large mural called *The Fire Next Time II* for two adjacent walls of the Joseph P. Lee Recreation Center. Flames and an African-style cloth link images of Africa with faces of African-Americans in the mural's two parts. (424)

students tried to convince the administration to sponsor another mural in the main building, but they met a bureaucratic stone wall. When Martin Luther King, Jr. was murdered, students carefully removed announcements from a hallway bulletin board and put up materials about black pride. When the school authorities responded with disciplinary measures, the students said they wanted their mural or they would destroy Arnautoff's work. The administration was not impressed, so the students tossed ink onto the frescoes, and this militancy eventually led to an agreement for the new murals. The students however, wanted Crumpler to paint the new murals while the school officials did not want a young black artist barely out of high school to receive such a significant commission. When they finally agreed on Crumpler, they offered him the insultingly low sum of $1,000 for the job. This was finally raised to $17,000, on which Crumpler lived for four years while he researched and painted the three panels of the mural.

One panel is of Native American and Latino figures with cultural symbols such as the great pyramids in Mexico, the eagle and serpent, Cesar Chavez, and so on. Another shows the Asian American heritage, including for example, not only famous figures from Chinese history, but also a pile of army helmets, one with "442" written on it. Students who pause to find out what this means learn that this mural, like many murals, has a strong didactic content which can teach viewers about their own and others' histories. In this case, the "442" stands for the 442nd Regimental Combat Rifle team, the Rainbow Division which fought in Italy during World War II and which was the most heavily decorated division in the U.S. Army. Most of the soldiers' Japanese-American families were locked away in detention camps while their sons were fighting. The central panel of the mural is a depiction of African American history, with the building's huge supporting beams effectively incorporated into the mural design, and an honor roll of famous black people coming out of the center, below an image of black rebirth. Crumpler's idea was to suggest to students that they too might have their names added to the list some day (#180).

This theme of the relationship between African and African-American cultures has persisted in Crumpler's work, and is the main idea of his next two major projects. In *The Fire Next Time* (#423) at the Joseph Lee Recreation Center in Hunter's Point-Bayview, Crumpler depicted three aspects of black people's lives in the United States: education, religion, and culture. The contemporary figures, a teacher and student, athletes, and dancers, are watched over by exemplary portraits of Harriet Tubman and Paul Robeson. Above them are two Senufo birds, which are mythical beings in Africa but here oversee the cultural and creative lives of the community. Two incidents during the painting of this project demonstrate how community relationships can interact with murals. In one case a young man came up to Crumpler and asked who the two portraits were, and when told, the young man listened and then responded by saying that "They don't live here, man. You should put up a couple of locals like Richard and Edwina. They're a stone couple." Crumpler tried to explain, but the young man would hear none of it. Several weeks later, he returned, and told Crumpler that he was right, that black people needed to know more about important leaders so they could have somebody to respect, and besides, Richard and Edwina had broken up.

In the other incident, a group from a local church came to question the propriety of the two nude figures in the center of the design, and in flames. Crumpler explained that the figures symbolized duality, which was important in Dogon and other African religions, and also in the Bible, as were the flames. The neighborhood had been a site of riots and burnings in the late sixties, but the mural showed flames not only as destructive but as purifying, their common meaning in African religions and the Book of Revelations. This satisfied the church delegation, and after a decade the mural remains untouched by any sort of marking (although the City of San Francisco has planted a tree and erected a tall light pole directly in front of it, reminding us of the discussion about the willow tree in the Minipark some years before). It was my privilege to work as Dewey's assistant in this project.

By 1984, Crumpler continued the mural on the adjacent gymnasium at the Recreation Center (#424). More stylized than the first part of the mural, it continues the same visual motifs, with large portraits of black leaders and a background of dualistic flames.

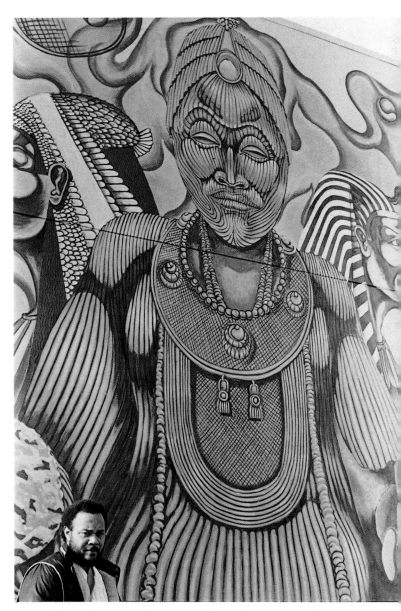

Dewey Crumpler poses beside the Oni of Ife figure in the center of his mural, *The Fire Next Time II*. (424)

Wrapped around the northern corner is a hand holding a quilt from Alabama. Up Newcombe Street is another hand, but with a section of cloth with an African textile design on it. The manipulation of architectural space obliterates the corner, and brings the mural into a dynamic unity. Between the two hands is a giant replica of a 16th-century Ife bronze figure against a background of Egyptian and United States figures: King Tut, Muhammed Ali, Willie Mays, Wilma Rudolph, Arthur Ashe. The second part alone measures over five thousand square feet.

In the same year, with the assistance of Kemit Amenophis, Bonnie Long and Sandra Roberts, Crumpler painted *A Celebration of African and African-American Artists* at the Western Addition Cultural Cen-

Two figures in outline leap into the intricate African-inspired patterns of James Phillips' *Sunflowers of Nature*. Photograph by Ted Pontiflet. (422)

ter (#135). This, too, is a huge wall, even larger than the one at Hunter's Point. The mural design incorporates a number of difficult architectural characteristics of the building (primarily large screen-covered windows), and is anchored by a large stylized portrait of Duke Ellington. He is surrounded by artists in music, dance and painting—a perfect theme for the use of the center and the cultural heritage of the location.

In 1976, David Bradford painted a spectacular wall of respect for black leaders on the WAPAC building in the Western Addition (#112). It stood as a beacon in an area on the verge of urban renewal until the mid 1980s, when it was removed. In the late 1980s two other murals were painted in Hunter's Point. One was a geometrical design by James Phillips. The other, *Tuzuri Watu/We Are a Beautiful People* (#425), was painted by Brooke Fancher two blocks away from *The Fire Next Time*. It is a beautifully painted tribute to Afro-American culture inspired by black women writers. The design shows scenes of black peoples' lives, rural and urban, with a strong emphasis on community and family life. Quotations from the works of five black women authors appear throughout the mural. Fancher explains her choice of location and topic by saying that "A lot of people don't even know about black women writers. Their work is a part of the self-affirmation of people learning about their culture, and the mural seems a good place to proclaim it."

THE BICENTENNIAL

In addition to the three Federal Bicentennial Neighborhood Beautification Fund murals painted in Haight-Ashbury, two other multiple mural projects were produced in 1976.

The Bicentennial Show at the San Francisco Museum of Modern Art (SFMMA), was curated by Rolando Castellon, a man whose abilities and enthusiasm opened the doors of that august edifice to community artists of color. This show, devoted entirely to murals, was the first such exhibit at any San Francisco museum.

The murals for this show were painted with acrylics on plywood panels, and most measured eight feet high by twenty feet wide. The show provided the public with a chance to observe the work of a significant number of the most influential community muralists of San Francisco at that time, without having to go into the poorer neighborhoods where the muralists' work was usually located. Some found this a favorable development, some deplored it because of the lessening of impact murals have when wrenched out of their social contexts. The murals were *Two Hundred Years of Children's Toys and Games*, directed by Shoshana Dubiner with the Creative Arts Workshop at Bessie Carmichael Elementary School (#240); Horace Washington and Caleb Williams' *Crispus Attucks: The Boston Massacre, March 5, 1770* (#154); Dewey Crumpler's untitled piece showing working people nurturing a living plant from the bonds of racism (#132); the Haight-Ashbury Muralists' *200 Years of Resistance*, which was later mounted on Uganda Liquors at the corner of Masonic and Haight Streets (#155); Jim Dong and Nancy Hom's International Hotel mural, *The Struggle for Low Income Housing* (#406) which measures 14' x 22' in a "V" shape; and Robert Mendoza's *The Struggle of Native American People for Sovereignty*, a rare Native American mural depicting traditional images alongside contemporary scenes of alcoholism, drug abuse, and Indians occupying Alcatraz and fighting against U.S. government attack forces. On the lower right is a "holy" Native American family, including two smiling, happy children and two parents armed with guns.

Perhaps the most shocking image was Michael Rios' and Tony Machado's depiction of fascist pigs dragging an American flag on the ground (#408). It has a swastika in place of stars. It was titled *Esta Gran Humanidad ha Dicho Basta!/This Great People Has Said Enough!* (an image ironic by the late 1980s, since Rios has become a serious student of Buddhist pacifism).

Next to it was Graciela Carrillo and Irene Perez's untitled piece showing a dual image of Latino/Native American people engaged in traditional food gathering/preparing and also holding rifles in preparation for armed struggle (#EB31). These murals are only twelve feet wide.

Several of these pieces found their way into community display after the show closed, but some remain untraced.

The other bicentennial mural production was located at Fort Mason, in an abandoned military supply warehouse now used as part of a cultural activities center run by the Golden Gate National Recreational Area. Inside local artists painted thirteen 10′ x 35′ panels just below the ceiling. Since they were located between large windows, they were difficult to see clearly. The images depicted a wide range of San Francisco scenes, from early Golden Gate Park and Chinatown, to the building of the city's skyscrapers. The styles tended more toward the artistic expressions of the artists than to any community involvement, and few other murals were painted by these artists. All the murals were destroyed in 1987 in an "upgrading" of the space (#1–#13).

A CHANGE OF TONE: THE LATE 1970s

In the late 1970s, community murals changed. The struggles and the concerns of many of the early muralists were generated by their political activism and resulted in collectively developed images. Potentially volatile themes still remained, but became muted. The early muralists were growing older, setting up house, having children, sometimes getting tired of living hand to mouth. Also, the mass political activity of the previous decade waned, (with a solid shove from the government) and many political organizations expired, their issues no longer having mass appeal. As one disgruntled veteran of the 60s put it, "We may have been beaten, but we weren't wrong. The causes still exist and the problems will be back again in some form or other." In short, there was a lack of civil rights, antiwar and feminist actions to which a community muralist could relate. The issues' publicity (not the issues themselves) receded, and muralists' work became accordingly less volatile. To this must be added the gentrification of San Francisco neighborhoods and a change in mural financing. As relatively upscale residents moved into older, physically upgraded neighborhoods, early murals were painted over or destroyed in renewal projects. Funding sources narrowed to the point that the Mayor's Office of Community Develop-

Michael Rios and Anthony Machado painted *Esta Gran Humanidad ha Dicho Basta!* for the Bicentennial Mural exhibition at the San Francisco Museum of Modern Art. Their mural, painted on panel, is seen on display in the museum. (408)

ment (OCD) was almost the only source available to local muralists except for an occasional foundation grant. What is more, as with everything else, the costs of painting murals rose.

One other reason for this shift in mural images is the direct result of the early murals themselves. People had come to accept them. When trying to gain permission to paint on a wall it was no longer necessary to justify the idea of a mural, only to satisfy the wall's owner that a particular image would not have anything objectionable in it, and then to receive design approval from the Visual Arts Subcommittee of the San Francisco Art Commission (sometimes a daunting prospect). Murals were OK. Younger, "second generation" muralists came onto the scene as murals became an acceptable art form, an approved forum for expression. This and the lack of concurrent political activity (hence lessened opportunity to learn to think in political terms) contributed to the increase in numbers of "apolitical" images. Since murals were OK, a young artist could turn to community walls for self-expression, and some commented privately that this was their road into the galleries, which otherwise were not interested in their easel work.

The proliferation of images made each image seem less significant than before. It took something special to get people's attention. The mural movement as a whole had developed three separate currents. At its heart remained the socially active artists and processes (the community muralists). However, a growing number of artists did not see murals as a part of a larger social process, but rather as vehicles for self-expression. A third well publicized strain developed commercially, as businesses hired muralists to paint attention-getting images for them. Still, community-based works continued to be produced, and competed with some potentially significant innovations.

THE EIGHTIES

In 1982 the Galeria de la Raza sponsored a show titled "In Progress." Twenty San Francisco muralists painted fourteen murals on panels of various sizes in the gallery space, which was open to the public during the painting. The show then travelled to Sacramento, to the Social and Public Art Resource Center in Venice, and to the Centro Cultural de la Raza in San Diego, where local artists painted their own pieces for the show. At every site the show was exciting for artists and the public, who were able to witness the process of painting in person. Some of the images were very strong politically. But that the murals were painted in gallery spaces suggested a shift from the earlier artworks "on the streets."

In 1986 the San Francisco Art Institute (SFAI) sponsored a similar show called "The Murals Project" in one of its galleries. Since the Art Institute had not been known for its support of muralists in the past, some said the artists were making a statement by working in a location where their mural work has not been traditionally accepted. The idea was that the meaning of this show could be extended to society as a whole, i.e., people initially turned to murals because their art and cultures were not acceptable in the mainstream. Now even mainstream institutions were recognizing their significance. This was continued at the end of the decade as SFAI sponsored a series of excellent forums on the problems and potentials of artists of color.

Many murals continue to be painted, and if we look back on the past two decades of community mural painting in San Francisco, we can see that in one way or another the city has continued to support murals, in spite of a complex and often infuriating bureaucracy that has driven some muralists away from seeking its help. OCD (sometimes referred to at the end of the decade as "MOCD," recognizing publicly the mayor's titular position) has the best record in the country of recognizing that communities can be developed by means other than massive construction projects. In its con-

tinued sponsorship of community murals OCD demonstrates that it has recognized the importance of culture and the existence of social, not just geographical, communities. Also, the role of the Mural Resource Center (MRC) cannot be overlooked. It has developed from being engaged in a constant fight for existence to acting as the major facilitator of city murals, especially in its function as administrator of the OCD mural projects. From its earliest days under the leadership of Kathie Cinnater to its present director Conrad Okamoto, it has grown in stature.

One muralist, Johanna Poethig, is difficult to place in a particular district because she has painted murals in several. She has painted with Southeast Asian refugees in the Tenderloin (#86), youth in the Mission District, a wall in honor of slain gay Supervisor Harvey Milk (#146), and a stunning multi-cultural mural, *Artifact*, at the South of Market Cultural Center (#248). She is perhaps best known for her work with the Filipino community. She has painted their history on Dimasalang House, a residence for elderly Filipinos

Johanna Poethig titled her mural of Filipino history, *Descendants of Lapu-Lapu*. It was painted on Dimasalang House by Poethig, Vic Clemente and Presco Tabios. (225)

(#225), and *Lakas Sambayanan* (#431) which deals with the coming to power of Corazon Aquino, painted near the intersection of Highways 101 and I-280. Fluent in Tagalog, tall and very fair-skinned, Poethig is a striking presence among groups of Filipinos, but that too is emblematic of the mixture of cultures in San Francisco's varied population.

The middle of the decade saw the creation of Balmy Alley and the *I.L.W.U. Mural-sculpture*. Although the latter had OCD funding, most of its cost was raised from union donations. That example and the subsequent increase in foundations' willingness to fund mural projects suggests the development of a new direction for funding in the nineties.

In 1990 a group of new murals was painted in Balmy Alley to replace those which had been destroyed. Patlan had plans to gain sponsorship for a similar project in the next alley to the west, Lucky Alley, and in addition he refurbished the PLACA murals in Balmy. The summer of 1990 saw Miranda Bergman begin restoration of the *Minipark* at 24th and Bryant Streets, too, with official funding.

The news was not all good. *Community Murals Magazine* had been edited and published by local muralists since 1978. It had become a respected and authoritative source of information about murals, written by muralists for each other. It was collected by libraries, universities and individuals. At the end of 1987, due to lack of funds, it ceased publishing. It was one of many arts publications to bite the dust in the decade, and represented a loss to muralists internationally as well as locally. Suitably, its demise was publicly announced when three of its editors created an altar at the annual Day of the Dead ceremonies at the Mission Cultural Center. The altar paid tribute to *CMM* and other arts magazines which had recently passed away.

In the Mission District, Chuy Campusano's massive abstract 1987 mural at 17th and Harrison Streets was a departure for the Mission District, at least in scale (Tomas Belsky had painted an abstract mural at the other end of the inner Mission District in the early 70s). Johanna Poethig, Susan Cervantes and Juana Alicia continued to produce spectacular murals. Alicia and Cervantes worked together on two in particular, *New World Tree* (#277) on Linda Street at 19th Street, and a truly massive project at Hawthorne School. *El Lenguaje Mudo del Alma/The Silent Language of the Soul* (#302), was painted on Shotwell Street between 22nd and 23rd Streets in 1990.

In 1989 Keith Sklar completed *Learning Wall* (#107) on the west side of the San Francisco Unified School District building on Franklin Street at Hayes.

Children of various ages painted *My Journey*. Muralist Johanna Poethig can be seen watching their efforts. (228)

Fittingly, this is the building in which the offices of the Alvarado School Arts Project were located at the beginning of the 1970s. Sklar's wall is so highly stylized that it borders on being abstract, and in several places is completely non-representational. The bright narrative panels, extending some fifty feet up the building, are placed within arches which Sklar has extended from ornaments on the building. The result, bolstered by art historical references within the mural (e.g., Michelangelo's "Cumean Sybil" from the Sistine Chapel frescoes) is a stunning combination of classical and modern—perhaps the muralistic equivalent of postmodern. In any case, it shows that the muralists have learned from their traditions, and that we can learn from their work on San Francisco's community walls.

FUNDING

Significantly, neither the Balmy Alley murals nor the *I.L.W.U. Mural-sculpture* were sponsored by the normal city-oriented community development process. The Balmy Alley project was completely ad-hoc, involved dozens of people who live/work in the immediate area, obtained permission only from owners whose fences or garages were painted, and held its own meetings to discuss designs. Suggested changes in designs were shared at these meetings, and changes were often made, but the city's official bodies had no role in the project. Muralists worked for free, however, putting in time after work or on weekends, or during their yearly vacations from regular jobs. One wonders if such a project, with such a theme and diversity of styles and technical levels of participants could ever have received approval from all necessary committees, or, if so, how many years it might have taken.

The I.L.W.U. project did receive OCD funding, but from a different part of its budget than was normal for murals. The key to the project's success was support from the union, both administratively (through the efforts of Director of Communications Danny Beagle) and through the donations of the rank and file membership. It received official approval of the design by both the Parks and Recreation Department and the Art Commission and was administered financially by the normal city arts channels in a frustrating, Byzantine manner.

In the mid 1970s, block grant money from Housing and Urban Development funds (HUD) became available to mural projects through the local Mayor's Office of Community Development (OCD, or MOCD). The specific agent was the Neighborhood Improvement Initiative Program (NIIP), which paid only for materials through the San Francisco Art Commission. The grants were small, only one to three thousand dollars, but supported about a dozen murals/training programs a year.

From 1975 until 1980, the Comprehensive Employment and Training Act (CETA) enabled muralists to receive salaries for conducting training programs, and thus CETA artists could apply for NIIP grants to paint murals. In many ways, CETA was modelled on the WPA of the 1930s. CETA artists' salaries were around $700 per month. When the CETA funding drew to a close at the end of the decade, muralists requested a follow-up, and this led to the establishment of the Mural Resource Center (MRC) which was funded by CETA until 1981. The MRC began to administer the OCD funds, and to move away from the Neighborhood Arts Program as the NAP was phasing out mural projects and putting its resources into the Neighborhood Cultural Centers, of which there were five in the city. This relative centralization put money into neighborhood centers, but reduced more widely-dispersed funding which had supported a wide variety of small projects throughout neighborhoods. Because of this shift in priorities by NAP, and because it was obvious that community mural projects in fact did develop communities, especially if one understood by "community" a social, not just a neighborhood grouping, OCD became the major mural funder in the city.

When CETA ceased to exist, OCD undertook on a cost per square foot basis the funding of materials and salaries, beginning with $1.75 per sq. ft. in 1975 and moving up to $5.75 per sq. ft. in 1986, where the figure remained through 1987. The current breakdown, as understood by muralists, was $3.25 per sq. ft. for materials, $2.50 per sq. ft. for salaries, but this was never made a clear policy, and OCD has resisted paying any salaries. Beginning in 1983, muralists are classified in a category that prohibits their being paid salaries. For reasons such as these, muralists and groups prefer to gain funding outside official city channels, continuing to search for independence. The MRC itself was always under pressure to raise its own funding, even after moving under the autonomous umbrella of the Friends of Support Services for the Arts, the governing body of the South of Market Cultural Center, where the MRC is located. This pressure kept the MRC's director working on funding the MRC instead of developing murals.

There is a built-in difficulty in the tension between truly community murals, independent funding for the MRC (which is virtually non-existent), the requirements of governmental funding groups such as OCD, and the MRC's acting as an agent for commercial jobs. These are not, of course, mutually exclusive, but establishing the proper balance has been difficult. If the MRC administration is supported by city funds released for mural projects, those funds are deducted from already underfunded muralists, while increasing commercial activity removes the MRC from the sort of advocacy and administration of community projects. Amid such problems it is easy for muralists to grouch about being ill-treated, which they are. But it is also important to keep in mind the admirable fact that there are an MRC and an OCD which have continued to support community murals for over a decade. Only Los Angeles provides comparable mural support.

In the 1980s there were few non OCD-funded murals in San Francisco, of which Balmy Alley is the leading example. Some of Precita Eyes' projects, for instance, have been corporately funded, some privately. The city's Department of Parks and Recreation has also been a steady source of mural support over the years. The MRC's involvement differs according to the project, sometimes acting as fiscal agent, sometimes as a technical resource, but always being available to bring muralists in contact with potential sponsors. Funding has ranged from $40,000 per year to around $186,000. In general, it is accurate to say that there is a tension between community-based murals, independent funding for the MRC, and commercial agentry.

As community muralists increasingly look "downtown" for funding, one problem has been the amount of unpaid work the current procedures demand. For community artists, it is particularly difficult to explore a community, develop a design, and prepare the presentation for free. It requires months, even years of meetings, design alterations, research, more meetings, etc. Official agencies have a tendency to approve a project on Friday and want to see paint on the wall on Monday. For the process to be as inclusive as possible, the muralist should begin the process of development only after some financial support frees him or her from other jobs.

LEGALITIES

When OCD took over paying salaries upon the withdrawal of CETA mural support, a contract was developed between muralists and the city which has served as a model for similar contracts elsewhere. At considerable personal sacrifice, the city's muralists fought for the retention of copyright, allowing the city to use images for non-commercial purposes. This was a small acknowledgement of the lack of adequate financial support given muralists. Also, provision was made that muralists must be notified if their works needed restoration or in case of proposed alteration or destruction. Unfortunately, the city unilaterally dropped these latter provisions in 1987.

The execution of a formal contract in itself tells us something about community murals and the law. On the one hand, increasing bureaucratic requirements are imposed as a matter of course when official agencies take a greater role in funding and administration. This in itself is a recognition of the murals' significance in the city. On the other hand lies the reality of muralists' inability or disinclination to support a formal legal challenge to any breach of contract or of law. Many muralists believe that their work belongs not to them but to the public, to the community, and they consequently believe that the image is not theirs to copyright. Others simply do not want any involvement with the legal system. Still others believe that it is important to copyright their work to protect it from a use opposed to their purposes for the project.

The basic motivation for copyrighting a mural image is to protect the artist's financial interests. While many muralists formerly believed that publication of a photograph of a mural image somehow meant the author or publisher was making a lot of money, most have come to realize that while this is not true, still, there is a principle involved saying that someone should not benefit financially from others' work without their permission. Copyright is a means to that protection. It is always ethical and appropriate, therefore, to get the permission of the artist before using images of his work.

In one instance, a member of the Haight-Ashbury Muralists discovered an airline's in-flight magazine in which their mural was portrayed as representing the cultural diversity of San Francisco. After numerous letters, the airline paid the muralists a total of $500. In another case, a textbook company used a detail of a mural for the cover of one of their texts, and paid a similar amount.

In addition to copyright protection, the California Arts Preservation Act (Civil Code Section 987) declares that "there is a public interest in preserving the integrity of cultural and artistic creations." This law gives muralists certain rights concerning protection of their work, and codifies several legal remedies if it is destroyed or damaged without permission. I know of no case yet which tests this law, although there are tests underway in two other states with similar laws.

CENSORSHIP

The question of legalities raises the problem of censorship. Censorship is illegal and abominable. But what exactly constitutes censorship, and what might be done about it? Asking these questions exposes a distinction that has played an uncomfortable role in San Francisco mural history. Speaking generally, muralists understand censorship to occur when an official demands alterations of an artist's image for reasons of disagreement with content. I know of only one public instance in San Francisco. Privately, I have been told of several where the artists chose to accept the censorship because they needed the money from the project, or thought there was no way to gain approval of an image if the official was challenged. One muralist told me, "They never say, 'I don't like the content of that.' What they say is, 'On purely aesthetic grounds I wish you would change that figure (or remove it). Then the design will be acceptable.' " Officials always deny such intentions, of course, and it is extremely difficult to prove otherwise, which is why instances of proven censorship, here or elsewhere, are so rare.

Also worth noting is the artists' self censorship. This occurs when an artist "knows what they will accept," and alters a design before showing it to an official body. It has been argued that officials certainly cannot be blamed for something that existed only in the mind of the artist, and on one level this is so. But there may well be good cause for the artist to have such suspicions, and in any case this scenario evidences something other than encouragement of unfettered artistic expression of the sort that civic arts bodies are charged to promote.

The instance of blatant public censorship in San Francisco occurred in 1981, at the time of the opening of the Moscone Convention Center building. A number of artworks had been commissioned for the space, including what has become a cause celebre, a bust of assassinated Mayor George Moscone by Robert Arneson. It was declared unacceptable because of its "tasteless" references— revolvers, bullets, and Twinkies—all elements in the mayor's murder. What went relatively unnoticed was the San Francisco Art Commission's rejection at the same time of another piece it had commissioned for the building, a mosaic mural by Katherine Porter. "It makes a political statement and I don't think any kind of political statement is appropriate," a *San Francisco Chronicle* article of December 1, 1981 quoted Art Commission chair Dimitri Vedensky as saying. Porter had put eight names on her ten by twenty foot piece: Martin Luther King, Jr., Cesar Chavez, George Jackson, I.F. Stone, Paul Robeson, Dorothy Day, Emma Goldman and Wounded Knee. Vedensky is quoted as saying that this "Is a very bizarre and personal list of people." Also according to the *Chronicle* article, although other artists had made similar changes to their works without consent of the committee, "they objected to the aesthetics of Porter's new frame." Thus does censorship operate in San Francisco when it is overt. The piece was not placed in Moscone Center (and remains untraced).

It is worth emphasizing that "censorship" in the sense being used here refers to actions taken by officials or official bodies. This is vastly different in results and implications from influences/pressures stemming from people in the community acting without the clout of the government. In fact, responding to such pressures is at the very heart of the artist-community interaction of community visual arts. Timing is crucial here, with community involvement occurring at a point in the mural's design process before the image is completely developed. It is part of the development. Official censorship imposes a different set of criteria than the community's, and thus functions negatively. I believe that in trying to satisfy official agencies, muralists may allow elements of censorship to intrude into a mural's design, possibly without even being aware of it.

BILLBOARDS AND "BILLBOARD CORRECTIONS"

Occasionally, someone mentions how billboards deface communities, but the ensuing discussions do not use art terms because billboards are not considered art; cynics point out that they have too much effect on our lives to be considered art. The fact remains that they are large, carefully placed for visual impact on their audience, and they offer possibilities of scale and subject matter which muralists are well qualified to utilize.

In 1975 a group of artists at the Galeria de la Raza became fed up with the imposition of advertisements on their community, in particular ads for liquor and cigarettes across from schools, and in general ads for products where purchase would help a corporation but not the community. For years there had been a Foster & Kleiser billboard on the Bryant Street wall of the Galeria, at street level, and so some of the artists stepped outside and "appropriated" the space. What they painted was an "ad" for *Tin Tan*, an arts magazine produced and sold in the Mission District, featuring the work of local artists. More than an ad, the magazine and the billboard were celebrations of local culture, and that was the beginning of the Galeria billboard.

Since then, dozens of versions of the Galeria billboard have been painted by local (and occasionally guest) artists. For a few years, the practice was semi-clandestine and fraught with uncertainty. One day, for instance, a Foster & Kleiser truck pulled up in front of the billboard and two young workers got out. Some folks from the Galeria came out to meet them, and a crowd began to gather on the sidewalk in front of the billboard. Suffice it to say that the local residents convinced the workers that they should not paint out the current design to prepare for more ads, and the workers got in their truck and drove off. The director of the Galeria, Rene Yanez, tried unsuccessfully for over two years to talk with the billboard company, but telephone calls were not returned, or he was put on hold and then cut off. Letters went unanswered.

Finally, the company took the billboard down. Someone from the Galeria asked what they were going to do with it, and was told, "Probably throw it away." They responded by saying, "Oh, we'll do that for you," so the company gave the disassembled billboard to them and drove off. The Galeria artists then set about putting the billboard back in its place. At that point, the company responded to Yanez's efforts, and erected a frame on the building onto which plywood or masonite panels may be affixed, combining to make a full-sized billboard lacking only the frame of the original (and the company logo). The space is now used exclusively by community residents who have a particular image to share, sometimes of community-interest messages. The billboard usually announces the current show at the Galeria, a storefront gallery which has become not only an important part of Mission District community life over the years, but a significant model for Latino and community-based arts throughout the country.

Unfortunately, it is impossible here to reproduce color photographs of every incarnation of the Galeria billboard, which is the best way to let readers see for themselves the changes in style and content over a prolonged period of time. Some information on particular examples will have to suffice to give some idea of the billboard's relationship to the community.

The third billboard in the series was painted by Michael Rios. In many ways it represents the heart of the project: immediately understandable to the people who saw it on a daily basis, bright, positive toward its community, celebrating the Mission's own culture, it depicted a laid back, stylized guitarist, with the large slogan across the top, *Salsa Ahora* (Salsa now). Over the years, Rios painted many of the billboards, including the spectacular *Homage to Frida Kahlo* in 1978 and the *International Year of the Child* in 1979.

In 1976, Xavier Viramontes embarked on the longest series of "linked" billboards. The initial design featured a large portrait in the center, with a word balloon off to the upper left of the billboard. The day Viramontes completed the portrait, he left the balloon empty, in-tending to return the next day and put in the telephone tree number for those who were prepared to protest the imminent eviction at the International Hotel across the city in Chinatown, where over a hundred mostly elderly and mostly retired Filipino merchant seamen lived. The Hotel had been purchased by a Hong Kong corporation which planned to wreck the building. The hotel represented not only the last stand of its residents to continue their inexpensive lives together, but had been taken on by activists as a symbol of urban renewal and its ravages on poor people. When Viramontes returned the following day to his mural, he found that someone had already written in the balloon, with spraycan, "Que Viva Danny Trevino?" Trevino, as nearly everyone at that time knew, was a young Latino who was stopped by San Jose police and then shot eight times in the back of the head for "trying to escape," or some such excuse. There had been no particular reason for his being stopped, other than he was roughly similar in appearance to a current suspect, i.e., he was a Latino youth. Viramontes understood immediately that this alteration of his design was completely in keeping with the spirit of his work and the spirit of community arts in general, and he let it stay for several weeks, adding the I-Hotel telephone tree number only in the week before the actual eviction occurred.

Xavier Viramontes used the Galeria de la Raza billboard for some advice about health in his temporary mural, *Avoid Junk Food*.

Some weeks later, Viramontes returned again and, using the same portrait, changed the surrounding areas to depict 24th Street with a legend reading "It's your neighborhood, keep it clean, por favor." Finally, almost a year later, the billboard was repainted by another artist, and the current string of incarnations began.

Billboard variations have included some painted by visiting artists, such as ASCO, a punk performance art group from East Los Angeles ("ASCO" is Chicano slang for "vomit" or "nausea"). The group painted not only the billboard, but the entire interior wall of the Galeria in preparation for their weekend shows. The Border Art Workshop from San Diego also painted a billboard, continuing the design into the adjacent Galeria storefront window, complete with a chain link fence to announce their show focusing on issues of immigration and border control in their part of the state (and thus figuratively moving the Mexico-U.S. border into the Mission District).

Other Galeria billboards have included the *Homenaje a Frida Kahlo*, and the *Low n' Slow* billboard for a lowrider art show (designed by fourteen year old Derrik O'Keefe). Billboards have been painted by Native Americans (for the American Indian Movement photography show), by Graciela Carrillo for *La Mujer Nueva/The New Woman* show, and a Day of the Dead altar for victims of the Mexico City earthquake, Ralph Maradiaga (who had died suddenly that year), and AIDS victims (a courageous gesture by the Galeria in a neighborhood which had often been hostile to gay and lesbian people).

The notion of changing billboards takes another form as more and more artists and activists have "corrected" advertisements on prominent advertising billboards throughout the city. The trick here is to alter the advertising image as elegantly as possible so that the ad's own message is turned against it. Sometime, new words are added to the billboard to change the message people glimpse as they drive by. A cigarette ad showing a cardboard box was quickly "corrected" when red dots were put on the face of the smiling portrait and the wording was changed from "the Box" to "the Pox." Another cigarette ad was changed by the beheading of the man shown relaxing with a smoke. A concern with alcoholism motivated the correction of the slogan "The Silver Bullet," to "The Liver Bullet," and so on.

In 1977 the Eyes and Ears Foundation sponsored a group of 14 billboards in the Embarcadero-Fisher-

Billboard corrections change the intended message of a cigarette company.

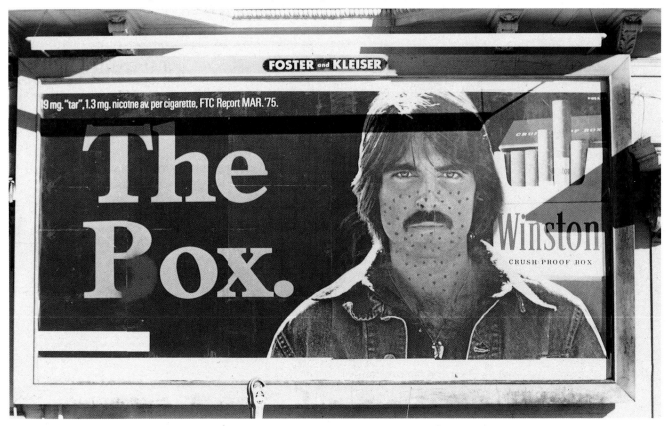

man's Wharf area. These billboards were each painted by a single artist, a few of whom were muralists. The project reflected more of a gallery-orientation than a community perspective, since they were divorced from any community input. When asked what it was these billboards were advertising, one observer answered, "Billboards."

The use of billboards for non-advertising has been discovered in other cities in the United States and Europe, and billboard corrections are popular in England and Australia as well as here.

LOST MURALS OF SAN FRANCISCO

In the two decades since the inception of community murals in San Francisco, many have been destroyed. In some cases, this was planned or at least expected because the images were in a space such as the *Mini-park* on 24th Street near Bryant where it was understood that they would be replaced periodically. The Galeria billboard mural is the most extreme example here, but Bill Wolf paints murals on his studio at 14th and Natoma Streets every 18 months.

In some cases murals have been destroyed by "routine maintenance." After a mural has been painted out, the landlord/owner defends the action by saying the destruction was merely the result of regularly scheduled painting. Although it is rarely possible to discover for certain, most muralists believe that many such cases are political attacks. They believe that when property owners or administrators don't like the politics of a mural they have it painted out. Important murals which have been destroyed include those painted at the city jail by Mosher and one painted by Ray Patlan and students in the central stairwell of the Humanities building at San Francisco State University. (Statewide, school administrators have been responsible for painting out dozens of murals, often in the early weeks of August, when virtually everyone is away on vacation or preparing for the beginning of the school year. At San Francisco State, the mural was ordered painted over by the Dean of the School of Humanities).

Most other cases of mural destruction stem from gentrification, or from real estate transactions where a building changes owners, and the new owners, having no obligations to neighbors, residents, the community, or the artists, simply choose to paint over a mural on one of "their" walls. This is perfectly legal unless there is a formal agreement specifying that a mural may not be covered or removed without the artist's permission. Since such agreements encumber the title to their property and hence make it more difficult to sell, property owners are understandably reluctant to enter into such agreements unless they plan to retain title themselves well into the foreseeable future.

In some instances, entire buildings have been demolished, and their murals along with them. The LULAC building (#394) at Folsom and Army Streets is an example, as were the mural on the front of the African-American Cultural and Historical Society (#102) on McAllister Street near Gough, and the mural at Hunter's Point II school (#427). Perhaps the most publicized of such destructions was the demolition of the International Hotel and its mural (#73). As the photographs show, destruction of murals by wrecking balls often provides a striking, albeit momentary, literalization of the destruction of poor and working class neighborhoods and communities by developers.

Sometimes the murals are not actually destroyed, but another building is constructed so close to the mural that it can no longer be seen. Neighboring buildings now prevent viewing of the Puerto Rican mural on Mission Street near Valencia (#410) as well as James Dong's Chinese American mural (#111) at 1834 Sutter Street.

Sometimes, the reasons for a mural's destruction involve complex community forces. Each such incident mirrors the vitality of our city, and the nature of conflicting interests. Some examples will help give an idea of the variety of forces interacting around community murals. One is Domingo Rivera's mural at Garfield Park (#364). According to local residents who frequent the park, the reason it was covered with graffiti when adjacent murals are left untouched is simple. Local people had no say in the image, never liked it, felt that it did not in any significant way pertain to them, and found it an arrogant visual imposition. The basic feeling seemed to be, "If the artist doesn't care about us, why should we care about what happens to his mural?" But this mural is more than simply an example of what can happen when community members are not adequately involved. It is also an example of a difficult and very real problem: under what circumstances should a mural be painted out? In the previous examples the murals were obliterated on the orders of a single authority. In the Garfield Park case, the muralist was unwilling to allow another mural to be painted on the wall. In spite of surveys of residents who saw the wall every day, it was not painted out until 1988. The artist's integrity, even though it was destroyed in the attacks on the wall, held priority over the expressed desires of the community audience.

Curiously, however, there was no such difficulty

Fran Valesco's two panel mural in Balmy Alley called *The Contest between the Sun and the Wind* was defaced by a spraycan-wielding vandal. (344)

when the art commission wanted to paint out a mural on the top of Twin Peaks shortly before the Democratic National Convention. The mural depicted a history of San Francisco (#208), and was painted on a service building at the base of the Sutro tower. Since no one staffs the building or regularly patrols the parking lot, the mural was a natural target—interesting but not on anyone's "turf." Or, it may have been the building itself, against which a series of fires were set. At any rate, the artist agreed, reluctantly, to allow the mural to be painted out under the condition that she be given support for another project. The mural was painted out. The convention came and went, and the artist has not received the promised support to date.

In 1980, murals were painted at the Holly Courts housing project (#413) after extensive discussions and design sessions with residents. At the dedication, the muralists experienced a tremendous outpouring of gratitude for their work and for the murals themselves. But within a couple of years, new leadership was selected for the tenants' group, and apparently as a demonstration of their power and of their need to "start with a clean slate," the murals were painted out. Five years later, another mural by one of the artists, Mike Mosher, was destroyed at Albion and 16th Streets, without notifying the artist or the art commission, for reasons of "routine maintenance."

Two other cases of calculated defacement are worth noting. As we have seen, the Haight-Ashbury seems to harbor one or more people politically opposed to community murals. They are apparently unable to organize a project articulating what they do like, and their only response to others' murals is destruc-tion. Thus have two Haight-Ashbury murals and Eugene Curley's Native American landscape been systematically defaced over the last decade. This includes the red-baiting, racist attacks on *Our History Is No Mystery* (#151), and an earlier attack on *Rainbow People* (#156). A third mural was also attacked. It was originally painted for the Bicentennial Exhibition and titled *200 Years of Resistance* (#155), but subsequently retitled *Uganda Liquors* when erected on the side of a liquor store by that name at the corner of Haight and Masonic streets. In 1986, someone completely covered it with thrown paint, destroying it. The mural had been instrumental in causing removal of an unsightly billboard which was originally adjacent to it. The owner of Uganda Liquors had even installed lighting to illuminate the mural at night, which was certainly a contribution to the enjoyment and safety of the area. There is no recourse for this sort of destruction other than to repaint the mural or to paint another mural in the same location. But the 1980s are more difficult economically for community artists than the 1970s, and what cost a few hundred dollars to paint then would undoubtedly cost several thousand to paint now, and so the corner remains without decoration of any sort save the dark brown paint on the side of the building.

Generally speaking, if a mural is the product of its immediate community, it will not be defaced, let alone destroyed. The most active enemy of community murals is gentrification, the "upgrading" process when a building changes owners. Political destructions are frequently masked as "routine maintenance," although there have been blatant attacks on some murals, almost always motivated by pig-headed racism.

What this adds up to is the fact that we live in a society/socio-economic system that values several things more than art or cultural expression. Until we can create a society in which all cultures are accepted, in which all people have the chance to develop self-confidence and sensitivity, the destruction of murals (not to mention other forms of cultural expression) will, sadly for us all, continue.

When chronicling the sad tale of mural destruction, we should end by remembering the experience of Balmy Alley. About two weeks before the murals were to be dedicated, several were defaced with pro-Nazi slogans and symbols. The muralists repainted their works within a week, but even before they could repair the damage, local children who had been a constant audience for the muralists, borrowed paints from them and wrote in front of their favorite murals a warning to any future vandals. The children's assertion of community support was simple: "No touching these."

Technical Considerations

At the most basic level, a mural is simply a painting on a wall. It makes a difference, however, what the wall is made of and what type of paint is used on it. Failure to prepare the wall surface properly or the use of incompatible paints may lead to an early demise of the mural through flaking, peeling, fading, or falling off the wall through weathering action (usually of water) beneath the paint. What follows is a brief outline of technical aspects of mural painting as practiced in San Francisco.

SURFACES

Walls are made of stone, brick, plaster, stucco, wood, concrete, or sometimes a combination, including even glass and tile in some instances. Basic wall preparation insures that the paint will adhere properly to the surface, and that normal aging of wall and paint will not cause problems. No matter what the surface, it must first be checked to be sure it is structurally sound, and that repairs will not have to be made to it or its drainage system once the mural is painted. Then, the wall must be thoroughly cleaned, using trisodium phosphate or some other cleanser followed by a thorough rinsing. If the surface is wood, careful filling and sanding are required. The surface is normally sealed with a clear sealer, then painted with a white gesso to give the most luminous background to the color.

PAINTS

Ancient cave painters made their own paints, grinding pigments for color. Today, muralists buy their paints. In between, paint technology continued to provide the "right paint for the job." New Deal artists worked mostly in oil paints and sometimes in fresco (a process of applying colored pigments to wet plaster which makes the final image literally part of the wall). Of the Mexican muralists, Siqueiros was a great experimenter, trying such innovations as airbrushes and automobile paints (for longevity and brightness).

Windows, doors, and heating vents are among the structural devices confronted by a muralist when he designs his painting. Dewey Crumpler is seen standing on the scaffolding next to his mural, *The Fire Next Time II*. One figure in the mural seems to be lifting a heating vent into the flames. (424)

San Francisco muralists have occasionally executed frescoes, and have tried other media, but the vast majority of local murals are done with modern acrylic paints. Until the late 1980s, when the local distributor went out of business, the brand of choice was Politec, which, like all acrylics, was easy to work with

A wood frame apartment building above the House of Brakes offered the setting for the mural, *Carnaval*. (314)

In *Carnaval* the walls of the apartment building are tranformed into city blocks. Between the houses the Carnaval parade explodes down each imaginary street. The mural was designed by Daniel Galvez and painted with the assistance of Dan Fontes, James Morgan, Jan Shield, and Keith Sklar. (314)

and terrifically durable, even in the California sunshine. It was specially formulated, with additives that help the colors resist fading due to the ultraviolet rays of the sun. Politec was developed in Mexico by Jose Gutierrez and had been sold locally since 1973. An advantage of working with acrylic paints is that as long as they are wet, they are water soluble, so spills and "errors" can be corrected easily (a major consideration when working with children or inexperienced painters). Once dry, the paint becomes plastic and resistant to nearly every kind of attack. Since the demise of Politec, muralists tend to work with Novacolor or, sometimes, Liquitex, both of which are excellent acrylics.

The murals are normally coated with clear sealer after they are finished as a final protection against the elements and graffiti. (If graffiti is put on the mural, it can be washed off with the right solvent without removing the mural paint itself. Manufacturers are searching for an ideal "graffiti protection" covering, but as of mid 1990, no product has found general acceptance among muralists).

Some artists have used oil-based paints, mostly because they are familiar with them from their easel painting. Any moisture beneath the paints, however, will cause them to peel. This familiarity has obvious advantages for the artist, but the oil paints will crack, however, and not weather as well as the acrylics. Still, Bulletin sign painter's colors have been used with great success in other parts of the country, especially in Chicago, with its harsh winters and hot, humid summers. (In Chicago, sometimes the paint holds up well, but the wall beneath deteriorates and crumbles away beneath the mural, destroying it). In Chicago these days, the medium of choice is Keim Paints, made in Germany, which are exceptionally durable, second only to fresco. They have been used sparingly in San Francisco, perhaps because of difficulty in availability.

Cynthia Grace's *Tactile Mural* is a fabric collage intended to be touched by those who come to the Rose Resnick Center for the Blind. (94)

The entire community (children, their parents, and the buildings in their neighborhood) was presented in this mosaic mural by Nancy Thompson at the *Alvarado Elementary School*. (216)

OTHER MATERIALS

For some reason, San Francisco muralists are curious and experiment with different materials. In 1984, Horace Washington installed a series of mural panels at the Martin Luther King, Jr., swimming pool (#428). Each panel consisted of individually painted and fired tiles. Several tiles made up the portrait of a figure. Although painted tiles and even mosaics had been used in community murals elsewhere, this is the first such instance in San Francisco. Tiles have the special value of being virtually immune to weather, and will retain a high gloss for decades.

Another unusual material was used for the *I.L.W.U. Mural-sculpture*, a group of three panels made out of 3/8″ structural steel with a narrative mural painted on both sides. The type of paint used was polyurethane epoxy. Extremely bright and durable (it is commonly used to paint automobiles, trucks, and airplanes), it should weather for an extended period of time. The drawback to using it is that it is a cumbersome medium to mix (short pot life of about four hours) and extremely toxic. Protective garments, such as respirators, gloves, goggles, and earplugs must be worn at all times when working with it. "Normal" paints, especially acrylics, are much more user friendly.

PORTABLE MURALS

In San Francisco, muralists have painted backdrops for rallies and speeches, and more permanent backdrops for stages. Also, many "portable" murals have been painted. These are usually painted on 4′ x 8′ masonite panels, or sometimes on marine plywood. The panels are then grouped into, commonly, an eight foot by sixteen or twenty foot rectangle, about the size of a small billboard, painted in a studio space, and then erected wherever an appropriate location is found. This style of working has the great advantage of not being subject to weather while being painted, and the relative calm of a studio environment.

Portable murals also have a tendency to be little more than large easel paintings, and often seem imposed on their exterior sites since they are rarely painted with a particular architectural (or social) environment in mind. In a few instances, portable murals have been executed in "unusual" shapes. Jane Norling created a portable mural in an accordion shape made by placing panels in a zig-zag pattern. This gave the structure a depth that created a visual variety not possible on a flat rectangular surface. There is no reason plywood cannot be shaped in virtually any way, and this has in fact been done by Leo Tanguma in Denver and Raul Valadez in Austin, Texas. Their inevitably small scale (they can be disassembled and stacked in the back of a station wagon for transport) also limit their potential as murals.

All of the M.E.T.A.L muralists needed to wear protective masks and clothing while they worked on the *I.L.W.U. Mural-sculpture*. (220)

Folding screens show the possibilities an artist can utilize in creating a portable mural. This untitled work with its effective sense of depth was painted by Jane Norling.

Introduction to East Bay Murals

The "East Bay" consists of towns and cities on the eastern shore of San Francisco Bay. Like San Francisco, most were founded in the nineteenth century and grew up as the gold and silver booms brought expansion to the area. Few New Deal murals were painted in the East Bay, although there were some public art projects, especially at schools, including the massive University of California campus in Berkeley. Still, the impetus for mural work came in the 1960s in the midst of the political activism for which the area is so famous. Nor were murals the only form of public visual expression of the times. Especially notable were the hundreds of posters announcing political events, and silkscreens dealing with ethnic or political themes which led to the Bay Area becoming the preeminent poster/silkscreen production center in the country.

The first political murals in the Bay Area were painted in 1968–1969 by students at Oakland's Grove Street Community College (#EB101). Murals were painted celebrating black, Latino, and multicultural concerns of the student population. They were painted by Shirley Triest, Wilma Bonnett, Joan X, David Salgado, David Bradford, Manuel Hernandez and Malaquias Montoya. These murals were admired by activists and activist artists throughout the area, and encouraged others to turn to public walls for artistic expression.

The most prolific of East Bay muralists has been Malaquias Montoya. Montoya's primary medium is silkscreen, and examples of his work are seen on office and apartment and home walls throughout the area. As a teacher of Chicano culture and art at several local colleges his method was to work collectively with students. In the seventies they produced a group of outstanding murals, such as: *The Limits of Tyrants* (#EB37), *Nuestra Historia* (#EB32), *No Hay Rosas Sin Espinas* (#EB33).

Other Latino artists active in the late seventies included Ray Patlan and Patricia Rodriguez, who worked with groups and painted murals in the Latino neighborhood of Fruitvale and East 24th Street in east Oakland. Rodriguez and Patlan also taught a course together at the University of California which generated a handful of murals close to the university campus.

In Berkeley the most influential group was Commonarts, the members of which were Osha Neumann, O'Brien Thiele, Patlan, and Anna de Leon. They painted half a dozen murals, such as *Winds of Change* (#EB114), and the spectacular *Song of Unity* (#EB99) at La Pena Cultural Center. *Song of Unity* is a magnificent example of a community mural. It was executed by a group of artists working in conjunction with the immediate community and the staff at La Pena. It is executed on plywood panels shaped at the top to conform to the outline of the images in the mural, giving the piece a dynamic presence along an otherwise routine one-story roofline. On the right stemming from a ceramic eagle are figures in U.S. culture, such as jazz and folk musicians. On the left, stemming from a South American condor, are figures of Latino culture, such as musicians playing Andean pan pipes and guitars. They come together at the entrance to La Pena, inviting everyone inside. On the larger left side is a figure of a guitarist in low relief (made of a wire armature and papier mache soaked in acrylic plastic sealer instead of paste). The musician is Victor Jara, a Chilean poet and folk singer whose hands were chopped off by Pinochet's police before they murdered him. The mural's concept is that Jara joins with artists and musicians from both continents in creating the culture inside La Pena. In 1986 the mural was refurbished, and a quetzal bird, symbolic of Central America, was added to the center in reference to the intensity of the current struggles there. Its painted tail spread down the mural and out across the adjacent sidewalk.

Another major mural of the seventies was *A People's History of Telegraph Avenue* (#EB79), located at the corner of Haste Street and Telegraph Avenue near People's Park. In it, Osha Neumann designed a political history of the area, much of which occurred at the site of the mural itself, from the Free Speech Movement of 1964 through the anti-Vietnam War and police riots of the early seventies. The mural ends on the right side with a scene of utopian frolic—and a life-size panhandler, who is often obscured by homeless people who stand on the spot asking for help.

The other well-known mural from the seventies is

Stefen's *Dutch Boy Mural* (#EB115), which was painted on the west-facing wall of a paint store at Milvia and University Avenues. It depicted a futuristic view of San Francisco Bay from Berkeley, a theme appropriate to the "new age" segment of the counterculture. Stefen included a figure on a ladder painting the wall, who looked at first glance like the Dutch Boy of paint advertising fame . . . or perhaps like Stefen himself. When the mural was destroyed in the process of renovating the building for a new tenant, many people in the community were upset, but the mural was not replaced.

Other muralists active in Berkeley and Oakland were George Mead, Gary Graham, Lou Silva, and Deborah Greene and Ariella Seidenberg. Of particular note among their work is *Oceanus* (#EB68), painted by Silva and Graham. Its underwater scene (excellently situated beneath a freeway overpass) contains drums of radioactive waste. This is a reference to the discarding of such waste near the Farrallon Islands, a marine life refuge just outside the Golden Gate. Strange, un-

The subject is education in this Oakland school mural by Malaquias Montoya and his mural students from the California College of Arts and Crafts. The Spanish title can be seen in this detail from *In Knowledge There is Liberation*. (EB36)

Detail from a destroyed mural painted by Malaquias Montoya and students from the California College of Arts and Crafts in Oakland. (EB59)

The hands and guitar of murdered musician Victor Jara emerge from the top of the La Pena mural, *Song of Unity*, painted by the Commonarts muralists in Berkeley. (EB99)

known plants, clearly mutations, are seen growing from the mural's drums.

The East Bay contains many examples of school murals, especially in high schools in Oakland, Berkeley, and El Cerrito. The Brigada Orlando Letelier, a Chilean refugee group, painted a mural at *Oakland Technical School* (#EB68) and another at *Berkwood-Hedge* School, an elementary school in Berkeley (#EB94).

In the eighties, Daniel Galvez painted three murals in Oakland using the popular photorealist style. He used photographs of local residents for his images, thereby linking the murals indelibly to the community. One of these murals, *Grand Performance* (#EB 53), by Keith Sklar and Galvez, is painted on a freeway underpass, and is a tribute to Bay Area artists including jazz pianist Mary Watkins, the San Francisco Mime

Troupe, Oakland Symphony conductor Calvin Simmons, folksinger Malvina Reynolds, and muralist Ray Patlan. Both Sklar and Galvez have painted major walls in San Francisco.

Also prominent in the decade was Dan Fontes, whose animals painted on freeway support pillars gained instant popularity (#EB54, #EB55). A number of muralists have painted on both sides of the Bay, among them Miranda Bergman, Ray Patlan, Dewey Crumpler, James Morgan, Edythe Boone, Kim Anno, and John Wehrle. So has Eduardo Pineda, who has begun what may prove to be a major outpouring of community murals in Richmond.

In 1985 a group of artists who had worked on Balmy Alley in San Francisco joined with East Bay artists active in Art Against Apartheid and formed Wallspeak! (originally Oakland Wallspeak!). Over the next four years the group painted five murals in Peralta Village (#EB43-#EB47), a poverty-stricken housing project in west Oakland next to the Cypress Freeway. The murals all celebrate black pride or try to make a connection with conditions in the local housing projects and apartheid in South Africa (although in their effort to paint this observation the artists were constrained by interference from the Oakland Housing Authority, on whose walls the murals were painted). Still, the brightness, hope and generally positive feeling the murals impart to their locations is impressive. Members of Wallspeak! include Edythe Boone, Dewey Crumpler, Kim Anno, Miranda Bergman, Tim Drescher, Roi Brown, Karen Bennett, Sam Shuchat, Nzinga Kianga, Jimi Evins, and Joel (Phresh) Freeman (a spraycan artist who combines graffiti-style with more traditional community murals).

The cutaway interior of a synagogue forms the setting for *Mitzvah: the Jewish Cultural Experience* painted by Keith Sklar, Brooke Fancher and Dan Fontes in Oakland. (EB43)

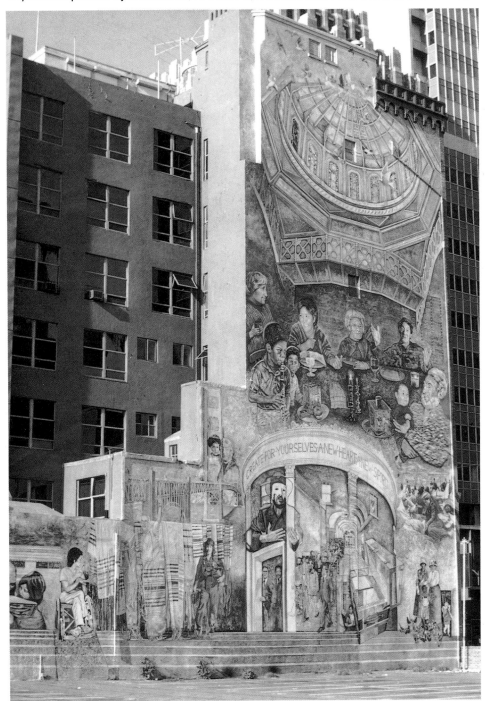

Bay Area Murals
in the Nineties

The nineties are a watershed in the mural movement. Murals are being painted in larger numbers than ever, there are many new faces in the movement, and a wide variety of media and ideas are being used in monumental community-based images, from hip-hop to poetry, to mosaics and ceramic materials and collage. The mural cluster, developed twenty years ago by Michael Rios in the Minipark project, finds its current embodiment in the Clarion Alley Mural Project (CAMP), while Lucky Alley, a block west of Balmy, looms on the horizon as the next alley waiting to be turned into an outdoor community art gallery. By 1994, community murals in San Francisco had established an important tradition of public works. For example, in 1991 the Muros exhibition at Capp Street Project included not only designs for unrealized mural projects, but actual panels from murals that had been taken down, including pieces of Paco's Tacos, *Para el Mercado* (313) and murals from Balmy Alley (1984). Murals from the early period, which in the Bay Area covered roughly 1968 to 1974 (the other two periods are 1974 through the 1980s, and the 1990s), are now viewed nostalgically as icons from an earlier age.

Unfortunately, there is no master plan for the preservation of these stunning works of community expression. Unlike Los Angeles, which has begun a systematic cataloguing of the conservation needs of all its thousand-plus murals, San Francisco is now just beginning to think about the importance of its more than five hundred-plus murals. All effort is going into painting new works, and in that regard the Bay Area is witnessing the greatest explosion of community murals in its history.

New artists with new attitudes toward murals are producing exciting work in addition to the new work by the "veterans." These veterans (artists such as Ray Patlan, Miranda Bergman, Johanna Poethig, Irene Perez, Horace Washington, Susan Kelk Cervantes, Ester Hernandez, Chuy Campusano, and Selma Brown) are all busy and earn enough money and satisfaction through painting murals (and from their day jobs) to keep them involved.

The politics have changed a bit, but monumental public images on community walls continue to articulate community concerns. Also, spray can pieces appear more often and need to be taken into consideration when assessing the area's community art. Bay Area muralists have already produced over 150 murals in the nineties. Although the first edition of this book ended with the murals created in 1991, that year is included again because it is now possible to assess all the murals painted in that year, as well as those produced in 1992, 1993, and some of the productions of 1994. This book remains the only complete guide to San Francisco and East Bay murals, but mural awareness has grown through articles in general magazines such as *Sunset, Travel and Leisure,* San Jose's *Artweek,* and even a feature on television's "Good Morning America."

Perhaps the most controversial mural in recent years was Senay's *Malcolm X* (585). Painted on a wall of the San Francisco State University student center it was attacked at its unveiling on May 19, 1994, the anniversary of Malcolm X's birth. University president Robert Corrigan ordered it painted over because of its anti-Semitic symbols. The overpainting was then washed away by students so the campus authorities had the mural sandblasted from the wall.

NUMBERS TELL (SOME OF) THE STORY

Since 1968, roughly 229 women and 294 men have painted on San Francisco walls. Many have worked on several projects over the years although exact figures are not possible because of uncertainty in the composition of some groups. In the nineties, approximately 87 men and 64 women have had leading roles on local murals, about half the murals were team projects, and half of those teams were multi-racial. Virtually all the teams include both men and women. In the East Bay, twice as many men are painting as women (47 and 23) in the nineties. One conclusion drawn from these statistics is that women have played a major role in designing, organizing, and painting murals. During the 1980s, with the exception of 1984, more women artists painted San Francisco murals than did men. It is to the

In *To Cause to Remember* (492) Johanna Poethig captures the bitter irony of current attitudes towards immigrants, homeless, and disenfranchised people. The Statue of Liberty, whose torch has left her outstretched hand, seems tired, suggesting that traditional notions of liberty may no longer be as respected as they once were.

Time After Time (483) faces a playground where its brightness and abstraction give a flair of visual excitement to the space. Betsie Miller-Kusz's mural is an example of the variety of images being painted in the city.

This Women's Building mural (528) is one of the most talked about murals in years, both because of the spectacular impact of the image, and because of the stunning team of skilled painters involved in the process. The mural celebrates the accomplishments and struggles of women today and throughout history, and proclaims a universal sisterhood.

credit of the mural movement and its motivating principles that its productions reflect so well the make-up of our society.

FUNDING

In the 1980s, funding for San Francisco murals came primarily from MOCD (the Mayor's Office of Community Development), which administers the federal Housing and Urban Development money. In the 1990s, the range of funding sources is much wider. MOCD still plays an important role, but private businesses, corporations, individuals and foundations are all expanding their support of mural projects. This is one result of the mural movement: the funders are aware now of what murals can offer to a community. The projected budget for the Lucky Alley mural project, a block away from Balmy Alley in the Mission District, is between $30,000 and $40,000. By contrast, in 1985 more than two dozen murals were painted in Balmy for a total cost of $2,500. Ray Patlan, who is leading the Lucky Alley project, says raising the money "shouldn't be a problem." This statement indicates the impact murals have made on many parts of our society.

Muralists engaged with their communities still need other sources of income (although Fresco and

Precita Eyes now receive enough funding to enable some members to live on it if they are frugal, and commissions/competitions are sufficient to sustain Oakland's Daniel Galvez). While all muralists have outside sources of income through regular jobs, many find funding support by working with students in schools, with Fran Valesco's Quilt Mural (460) or Johanna Poethig's William DeAvila School project (472) as examples. Mural work must be wedged into lives already occupied by "regular" jobs and families. In a project like the Women's Building (528) where seven artists comprise the painting team, the scheduling complexities are staggering, and the level of sacrifice rises to match the scale of the project. The women paint on Tuesdays, Thursdays, and all day Saturday, much as the dozen painters did on the I.L.W.U. Mural-sculpture (220) in 1986.

Funding in the second period of mural painting, from 1974 through the eighties, depended primarily on federal money, beginning with CETA, the federal Comprehensive Employment and Training Act which paid artists, among others, to teach usable skills to low-income residents, especially youth. In San Francisco, CETA monies supported 101 murals. When CETA was phased out (its last support is listed in 1982), the local Office of Community Development (OCD) stepped in and supported several mural projects every year. OCD, which became the Mayor's Office of Community Development (MOCD) in the eighties, works with federal HUD money which it administers locally. From 1979 to 1994, OCD supported 91 murals. The city's record of unbroken support for murals is unmatched anywhere in the world.

In the nineties, the biggest change in mural support lies in sources other than federal/MOCD: businesses and foundations, especially. In the nineties, over twenty private businesses have already contributed to mural projects, as opposed to only twenty-five for the entire decade of the eighties and twenty-one from 1968–1979. Clearly, businesses are realizing that mural projects can be a healthy part of maintaining a stable community. In the case of the Clarion Alley Mural Project, nearby businesses, owners of property in the Alley and residents all agree that an alley-full of murals will attract visitors and this increased attention to the area will encourage drug dealers/users to go elsewhere.

A similar funding pattern is true of foundations. In 1984, the Zellerbach Foundation contributed $2,000 to PLACA for the Balmy Alley mural project which painted over two dozen murals in a one block long Mission District alley. Three foundations supported mural projects in 1986, five in 1990, seven in 1993, and the number is already at six for 1994. Foundations, too, have seen that mural programs involving communities are worthwhile projects deserving their support.

Municipalities remain an important source of mural funds. In San Francisco, agencies such as the Mural Resource Center and the San Francisco Art Commission continue to support murals, and the recent availability of anti-graffiti funds administered by the Neighborhood Beautification and Graffiti Cleanup Fund (NBAGCF) have played a major role in funding recent murals (twelve since 1991). Significantly, the wider variety of funding sources in this decade has meant that individual projects are funded from several different sources. Whether this means muralists are freer because they are not beholden to a single funder, or whether they are even more constrained because they must not antagonize several funders, is yet a matter of discussion. But the relatively small size of the city and its tradition of support for community artworks does not appear to have greatly constrained the mural images themselves. While the muralists in the eighties had to "satisfy downtown," meaning MOCD, they nevertheless kept their focus on the communities with which or for which they painted. In the Bay Area, neither censorship nor lack of government funding have exerted significant limitations on recent mural work. What changes have occurred are due to shifts in, and lessening of, political activism.

TECHNICAL PROFICIENCY

The technical proficiency of the murals has improved over the almost three decades of the movement's existence. Partly this is due to greater artistic skills on the part of artists who have been painting now for ten to twenty years. Partly it is due to the higher expectations generated by constantly improving projects. Also, artists are now sometimes actually trained to paint murals in art schools such as the California College of Arts and Crafts in Oakland, or through workshops at Precita Eyes Mural Arts Center. In addition, artists have over five hundred local examples to study.

THEMES AND NUMBERS

Mural themes have remained more or less constant over the years. The two main topics have been destruction of communities by "urban renewal" or other gentrifying projects, and declaration of group identity, primarily ethnicity. In the nineties, too, these themes continue, but AIDS as a theme has appeared in three recent works. Ecological/nature themes continue to proliferate at an even greater rate.

Latino-theme murals have been painted at a rate of about half a dozen a year (except for Balmy Alley in 1984, when two dozen Latino themes were painted). The number of African-American images was comparable (from six in 1975 to ten in 1993). But, significantly, the number of murals with multicultural images has always been greater than those identified with a single group (again, with the exception of Balmy Alley). In 1976, eleven multicultural-theme murals were painted. There were six in 1990, ten in 1992, seven in 1993, and eight thus far in 1994. Of course, the actual numbers in this sort of survey will vary depending on individual definitions, but the primary fact remains: the themes of San Francisco's community murals reflect its multiethnic population.

There were three high points of mural painting over the years. First, recall that 1976 was the nation's bicentennial celebration, and unusually large amounts of money were available for communities to spend on art. In the Haight-Ashbury neighborhood, a battle raged for months between a group of merchants which wanted to paint fire hydrants red, white and blue, and another group which supported the painting of community murals. The group preferring murals won, so

In this mural Susan Greene and Meera Desai have captured Reverend Martin Luther King Jr.'s concern for the future and for commitment to moral principle and historical reality. Called *To Ignore Evil is to Become an Accomplice to It* (EB 183) the mural was painted in an underpass under Highway I-580.

Isaias Mata's *500 Years of Resistance* (555) is a spectacular mural wrapped around the corner of a Catholic church in the Mission District. The east wall shows the positive spirit of working people, their demands, and their heroes. Note the children in the lower corner, reminding viewers that the work we do is also for future generations.

three were painted, each receiving one-third of the $10,000 grant.

The next burst of murals came with the Balmy Alley project in 1984, in which all the images either celebrated Latin American cultures or opposed United States intervention in Latin America. The final highpoint in mural production occurred in 1993 with the *Clarion Alley Mural Project.* Twenty murals were painted in that year and another twenty are planned for 1994.

In the East Bay, the pattern is basically the same, but the numbers are smaller.

Let us take a quick glance at some of the most productive muralist groups over the past three years.

PRECITA EYES MURAL ARTS CENTER

The most prolific group of muralists over the past three years has centered around the Precita Eyes Mural Arts Center, located facing Precita Park on the northern slopes of Bernal Heights. Precita Eyes is led by Susan Kelk Cervantes. In addition to sponsoring mural workshops for participants of all ages, that workshop schedules regular lectures about all aspects of mural painting, and has developed Mural Awareness Week, held yearly in late spring to honor local muralists and help call attention to the beauty and variety of the city's community murals.

Part of the program at the workshop is called Precita Eyes Youth Artists or PEYA, which has forged a strong bridge between spray can artists and more traditional mural approaches. The integration seems to be working well.

Another of its contributions is the guided tours of Mission District murals (near the workshop's location) offered every Saturday, and on other days by special arrangement. These tours begin with a brief slide show on mural history and then visitors take a walking tour of several of the most exciting mural sites in the area, including Balmy Alley. Details and reservations are available by telephoning the workshop.

FRESCO

Taking a different approach, one of the leading muralists of the first generation of painters, Ray Patlan, has joined with muralist Eduardo Pineda to form "Fresco," a private partnership. Fresco provides consultation, slide shows, and most importantly, the painting of murals by the two professional community muralists. It is funded by businesses, MOCD, and foundations, allowing it the freedom to pursue its own

The giant tree in Susan Kelk Cervantes' *Keep Our Ancient Roots Alive* (579) soars above a school playground. Climbing the tree and behind it are students of various ethnic backgrounds. Framed by borders of masks, these motifs illustrate how the school helps students treasure their traditions while living and working productively together.

vision. Even though it is a professional endeavor, Fresco's orientation remains rooted in working with members of different social communities. In the past two years Fresco has completed over a dozen mural projects, ranging from large outdoor walls in Oakland, to relatively small portable murals for indoor locations.

CLARION ALLEY MURAL PROJECT

Of all the recent mural activity, the *Clarion Alley Mural Project* (CAMP) is among the most exciting. Inspired by the Balmy Alley project of the mid 1980s (itself inspired by Michael Rios' *Minipark* project of the mid 1970s), Clarion Alley was planned in October 1992 to take two years with twenty murals painted each year. CAMP is exciting for a number of reasons. Its concept

A good example of the work by Fresco artists Ray Patlan and Eduardo Pineda is *Universal Learning* (501). The diversity of people who see the mural as well as the many cultures represented by students at Marshall elementary school are stressed.

and execution are guided by a group of "new" artists, people who did not participate in the earlier periods of the mural movement, even though they were inspired by it. CAMP's original intention was that the work would be a "free field," but executed by people closely connected with either the North Mission area or the alley itself.

Funding comes from foundations, private donations, local businesses, and the city, but the group retains complete autonomy within the project. No problem is anticipated with Art Commission approval of any design, and if there were, it is likely the money would be refused rather than allowing funders to censor the artists. As one walks through the alley itself (somewhat warily because of the neighborhood) the variety of the artwork constantly surprises. If a piece is not to your liking, walk on a few paces and see what's next. CAMP includes spray can art as well as cartoon pieces mounted on large panels, traditional murals (Fresco and Precita Eyes have pieces in the alley), and even collages and poems. In 1992–93, CAMP had a "poetry curator" to help select the poems mounted in the alley. There is talk of continuing the project for another year or two and of painting portraits of local residents and denizens on the several doors into the alley.

CAMP counters the misinformed opinion that "murals aren't political anymore." They certainly are, perhaps especially when the focus is on members of the immediate community. CAMP incorporates much of what gave the community mural movement its strength for the first quarter century of its existence:

the participants are ethnically and sexually mixed, the content is spontaneous and relevant to the visions and concerns of the people who live with the images on a daily basis, and it is supported financially by those same people. The variety of images, participants, and styles (from felt-tipped pen to spray can to paint and brush) is inclusive, not exclusive. CAMP speaks to the idea that we all now live in a multicultural world, a postmodern world where "everything is everywhere, all the time." CAMP exemplifies this reality by welcoming the diversity. Earlier mural cluster projects such as Balmy Alley, the Minipark, *La Lucha Continua* on New York's Lower East Side, or Chicano Park in San Diego had more focused themes which were appropriate to those times (and, sadly, still appropriate today). CAMP takes for granted much of what earlier muralists fought to legitimize, and moves on from there.

GRAFFITI/SPRAY CAN ART

Certainly a word is in order about graffiti/spray can art. Kids and lovers have carved their initials on trees or written them on walls seemingly forever, but today, such gestures of self declaration are more numerous than ever before, made possible by easy-to-handle, quick-to-dry, adhere-to-any-surface, spray can enamel paints. Its ubiquity demands attention, which, in the case of tags, is the whole point.

According to Martha Cooper and Henry Chalfant in *Subway Art* (New York, 1984), there are three types of spray can work. The simplest is the tag. Tags are

Is this escalator a way out of the deteriorated environment of Clarion Alley? Or is it a route into the alley from "up above"? Julie Murray's untitled mural (518) only suggests, but does not answer, these questions.

drawn with spray paint, felt-tip pens, magic markers, or pencils—anything which can quickly declare a writer's initials, "placa," or nickname. With tagging, the goal is to "get up" in as many places as possible, including walls, signs, busses, subway trains, mail boxes—any place to get your tag noticed. The Spanish word for tag, "placa," was the name used by the group that painted Balmy Alley, although in the original version only one piece was painted with spray enamel. Today, several Balmy Alley murals are spray can pieces. Nearly everyone finds tags unsightly, but to poor youths who see no other way of establishing a presence in their world, it passes for self expression, or at least a declaration of existence.

A name in large, quickly written letters done in one color with a single outline is known as a "throw-up." Large, multicolored, calligraphic tags, intricately lettered, and deliberately difficult (or impossible) to read, are known as "wild style." Many New York subway trains in the 1970s were covered with wild style spray can names.

The most aesthetically complex spray can works are "masterpieces" or simply, "pieces." They are often done with permission, since they require more time and space than other forms. Every city has locations which are at least tacitly permission spaces. Writers (all spray can/graffiti artists are known as writers) con-

gregate there to share ideas, and put up new works. In San Francisco, Silver Terrace Playground off Silver Avenue, and Psycho City, a series of interlocking parking lots on the south side of Market Street at Franklin, are major locations for spray can writers.

The artistic source for much spray can art is the comic book, in both style and content. The example of such spray can artists as Keith Haring and Jean-Michel Basquiat, who successfully moved their spray can work from subways to art galleries and museum exhibitions, is undeniable. Museums have continued to host shows of graffiti art, sometimes commissioning a site-specific example as San Jose's Museum of Art did when it sponsored a painting called "Fascinating Slippers" done by Los Angeles artist Gronk in 1992. In San Francisco, Brett Cook-Dizney, Twist, Reminisce, Estria, TWS, Neon, Krash, Benz, Nate, Omen, EFX, and Dug all gained tangible artistic reputation through their spray can work. Each is an accomplished artist, and some of them continue to execute "non-permission works," as Cook-Dizney calls them.

Anti-graffiti campaigns, whether initiated privately by irate property owners or sponsored officially by municipalities, often enlist racist stereotypes and become civic excuses for harassing or sometimes beating up youths who have been caught with spraycans. Graffiti, especially tags, are surely attacks on either

Rigo's mural is the third to grace this fence in Balmy Alley. Called *Colors* (546) its title refers to both the variety of racial groups in the neighborhood and to the way in which spray can artists bring color to otherwise blighted areas.

Twist's unmistakable figures elicit smiles whenever you run into them throughout the city. This untitled work (508) can be seen in Clarion Alley.

public or private property. This lack of discrimination seems to lessen any subversive effect the graffiti might have, although that is probably irrelevant to the ego-motivation of the taggers. But official outcries against spray can-using youths appear just as self-serving and hypocritical when the same voices are not raised against, for example, urban renewal programs which obliterate entire neighborhoods. The "solution" to graffiti is clear enough—build a society in which even poor youths can see hope for a decent future and a life with dignity instead of degradation, so that the writers might choose other venues than busses and walls. Unless this occurs, rampant tagging will continue. As a lifestyle and as a commentary on the decay of civic (but not of individual) spirit in our cities, spray can art will continue until youths recognize another outlet for their self-expression.

In the spring of 1994, a young tagger was caught in the act of writing in the Richmond District and charged with committing over $5,000 worth of damage. If convicted, he faces possibly years in jail and, when released, hundreds of hours of "community ser-

vice" erasing tags. Significantly, newspaper and TV stories identified him as a "muralist."

"TEMPORARY" WALLS

In the first decades of community murals, construction fence paintings were sometimes sponsored by contractors who wanted something more visually palatable on the fences surrounding construction sites than handbills and graffiti tags. In the past few years, construction fence murals have become part of the planning of large projects. Competitions are held and images are planned long before the fences actually are erected. The fences are often painted by classes of school children. These murals often remain in place for two or three years, sometimes longer. Then the fence murals are returned to the muralists or taken to previously selected locations for permanent installation. In San Francisco, recent construction projects included Yerba Buena Gardens (490), and the Muni turnaround at Mission and the Embarcadero (489). In Oakland, similar fences currently surround buildings

Spray painted on a fence surrounding an empty lot is Brett Cook-Dizney's 1993 mural, *Confused, Frustrated, Vandalized, Misguided, Active, Poor, Need Love, Gato, Desolate* (493). The people portrayed live, often homeless, in the immediate area, and the words are what they feel about their lives. The mural provides a public respect rarely given to those depicted.

damaged by the earthquake of 1989, and construction sites near City Hall. City-block length fences with works by several artists thus become temporary street galleries of community-inspired mural art. In any city these days, if you have an interest in murals, take a glance at large-scale construction projects.

EAST BAY MURALS

Several East Bay projects have already been mentioned, but it is important to note that there, too, community murals are undergoing a renaissance in the nineties. Numerically, the most murals painted in any previous year was eighteen in 1978. In 1992 and 1993 eighteen and seventeen murals were painted. Reasons include the rising popularity of community murals as a form of expression (perhaps particularly in a depressed economic period), a prolific and increasingly serious group of young spray can artists, and the support of two government funded sources, the Public Art Program of the Division of Cultural Afffairs of the

City of Oakland, and the East Bay Conservation Corps' Project YES (Youth Engaged in Service).

Project YES painted five murals in tribute to Reverend Martin Luther King, Jr. during the summer of 1992. The painting teams were each directed by an experienced muralist, and consisted of students from five local middle and junior high schools. Project YES has also sponsored several other projects, each involving students as painters. The Cultural Affairs murals are more formally produced, but nevertheless are always placed in locations beneficial to the general Oakland community. This demonstrates admirable support and enlightened understanding of the potential role mural projects can play in building and maintaining a strong sense of civic pride.

A further indication of Oakland's concern for its public spaces and communities is a major competition held to select muralists to paint three murals inside Oakland City Hall, which has been extensively renovated after serious damage in the 1989 Loma Prieta earthquake.

Seyed Alavi worked with high school students for months in designing four murals to be located at I-580 underpasses in Oakland. The task was to have the students articulate what was most important to them and then to reduce the ideas into words. *eRacism* (EB 186), created with outdoor paint and glass highway beads, is one of the powerful results of this process.

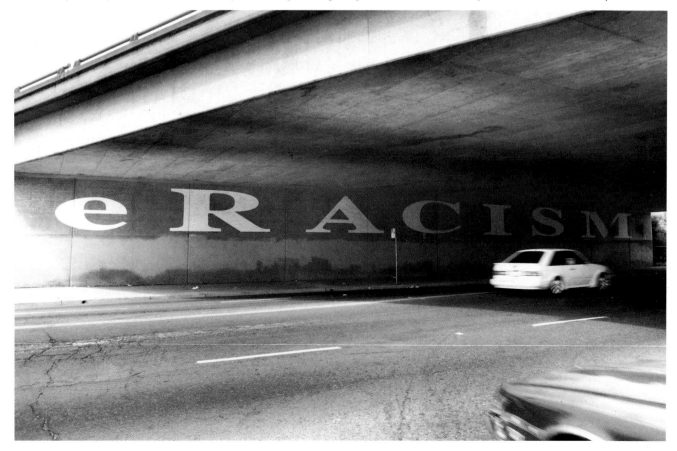

Phresh, Krash, Poem, Vogue, Dream, WIM, and Raevyn are examples of an increasingly sophisticated group of spray can artists working primarily in the East Bay. Each has also begun receiving formal commissions.

In Berkeley, while the City has not been sponsoring mural work, the People's Park area (see EB 192) has continued to be the location of ongoing, non-permission mural work. Murals were painted on the public bathrooms almost as soon as the walls were up. What these works lack in trained artistic skills, they offer in vitality. As spontaneous projects, they have also remained untouched by spray can tags for over two years.

OUT OF TOWN WORK

Local mural production would be even higher if several muralists had not been busy painting major projects in other locations. Sometimes this is because of funding inducements, but sometimes it is because an opportunity arises to paint in a particularly interesting location. Susan Kelk Cervantes, for example, painted a large project in St. Petersburg, Russia, in 1989, and expects to paint in the former Czechoslovakia in the summer of 1994. Foreign projects are painted in collaboration with local artists, and they, in turn, paint with Precita Eyes when they come to San Francisco. Thus do community murals continue to be painted by a widening community of artists.

The value of "expatriate" projects accrues both to the city where the murals are painted and to the Bay Area. Visiting muralists talk with other muralists, see other works, toss around new ideas about art, society, materials and techniques. In this postmodern world, murals and their ideas are everywhere in a continuing cross-fertilization. A 1991 mural in Belfast, Northern Ireland, for example, was based on an International Women's Day poster which featured a detail from Jane Norling's *Sistersongs of Liberation* (236), a mural originally painted in Berkeley in 1975, but later relocated to San Francisco.

Fresco has accepted commissions in the wine country north of San Francisco at the Gundlach Bundschu Winery, where they painted a history of wine industry fieldworkers. The four women of the *Break the Silence Mural Project* (296) have painted on the West Bank of Israel/Palestine as well as in San Francisco, articulating a theme that everyone deserves a homeland, a place to put down roots. Johanna Poethig won a major competition and last year painted a spectacular mural on Main Street in Los Angeles. This project was administered by the Social and Public Art Resource Center in Venice, and was one of a dozen murals painted in Los Angeles under its auspices. And Oakland's Daniel Galvez has spent considerable time in the past few years painting murals in Massachusetts, New York and Santa Monica.

List of San Francisco Murals

If a visitor is pressed for time, the most murals can be seen in the briefest period by walking from 24th and Mission Streets (a BART stop) down 24th Street to York, then turning to go up and down Balmy Alley, next stopping at the Galeria de la Raza/Studio 24 at Bryant Street, and then visiting the Minipark just past Bryant Street.

Longer tours will find an automobile useful. The murals are listed in a reasonable order for driving tours.

The Mural Resource Center at 934 Brannan Street has a lot of information on the murals, and coordinates most of the mural painting in the City. Precita Eyes Mural Workshop offers information, workshops, and tours (285–2287). The Galeria de la Raza/Studio 24 has information, and is located in the heart of the Mission District murals (826–8009). All these resources have up-to-date information on current mural projects.

> The information for each mural is presented in the following order:
> Title [unofficial titles in brackets]. An asterisk indicates that the mural no longer exists.
> Date completed
> Funding source
> Location
> Size, medium and wall type [height precedes width. Sizes are often approximations]
> Artist(s)

FORT MASON

1 *SAN FRANCISCO CHINATOWN 1890, 1976 (destroyed 1987)
CETA; NAP; National Park Service
Pier 2, Fort Mason
10' x 35', Politec acrylic on concrete
Judy Helsing

2 *SAN FRANCISCO'S GOLDEN GATE 1890, 1976 (destroyed 1987)
CETA; NAP; National Park Service
Pier 2, Fort Mason
10' x 35', Politec acrylic on concrete
Angela Berlingeri

3 *SUMMER REFLECTIONS, 1976 (destroyed 1987)
CETA; NAP; National Park Service
Pier 2, Fort Mason
10' x 35', Politec acrylic on concrete
Vincent Droney

4 *SAN FRANCISCO SKYLINE, 1976 (destroyed 1987)
CETA; NAP; National Park Service
Pier 2, Fort Mason
10' x 35', Politec acrylic on concrete
Richard Brown

5 *SAN FRANCISCO ORIGINAL LANDSCAPE, 1976 (destroyed 1987)
CETA; NAP; National Park Service
Pier 2, Fort Mason
10' x 35', Politec acrylic on concrete
Hilaire Dufresne

6 *SAN FRANCISCO MISSION DOLORES, 1976 (destroyed 1987)
CETA; NAP; National Park Service
Pier 2, Fort Mason
10' x 35', Politec acrylic on concrete
Adolfo Castillo

7 *1906 EARTHQUAKE, 1976 (destroyed 1987)
CETA; NAP; National Park Service
Pier 2, Fort Mason
10' x 35', Politec acrylic on concrete
Eileen Nelson

8 *BATTLE OF GOLDEN GATE, 1976 (destroyed 1987)
CETA; NAP; National Park Service
Pier 2, Fort Mason
10' x 35', Politec acrylic on concrete
John deLorimer

9 *CULTURAL PATTERN, 1976 (destroyed 1987)
CETA; NAP; National Park Service
Pier 2, Fort Mason
10' x 35', Politec acrylic on concrete
Diana Losch

10 *FLOATING CITY/BAY AREA WILDERNESS, 1976 (destroyed 1987)
CETA; NAP; National Park Service
Pier 2, Fort Mason
10' x 35', Politec acrylic on concrete
Lawrence Johnson

11 *SAN FRANCISCO RISING, 1976 (destroyed 1987)
CETA; NAP; National Park Service
Pier 2, Fort Mason
10' x 35', Politec acrylic on concrete
Louie LaBrie

12 *CALIFORNIA NATIVE AMERICANS, 1976
    (destroyed 1987)
    CETA; NAP; National Park Service
    Pier 2, Fort Mason
    10' x 35', Politec acrylic on concrete
    Pamela Maxwell

13 *BRIDGES, 1976 (destroyed 1987)
    CETA; NAP; National Park Service
    Pier 2, Fort Mason
    10' x 35', Politec acrylic on concrete
    Jack Frost

14 TEOTIHUACAN MURAL PROJECT, 1986
    Citicorp; M. H. de Young Museum
    Mexican Museum, Building D, Fort Mason
    8' x 16', Fresco
    Chuy Campusano with Stephen Dimitroff and Lucienne
        Bloch

15 POSITIVELY FOURTH STREET, 1976
    CETA; M. H. de Young Museum
    Pier 3, Fort Mason
    16' x 60', Oil on masonite
    John Wehrle and John Rampley

16 SEA FORMS, 1939
    WPA
    National Maritime Museum (promenade deck),
    Polk Street at Aquatic Park
    14' x 125', Commercial glazed tile
    Sargent Johnson

17 UNDERSEA LIFE, 1939
    WPA
    National Maritime Museum (main hall),
    Polk Street at Aquatic Park
    10' x 100', Oil on canvas
    Hilaire Hiler

18 PSYCHOLOGICAL COLOR CHART & DR. OSTWALD'S
        COLOR SOLID, 1940
    WPA
    National Maritime Museum (ceiling),
    Polk Street at Aquatic Park
    50' diameter, Oil on plaster
    Hilaire Hiler with Richard Ayer, Thomas Dowley,
        Lawrence Holmberg, and Sargent Johnson

19 [SOUTHWEST SCENE], 1940
    WPA
    National Maritime Museum (women's bathroom),
    Polk Street at Aquatic Park
    6' x 32', Oil on canvas
    Charles Nunnamaker

20 THE MAKING OF A FRESCO SHOWING THE BUILDING
        OF A CITY, 1931
    William Gerstle
    San Francisco Art Institute (gallery north wall),
    800 Chestnut Street
    18' x 32', Fresco
    Diego Rivera

21 ARTS OF MAN, 1936
    Albert Bender
    San Francisco Art Institute library,
    (north wall on east side), 800 Chestnut Street
    30" x 68", Fresco
    Fred Olmsted, Jr.

22 ARTS OF MAN, 1936
    Albert Bender
    San Francisco Art Institute library,
    (north wall on west side), 800 Chestnut Street
    30" x 68", Fresco
    Gordon Langdon

23 PRIMITIVE AND WESTERN ART, 1936
    Albert Bender
    San Francisco Art Institute library,
    (east and west walls), 800 Chestnut Street
    Two panels, 30" x 68" each, Fresco
    Ray Boynton

24 ART AND FREEDOM (THE MAN CHAINED, THE
        CREATIVE ACT, and MAN FREED), 1936
    Albert Bender
    San Francisco Art Institute library,
    (center of south wall), 800 Chestnut Street
    Three panels, 30" x 68" each, Fresco
    Victor Arnautoff

25 ARCHITECTURE AND SCULPTURE, 1936
    Albert Bender
    San Francisco Art Institute library,
    (east side of south wall), 800 Chestnut Street
    Two panels, 30" x 68", Fresco
    Ralph Stackpole

26 TWO ALLEGORICAL FIGURES, 1936
    Albert Bender
    San Francisco Art Institute library,
    (west side of south wall), 800 Chestnut Street
    Two panels, 30" x 68" each, Fresco
    William Hesthal

NORTH BEACH

27 [SEA LION SCENE], 1981
    NAP
    North Beach Housing Project,
    600 Francisco Street at Taylor
    Approx. 35' x 28', Politec acrylic on concrete
    Kym Sites

28 [LAKE WITH PYRAMID], 1977
    CETA
    North Beach Housing Project,
    590 Francisco Street at Taylor
    12' x 30', Politec acrylic on concrete
    Horace Washington

29 [YIN YANG MAN AND WOMAN], 1976
    CETA
    North Beach Housing Project,
    120 Columbus Avenue at Francisco
    35' x 15', Politec acrylic on concrete
    Carol Nast, Percy Chester, Paula Remkiewicz, and
        tenants

30 *UNTITLED, 1976
    North Beach Project
    North Beach Housing Project,
    Francisco Street between Columbus and Taylor
    Approx. 12' x 25', Politec acrylic on concrete
    Jackie Ortez

31 [FISH SWIMMING], 1986
OCD
North Beach Swimming Pool,
Lombard Street near Mason
16' x 135', Politec acrylic, Roy Anderson latex,
Triangle varnish on cement and wood on concrete
Fran Valesco

32 *TELEGRAPH HILL NEIGHBORHOOD CLINIC, 1975
NEA
Apartment, 550 Lombard Street
10' x 100', Politec acrylic and sealer on wood
Karen Ezekiel and Lee Hastings

33 THE RIGHT OF EDUCATION/THE SEED OF FREEDOM,
1987
OCD
Francisco Middle School,
Stockton and Francisco Streets
20' x 80', Politec acrylic on concrete
Arch Williams with Jose Antonio Ochoa, Anthony Senna,
Jo Tucker, Selma Brown, and Leo Frances Stevens

COIT TOWER, TELEGRAPH HILL

(First floor murals were restored in 1990.)

34 ANIMAL FORCE AND MACHINE FORCE, 1934
PWAP
Coit Tower (inner north wall)
10' x 36', Fresco
Ray Boynton

35 CALIFORNIA INDUSTRIAL SCENES, 1934
PWAP
Coit Tower (outer north wall)
10' x 24', Fresco
John Langley Howard

36 RAILROAD AND SHIPPING, 1934
PWAP
Coit Tower (outer west wall)
10' x 10', Fresco
William Hesthal

37 SURVEYOR AND STEELWORKER, 1934
PWAP
Coit Tower (outer west wall)
Two panels, 10' x 4' each, Fresco
Clifford Wight

38 INDUSTRIES OF CALIFORNIA, 1934
PWAP
Coit Tower (inner west wall)
10' x 36', Fresco
Ralph Stackpole

39 NEWSGATHERING, 1934
PWAP
Coit Tower (outer west wall)
10' x 10', Fresco
Suzanne Scheuer

40 LIBRARY, 1934
PWAP
Coit Tower (outer south wall)
10' x 10', Fresco
Bernard Baruch Zakheim

41 STOCKBROKER AND SCIENTIST-INVENTOR, 1934
PWAP
Coit Tower (outer south wall)
Two panels, 10' x 4' each, Fresco
Mallette Dean

42 CITY LIFE, 1934
PWAP
Coit Tower (inner south wall)
10' x 36', Fresco
Victor Arnautoff

43 BANKING AND LAW, 1934
PWAP
Coit Tower (outer south wall)
10' x 10', Fresco
George Harris

44 DEPARTMENT STORE, 1934
PWAP
Coit Tower (outer east wall)
10' x 10', Fresco
Frede Vidar

45 FARMER AND COWBOY, 1934
PWAP
Coit Tower (outer east wall)
Two panels, 10' x 4' each, Fresco
Clifford Wight

46 CALIFORNIA, 1934
PWAP
Coit Tower (inner east wall)
10' x 42', Fresco
Maxine Albro

47 MEAT INDUSTRY, 1934
PWAP
Coit Tower (outer east wall)
10' x 10', Fresco
Ray Bertrand

48 CALIFORNIA AGRICULTURAL INDUSTRY, 1934
PWAP
Coit Tower (outer north wall)
10' x 27', Fresco
Gordon Langdon

49 SAN FRANCISCO BAY, 1934
PWAP
Coit Tower (elevator lobby, north wall)
9' x 54", Oil on canvas in lunette
Otis Oldfield

50 SAN FRANCISCO BAY, NORTH, 1934
PWAP
Coit Tower (elevator lobby, north wall)
9' x 54", Oil on canvas in lunette
Jose Moya del Pino

51 BAY AREA HILLS, 1934
PWAP
Coit Tower
(elevator lobby, east and west walls)
Two panels, 9' x 54", Oil on canvas in lunettes
Rinaldo Cuneo

52 SEABIRDS and BAY AREA MAP, 1934
PWAP
Coit Tower (elevator lobby, south wall)
Three semicircular panels, approx. 2' x 4',
Oil on canvas in lunettes
Otis Oldfield

53 POWER, 1934
PWAP
Coit Tower (outer north wall)
3' x 3', Fresco
Fred Olmsted, Jr.

54 POWELL STREET, 1934
PWAP
Coit Tower (stairway to second floor)
Two panels, 6′ x 32′ each, Fresco
Lucien Labaudt

55 COLLEGIATE SPORTS, 1934
PWAP
Coit Tower
(second floor, by staircase)
9′ x 13′, Fresco
Parker Hall

56 SPORTS, 1934
PWAP
Coit Tower
(second floor, by staircase)
9′ x 10′, Fresco
Edward Terada

57 CHILDREN AT PLAY, 1934
PWAP
Coit Tower
(second floor, by staircase)
9′ x 6′, Fresco
Ralph Chesse

58 HUNTING IN CALIFORNIA, 1934
PWAP
Coit Tower
(second floor, elevator wall)
9′ x 12′, Fresco
Edith Hamlin

59 OUTDOOR LIFE, 1934
PWAP
Coit Tower
(second floor, outer wall)
9′ x 22′, Fresco
Ben F. Cunningham

60 HOME LIFE, 1934
PWAP
Coit Tower
(second floor, south alcove)
9′ x 34′, Egg tempera
Jane Berlandina

CHINATOWN

61 BRIDGE OF LOVE, 1988
OCD
On Lok House Senior Citizens' Center
Powell Street near Broadway
18′ x 60′, Novacolor acrylic on concrete
Miranda Bergman

62 THE SEEDS WE PLANT NOW WILL GIVE OUR
CHILDREN SHADE, 1990
OCD; On Lok House
On Lok House Senior Citizens' Center,
Powell near Broadway
10′-2′ x 108′, Acrylic on wood
Miranda Bergman

63 PING YUEN TAI CHI, 1982
OCD
Ping Yuen Housing Project,
795 Pacific Street at Stockton
20′ x 160′, Politec acrylic on concrete
Josie Grant

64 [BOK SEN AND IMMORTALS, THREE WISDOMS, AND
CHINESE ZODIAC], 1979
OCD; NIIP
Ping Yuen Housing Project,
895 Pacific Street at Trenton Alley
Five walls totalling 20′ x 160′, Acrylic on concrete
Josie Grant

65 FISH STRUGGLING UPSTREAM, 1983
MRC; OCD
Ping Yuen Housing Project,
895 Pacific Street at Trenton Alley
35′ x 30′, Various media on asphalt playground
James Dong

66 [CHINESE IN SAN FRANCISCO], 1987
OCD
Building, 950 Washington Street
between Stockton Street and Stone
50′ x 25′, Acrylic on stucco
K. S. Chan

67 HISTORY OF COMMODORE STOCKTON SCHOOL,
1974
Alvarado School Art Workshop
Commodore Stockton School, 950 Clay Street
Approx. 25′ x 70′, Housepaint on concrete
James Dong and the Kearny Street Workshop

68 UNTITLED, 1986
OCD
Wall, Spofford Alley between Washington Street and Clay
8′ x 29′, Liquitex acrylic on masonite
Gail Aratani

69 UNTITLED, 1986
OCD
Chinese Playground wall,
Sacramento Street between Stockton and Waverly
35′ x 45′, Politec acrylic, Liquitex acrylic,
and housepaint on concrete over brick
James Dong

70 [CHINESE-AMERICAN HISTORY], 1988
OCD
YMCA Playground,
855 Sacramento Street at Waverly Alley
8′ x 48′, Pictor acrylic on cement
Victor Fan

71 [PHOENIX], 1988
Private funding
Store wall at Walter U. Lam Place and Clay Street,
Portsmouth Square
12′ x 20′, Acrylic on stucco
K. S. Chan

72 [DRAGON], 1988
Private funding
Store (side wall), Clay and Grant Streets
10′ x 20′, Acrylic on stucco
K. S. Chan

73 *I-HOTEL MURAL, 1975
CETA; NAP
International Hotel, Jackson near Kearny Streets
8′ x 65′, Acrylic on concrete, brick, and wood
James Dong and the Kearny Street Workshop

Marina Green

Fort Mason

Aquatic Park

Fisherman's Wharf

Pier 39

The Embarcadero

Ghirardelli Square

Coit Tower

Washington Square

Grace Cathedral

Union Square

Jefferson Square

Golden Gate Park Panhandle

Duboce Park

Civic Center

Marina Blvd

Richardson Ave

Cervantes Blvd

Jefferson St
Beach St
North Point St
Bay St
Francisco St
Chestnut St
Lombard St
Greenwich St
Filbert St
Union St
Green St
Vallejo St
Broadway
Pacific Ave
Jackson St
Washington St
Clay St
Sacramento St
California St
Pine St
Bush St
Sutter St
Post St
Expressway
Olive
O'Farrell St
Ellis St
Eddy St
Turk St
Golden Gate Ave
McAllister St
Hayes

Jefferson St
Beach St
North Point St

Columbus Ave

Polk St
Octavia St
Laguna St
Franklin St
Gough St
Webster St
Buchanan St
Fillmore St
Steiner St
Pierce St
Scott St
Divisadero St
Broderick St
Baker St
Lyon St
Presidio Ave
Baker St
Lyon St

Hyde St
Leavenworth St
Jones St
Taylor St
Mason St
Powell St
Stockton St
Grant Ave
Kearny St
Montgomery St
Sansome St
Battery St
Front St
Davis St
Drumm St

Van Ness Ave
Polk St
Larkin St
Market St
Powell

Embarcadero

Montgomery

Vega Nido
Anza Vista
Golden Gate Ave
McAllister St
Fulton St
Grove St
Hayes St
Masonic Ave
Central Ave

Divisadero St
Broderick St
Steiner St
Scott St
Pierce St
Fillmore St
Webster St
Buchanan St
Laguna St
Grove St
Page St
Haight St
Waller St
Fell St
Oak St

Fourteenth St
Henry St
Fifteenth St
Beaver St

Hermann St
Duboce Ave
Church St

Map by Eurydice Thomas

Richardson Ave

101

Hollis
Willow

73

PACIFIC OCEAN

Golden Gate Bridge

Bay Bridge

GOLDEN GATE PARK

Lake Merced

101

101

446   NORTH BEACH SCENES, 1988
      Private funding
      Apartment building
      Broadway and Columbus Streets
      Facade of two story building, Kelly-Moore exterior
         housepaint on masonry blocks
      Bill Weber with Tony Klaas

FINANCIAL DISTRICT

74   [FIVE MAPS], 1939
     Golden Gate International Exposition
     World Trade Center,
     Ferry Building (entrance ramp), Market Street
     Various dimensions, Lacquer on wood
     Miguel Covarrubias

75   *MAP, 1962
     Funding unknown
     Ferry Building, Market Street
     5' x 10', Glass mosaic
     Edith Hamlin

76   *[SAN FRANCISCO HISTORY], 1965
     Private funding
     Fidelity Savings and Loan Association,
     260 California Street
     Three panels, Fresco
     Lucienne Bloch and Stephen Dimitroff

77   TRADERS OF THE ADRIATIC, 1922
     Federal Reserve Bank
     Kaplan, McLaughlin, Diaz Company (lobby),
     301 Battery Street at Sacramento
     9' x 40', Oil on canvas
     James Guerin

78   [SAN FRANCISCO SCENES], 1967
     Private funding
     Bank of California, 400 California Street (2nd floor)
     Three panels, 15' wide, Acrylic on canvas
     Don Kingman

79   ALLEGORY OF CALIFORNIA, 1931
     Private funding
     Pacific Stock Exchange Club,
     (stairway and ceiling outside dining room),
     155 Sansome Street near Pine
     142.5 square feet, Fresco
     Diego Rivera

80   [BEACH SCENE], 1984
     Private funding
     Galleria Park Hotel roof,
     Sutter and Kearny Streets
     15' x 20', Acrylic on roof
     Dick Fossleman and Karen Lusebrink

UNION SQUARE

81   LANDSCAPE, 1923
     Spring Valley Water Company
     San Francisco Water Department (north wall),
     425 Mason Street
     8' x 16', Oil on canvas
     Maynard Dixon

82   [WOMEN ROLE MODELS], 1979
     CETA; YWCA
     YWCA Downtown, 620 Sutter Street near Mason
     8' diameter, Politec acrylic on plywood
     Fran Valesco

NOB HILL

83   CALIFORNIA HISTORY AND LEGENDS, 1926
     Private funding
     Mark Hopkins Hotel, Room of the Dons
     999 California Street
     Four panels, 7' x 21',
     One panel, 12' x 7', Oil on canvas
     Maynard Dixon, Frank von Sloun

84   [CHURCH HISTORY], 1949
     Private funding
     Grace Cathedral (north and south interior walls),
     1051 Taylor Street between Sacramento and California
     9' x 105', Wax emulsion on plaster
     Jan Henryk De Rosen

85   ADORATION OF THE VIRGIN, 1946
     Mrs. James L. Flood
     Grace Cathedral (Nativity Chapel),
     1051 Taylor Street between Sacramento and California
     20' x 10', Wax and oil emulsion fresco
     Jan Henryk De Rosen

TENDERLOIN

86   [UNTITLED], 1989
     Parks and Recreation Department; SFAC
     Father Boedekker Park, Jones and Eddy Streets
     11' x 40' free form, Ceramic tiles painted with glazes
     Johanna Poethig and children of the area

87   FLYING DOGS BREATHING FIRE, 1990
     LEF Foundation
     Father Boedekker Park, Jones and Eddy Streets
     15' x 20', Acrylic, tile and wood on plaster
     Johanna Poethig

88   REFLECTIONS OF CULINARY WORKERS' STRUGGLE,
         1988
     Carpenters' Local 22; Local 2 H.E.R.E.
     Leavenworth at Golden Gate Avenue
     12'-1' x 117', Acrylic on concrete
     Ted Abraham, Kim Anno, and Marion Kendrick

89   [THE EARTH], 1979
     Private funding
     Central City Hospitality House (Art Department),
     146 Leavenworth Street
     5' x 8', Liquitex acrylic and oil on concrete
     Mike Mosher, Fell Williams, Claire Davidson, James
        "Spider" Taylor, and the Hospitality House Arts &
        Crafts Program

90   [TROMPE L'OEIL IONIC COLUMNS BEHIND
         DEMOLISHED BRICK WALLS], 1983
     OCD
     Building, Turk and Hyde Streets
     35' x 70', Unknown paint on brick
     John Russell Wullbrandt

POLK GULCH

91   [UNDERWATER SCENE], 1979 (south side restored
     and altered 1990)
     Mitchell Brothers Film Group
     Mitchell Brothers Theater,
     895 O'Farrell Street
     8,000 square feet, Acrylic on concrete
     Gary Graham, Ed Monroe, Todd Stanton, and Lou Silva

92 [FOREST SCENE], 1990
Mitchell Brothers Film Group
Mitchell Brothers Theater,
O'Farrell and Polk
20'-40' x 120', Acrylic on stucco
Lou Silva

93 STRONG ROOTS, HEALTHY TREE, 1989
Private funding; OCD
Center for Southeast Asian Refugee Resettlement,
Olive Alley at Polk Street
40' x 60', Acrylic on stucco
Johanna Poethig

94 TACTILE MURAL, 1976
CETA
Rose Resnick Center for the Blind,
1299 Bush Street
15' x 22', Fabric on plaster
Cynthia Grace

95 [TROPICAL BEASTS], 1977
Private funding
Redding Elementary School,
1421 Pine Street near Larkin
10' x 200', Politec acrylic on concrete
Karen Ezekiel, SFAI students, and elementary school
children

96 [OUTER SPACE AND ASTRONAUTS], 1978
Private funding
Redding Elementary School,
1421 Pine Street near Larkin
30' x 150', Politec acrylic
and sealer on concrete
Karen Ezekiel, SFAI students, and elementary school
children

CIVIC CENTER

97 PIONEERS LEAVING THE EAST and PIONEERS
ARRIVING IN THE WEST, 1914
Panama-Pacific International Exposition
San Francisco Main Library Reference Room
(north wall), Humanities Room (east wall),
Larkin Street at McAllister
Two panels, 12' x 50' each, Oil on canvas
Frank Vincent Dumond

98 THE SEA AND THE LAND, 1931; 1932
Private funding
San Francisco Main Library
(walls flanking main staircase),
Larkin Street at McAllister
Fourteen panels, 11' x 6' each, Oil on canvas
Gottardo F. P. Piazzoni

99 MAP OF SAN FRANCISCO, 1939
WPA
Assessor's office (3rd floor north wall),
City Hall, Civic Center
20' x 50', Oil on canvas
Marion Simpson

100 U.S. SIGNS THE CHARTER OF THE UNITED NATIONS,
JUNE 26, 1945, 1956
United Nations
Herbst Theater (foyer),
Van Ness Avenue at McAllister
6' x 10', Oil on canvas
Howard Chandler Christy

101 EARTH, AIR, FIRE, AND WATER, 1915
Panama-Pacific International Exposition
Herbst Theater (north and south walls),
Van Ness Avenue at McAllister
Eight panels, 18' x 10 1/2' each, Oil on canvas
Frank Brangwyn

102 *AFRO-AMERICAN HISTORICAL AND CULTURAL
SOCIETY, 1974
CETA; OCD
Afro-American Historical and Cultural Society,
680 McAllister Street
12' x 25', Politec acrylic on plywood
Arthur Monroe and students from Fillmore-Fell
Corporation

103 *UNTITLED, 1975
Fillmore-Fell Corporation
Building, 646 Gough Street
10' x 60', Acrylic on plywood
Bob Gayton

104 PRIME TIME/NO TIME, 1980
CAC
New College of California Law School library,
50 Fell Street near Market
Two triangular panels, approx. 8' x 30' each,
Politec acrylic on plaster
Ray Patlan

105 JUST US, 1980
CAC
New College of California Law School, second floor,
50 Fell Street near Market
Approx. 20' x 40', Politec acrylic on concrete
Ray Patlan

440 THE LINEAL DOMINATION OF THE SIXTH AGE, 1988
Funding unknown
New College of California Law School,
second floor, 50 Fell Street near Market
Four panels: two measuring 12' x 50' and two
measuring 12' x 6', Acrylic on sheetrock
Betsie Miller-Kusz and mural students: Liesbeth
Middelberg, Yung Shin, and Linda Tunner

106 VENCEREMOS, 1981
CAC
New College of California Law School,
Main stairway, 50 Fell Street near Market
1,500 square feet, Politec acrylic on plaster
Ray Patlan

107 LEARNING WALL, 1989
OCD; SFAC
San Francisco Unified School District headquarters,
Rear wall, Franklin and Hayes Streets
45' x 100', Art Guerra acrylic on stucco
Keith Sklar

UNION STREET

108 THE LIFE OF MARY, 1966
Private funding
St. Mary the Virgin Episcopal Church courtyard,
2325 Union Street near Steiner
Five panels, 8' x 4' each, Fresco
Lucienne Bloch and Stephen Dimitroff

UPPER FILLMORE

109 GARDEN, 1982
Learning and Education through the Arts
Cobb School, 2725 California Street near Steiner
3' x 80', House paint on concrete
Patricia Rodriguez and Fran Valesco

JAPANTOWN

110 YWCA-WESTERN ADDITION, 1979
CETA; YWCA
YWCA-Western Addition (interior),
1830 Sutter Street near Buchanan
Two panels, 12' x 50',
Two panels, 12' x 70',
Politec acrylic on plaster
Fran Valesco

111 *UNTITLED, 1981
CAC; MRC; OCD
Building, 1834 Sutter Street
35' x 150', Politec acrylic on wood
James Dong

FILLMORE

112 *WAPAC MURAL, 1975; 1977
OCD
WAPAC building, 1956 Sutter Street
26' x 24', Unknown paint on wood
David Bradford

113 UNTITLED, 1977
Funding unknown
Booker T. Washington Community Center,
800 Presidio Drive
Approx. 15' x 60', Unknown paint on stucco
Bob Gayton

114 *UNTITLED, 1973; 1974; 1975
Private funding
Building, 631 Divisadero Street
6' x 15', Oil on wood
Pyramid-it A. Kaaba

115 UNTITLED, 1977
Private funding
Westside Housing Project,
Post and Broderick Streets
5' x 12', Unknown paint on concrete
Reid

116 *SERGEANT HENDERSON PARK, 1973
Private funding
Building wall next to park,
Divisadero Street between Turk and Eddy
7' x 100', Unknown paint on concrete
Sondra Chirlton, Doug Huntley, Craig Moline, Milton
    Schueler, and Mark Soetaert

117 [A SALUTE TO ARTISTS], 1975
NIIP
Beidman Minipark, O'Farrell Street
near Divisadero and Scott
8' x 40', Politec acrylic on wood
Dewey Crumpler and Neighborhood Youth Corps

118 BENJAMIN FRANKLIN, 1985
OCD
Ben Franklin School, 1430 Scott Street
(best viewed from Geary Street near Scott)
30' x 60', Politec and Liquitex acrylics on concrete
Selma Brown

119 [MEDICAL SCIENCE], 1968
SFAC
District Health Center #1 (entrance facade),
1301 Pierce Street
8' x 6', Glazed tiles
Win Ng

120 THE CHILDREN OF SAN FRANCISCO, 1968
SFAC
San Francisco Public Health Center #2,
Steiner and Ellis Streets
8' x 20', Mixed media on masonite
Dewey Crumpler

121 UNTITLED, 1975
FSSA; Private funding
Raphael Weill Elementary School (interior),
1505 O'Farrell Street near Webster
8' x 20', Politec acrylic on plywood
Peretti and Park

122 [MATH GAMES], 1977
Private funding
Raphael Weill Elementary School,
1505 O'Farrell Street near Webster
14' x 60', Politec acrylic on plywood
Peretti and Park

123 THE PEOPLE'S GAME, 1977; 1980
Private funding
Raphael Weill Elementary School,
1505 O'Farrell Street near Webster
14' x 60', Politec acrylic and Roy Anderson
paint on concrete
Peretti and Park

124 [FACES, RAINBOW, BOXES, ANIMALS, AND
       FLOWERS], 1980
Private funding
Raphael Weill Elementary School,
1505 O'Farrell Street near Webster
Approx. 6' x 18', Politec acrylic on concrete
Peretti and Park

125 [CAREERS AND LANDSCAPE], 1980; 1982
Private funding
Raphael Weill Elementary School,
1505 O'Farrell Street near Webster
Two panels, approx. 25' x 30' each,
Politec acrylic on concrete
Peretti and Park

126 [THE LIFE OF RAPHAEL WEILL], 1982
OCD; Private funding
Raphael Weill Elementary School,
1505 O'Farrell Street near Webster
Four panels, approx. 20' x 8' each,
Politec acrylic on concrete
Peretti and Park

127 [BLACK HISTORY, AFRICAN MOTIFS, ROLE MODELS,
      AND FANTASY], 1975
    CETA; OCD; YMCA
    YMCA Western Addition,
    1530 Buchanan Street near Geary
    Two panels, 16′ x 60′ each,
    One panel 16′ x 30′,
    House paint on plaster
    Fran Valesco and teenagers from the YMCA

128 AFRICAN MASK, 1976
    SFHA
    Plaza East Housing Project,
    Interior staircases,
    1225, 1245, and 1265 Laguna Street near Eddy
    Nine panels, 8′ x 8′ each,
    Cal-Western acrylic on concrete
    Caleb Williams

129 [AFRICAN SCENES], 1973
    Alvarado School Art Workshop; SFHA
    Plaza East Housing Project,
    Laguna Street and Eddy,
    and Buchanan Street and Eddy
    Two panels, 8′ x 30′ each,
    Cal-Western acrylic on concrete
    Horace Washington and Caleb Williams

130 [AFRICAN SCENES], 1975
    CETA; NYC; SFHA
    Plaza East Housing Project, west wall,
    Turk Street and Laguna
    5′ x 30′, Acrylic on concrete
    Caleb Williams and Neighborhood Youth Corps

131 [UNTITLED], 1988
    SFAC
    Northern Police Station,
    Turk Street and Fillmore
    3′ x 8′, Community cast cement
    Horace Washington

132 UNTITLED, 1977
    CETA
    Minipark,
    Golden Gate Avenue and Steiner Streets
    Two panels, 20′ x 30′ and 20′ x 40′,
    Acrylic on wood
    Dewey Crumpler and Neighborhood Youth Corps

HAYES VALLEY

133 *A TRIBUTE TO BLACK THEATER, 1975
    Private funding
    Western Addition Cultural Center (interior),
    762 Fulton Street between Webster and Buchanan
    9′ x 45′, Acrylic on plaster
    Judy Shannon

134 [SAN FRANCISCO BREWING], 1935
    Acme Brewery
    Western Addition Cultural Center, third floor,
    762 Fulton Street between Webster and Buchanan
    Two panels, approx. 6′ x 18′ each,
    One panel, 6′ x 12′, Fresco
    Jose Moya del Pino

135 A CELEBRATION OF AFRICAN AND AFRICAN-
      AMERICAN ARTISTS, 1984
    OCD
    Western Addition Cultural Center,
    762 Fulton Street between Webster and Buchanan
    45′ x 131′, Politec acrylic on concrete
    Dewey Crumpler, with Kemit Amenophis, Bonnie Long,
      and Sandra Roberts

136 UNTITLED, 1978
    Funding unknown
    Hayes Valley Playground,
    Hayes Street near Buchanan
    Approx. 4′ x 120′, Acrylic on concrete
    Scott Guein

137 ART, NATURE, AND CIVILIZATION, 1934
    WPA
    John Muir School, auditorium foyer,
    Webster Street at Oak
    Two panels, 7 1/2′ x 15′ each, Fresco
    David Park

138 A DISSERTATION ON ALCHEMY, 1937
    WPA
    University of California Extension, Woods Hall,
    Laguna Street between Haight and Hermann
    10′ x 15′, Fresco
    Reuben Kadish and Urban Neininger

139 [CHILDREN AT PLAY], 1984
    Private funding
    French American International School schoolyard,
    Haight Street and Buchanan
    Dimensions unknown, Acrylic on stucco
    Marilyn Gaines Gayton

140 *NEIGHBORHOOD ARTS THEATER, 1974
    NIIP
    Neighborhood Arts Theater,
    220 Buchanan Street between Waller and Haight
    Approx. 15′ x 55′, Politec acrylic on concrete
    Art Grant, A. Fisher, and neighborhood residents

141 THE WALDEN HOUSE EXTENDED FAMILY UNDER THE
      TREE OF ENLIGHTENED WISDOM, 1989
    CAC; Private funding
    Walden House,
    Haight Street between Buchanan and Laguna
    23′ x 14′, Liquitex, Novacolor, and
    Politec acrylics on stucco
    Michael Rios

142 ODE TO ROUSSEAU, 1976
    CETA
    Page Street Minipark,
    between Laguna Street and Octavia
    Approx. 30′ x 70′, Politec acrylic on wood
    Josie Grant

143 *[ATHLETICS], 1976
    NIIP
    Red Shield Playground,
    340 Fillmore Street near Page
    8′ x 80′, Acrylic on plywood
    Camille Marvin Breeze

144 MILES DAVIS, 1976
Funding unknown
United Projects (interior),
137 Steiner Street between Herman and Waller
Dimensions unknown,
Cal-Western acrylic on plaster
Caleb Williams

145 UNTITLED, 1979
OCD
Home for Visiting Nurses,
401 Duboce Street at Church
9' x 101', Acrylic on concrete
Caleb Williams

146 HARVEY MILK MEMORIAL MURAL, 1988
OCD
Harvey Milk Recreational Center, Duboce Park,
Duboce Street and Scott
35' x 50', Acrylic on concrete
Johanna Poethig

147 [CAMPFIRE SCENES], 1982
Koret Foundation
Storefront, Scott Street and Haight
20' x 65', Politec acrylic on stucco
Chuy Campusano and youth

148 [CHILDREN'S SILHOUETTES], 1982
Private funding
Florence Martin Children's Center,
1155 Page Street
Two panels, 5' x 85' and 6' x 40',
Politec acrylic on stucco
Elizabeth Greene and P.T. Greene

149 WHALE, 1977
Private funding
San Francisco Fire Department warehouse,
1152 Oak Street
20' x 90', Unknown paint on wood
Kevin McCloskey

150 [STREET SCENE], 1975
Private funding
Church's Fried Chicken,
1309 Hayes Street at Divisadero
Approx. 15' x 25', Acrylic on stucco
Clarkston Peadee

44l THE SPIRIT OF RAOUL WALLENBERG, 1989
San Francisco Education Fund
Raoul Wallenberg High School,
40 Vega Street
12' x 30', Acrylic on stucco
Susan Cervantes and students

151 *OUR HISTORY IS NO MYSTERY, 1976
(replaced by #152 in 1988)
Federal Neighborhood Bicentennial
Beautification Fund; NIIP
Retaining wall at Hayes Street and Masonic
2'-12' x 390', Politec acrylic on concrete
Haight-Ashbury Muralists: Jane Norling, Miranda
    Bergman, Arch Williams, Jo Tucker, Vicky Hamlin, and
    Thomas Kunz

152 EDUCATE TO LIBERATE, 1988
OCD
Retaining wall at Hayes Street and Masonic
2'-12' x 390', Novacolor acrylic on concrete
Miranda Bergman, Jane Norling. Maria Ramos, Vicky
    Hamlin, and Arch Williams

HAIGHT-ASHBURY

153 UNTITLED, 1977
Private funding
Haight-Ashbury Children's Center,
1101 Masonic Street at Page
10' x 17', Acrylic on concrete
Consuelo Mendez

154 CRISPUS ATTUCKS: THE BOSTON MASSACRE,
    MARCH 5, 1770, 1976
SFMMA
William De Avila School (interior),
Haight Street and Masonic
8' x 20', Roy Anderson paint on masonite
Horace Washington and Caleb Williams

155 *TWO HUNDRED YEARS OF RESISTANCE, 1976
SFMMA
Uganda Liquors, Haight Street and Masonic
8' x 20', Politec acrylic on masonite
Haight-Ashbury Muralists: Miranda Bergman, Jane
    Norling, Arch Williams, Jo Tucker, Vicky Hamlin, and
    Miles Stryker

156 *RAINBOW PEOPLE, 1972; 1974
Private funding
Seeds of Life Grocery,
Haight Street near Masonic
8' x 20', Oil on plywood (1972);
Politec acrylic on masonite (1974)
Haight-Ashbury Muralists

157 *UNITY EYE, 1973
Private funding
Building, Haight Street and Ashbury
8' x 15', Politec acrylic on plywood
Miranda Bergman, Andrea Cole, Jane Norling, and Jo
    Tucker

158 EACH COME TOGETHER IN YOUR OWN PERCEIVING
    OF YOURSELF, 1976
Federal Neighborhood Bicentennial
Beautification Fund
Apartment building,
1815 Page Street near Stanyan
44' x 24', Politec acrylic on masonite
Selma Brown and Ruby Newman

159 *THE PHOENIX MURAL, 1974
Private funding
Building,
1818 Haight Street at Shrader
15' x 65', Acrylic on stucco
Eugene Curley

160 EVOLUTION RAINBOW, 1969; 1981; 1983
Private funding
Storefront, Cole Street at Haight
10' x 30', Latex house paints on concrete
Joana Zegri

161 *[NATIVE AMERICAN LANDSCAPE], 1976
Private funding
Storefront apartments
612 Clayton Street near Haight
45' x 7'-10', Acrylic on stucco
Eugene Curley

162 [UNICORN BILLBOARD], c. 1977
Private funding
Billboard on Belvedere Street and Haight
8' x 20', Oil on masonite
Artist unknown

163 THE SPIRIT OF YOUTH IN AMERICA, 1977
Federal Neighborhood Bicentennial
Beautification Fund
Paltenghi Youth Center,
1525 Waller Street near Frederick
2,400 square feet,
Politec acrylic on concrete and plaster
Charles Lobdell, Phil van Dalen, Wendell Jones, and
    Evelyn Messinger

164 [TIGER], 1980
Private funding
Residence,
3579 Frederick Street near Clayton
24' x 35', Unknown paint on wood
Charles Marchiori

165 A PLACE IN THE SUN, 1971
Private funding
Bradley's Corner,
800 Cole Street near Carl
13' x 30', Oil on concrete
Raymond Howells

PARNASSUS HEIGHTS

166 *UNTITLED, 1975
Standard Oil Company
San Francisco Polytechnic High School
Approx. 20' x 350',
Mosaic tiles and acrylic on concrete
Peretti and Park, and students

167 SUPERSTITIOUS MEDICINE, 1935
SERA
UCSF Medical Center,
Health Sciences West,
Classroom HSW 300,
Parnassus Street at 3rd Avenue
7' x 9'7", Fresco
Bernard Baruch Zakheim, Phyllis Wrightson, Leon Bibel,
    and Joseph Kelly

168 RATIONAL MEDICINE, 1935
SERA
UCSF Medical Center,
Health Sciences West,
Classroom HSW 301,
Parnassus Street at 3rd Avenue
7' x 9'7", Fresco
Bernard Baruch Zakheim, Phyllis Wrightson, Leon Bibel,
    and Joseph Kelly

169 HISTORY OF MEDICINE IN CALIFORNIA, 1938
WPA
UCSF Medical Center, UCSF Hospital,
Toland Hall, U142,
Parnassus Street at 3rd Avenue
Six back wall panels, Four front wall panels,
4' 5" x 14'2" each, Fresco
Bernard Baruch Zakheim, with Phyllis Wrightson, and Koi
    Anderson (plasterer)

170 UNIVERSITY OF CALIFORNIA MEDICAL CENTER, 19,
San Francisco Unified School District;
Private funding
UCSF Medical Center,
Parnassus Street at Fourth Avenue
8' x 28', Unknown paint on plaster
Nancy Thompson, Ruth Asawa, Phoebe Brown, and
    students

INNER RICHMOND

171 HARVEST AND LAND, 1934
WPA
Roosevelt Junior High School,
First floor lobby,
Arguello Street and Geary
5' x 20', Oil on canvas
Nelson Pool

172 EDUCATION, 1934
WPA
Roosevelt Junior High School,
Second floor lobby,
Arguello Street and Geary,
5' x 25', Oil on canvas
George Wilson Walker

LAUREL HEIGHTS

173 THE WEDDING CEREMONY, 1933
Private funding
Jewish Community Center courtyard,
3200 California Street
100 square feet, Fresco
Bernard Baruch Zakheim

PRESIDIO

174 PEACETIME ACTIVITIES OF THE ARMY, 1935
SERA
Military Chapel at the Presidio,
Fischer Loop near Infantry Terrace
10' x 35' 8", Fresco
Victor Arnautoff, with Suzanne Scheuer, B. Cunningham,
    Edward Terada, Richard Ayer, M. Hardy, P. Hall, P.
    Vinson, G. Serrano, M. Cohen, P. Zoloth, T. Mead,
    and W. Mannex (plasterer)

OUTER RICHMOND

175 ARGONNE ELEMENTARY SCHOOL MURAL II, 1976
1976
Alvarado School Art Workshop; CETA;
San Francisco Unified School District
Argonne Elementary School,
675 18th Avenue near Anza
Three panels: 16' x 3 1/2',
6 1/2' square, and 3' x 30',
Roy Anderson and Cal-Western paint on wood and metal
Fran Valesco and school children

176 LIFE OF WASHINGTON, 1935
WPA
George Washington High School lobby,
32nd Avenue and Anza
1,600 square feet, Fresco
Victor Arnautoff

PACIFIC

OCEAN

PACIFIC

OCEAN

Golden Gate
Bridge

Bay
Bridge

GOLDEN GATE PARK

Golden Gate
Bridge

Lincoln Blvd

Doyle Dr

Lincoln Blvd

Richardson Ave

Moraga Ave

Infantry Terr

174

Presidio Ave

Laurel St

Spruce St

Cherry St

Arguello Blvd

Euclid Ave

2nd Ave

4th Ave

6th Ave

8th Ave

Masonic Ave

173

Lake St

California St

Clement St

Geary Blvd

Point Lobos Ave

Park Presidio Blvd

California St

Anza St

171

172

Anza St

Balboa St

Turk Blvd

University of
San Francisco

Golden Gate Ave

181

176 180

476

175

32nd Ave

48th Ave

46th Ave

44th Ave

42nd Ave

40th Ave

38th Ave

36th Ave

34th Ave

30th Ave

28th Ave

26th Ave

24th Ave

22nd Ave

20th Ave

18th Ave

16th Ave

12th Ave

10th Ave

Cabrillo St

Fulton St

McAllister St

152

Grove St

Hayes St

Fell St

Clayton St

Cole St

Shrader St

Stanyan St

Oak St

Page St

Ashbury St

153

DeYoung
Museum

Asian Art
Museum

470

182

JFK Drive

GOLDEN GATE

PARK

Haight St

Waller St

158

160

163

Frederick St

Carl St

Arguello Blvd

165

164

Lincoln Way

Hugo St

Parnassus Ave

3rd Ave

Grattan St

Cole St

17th St

Irving St

Judah St

167 170

University of
California at
San Francisco
Medical Center

Carmel St

Belgrave Ave

Burnett Ave

Kirkham St

7th Ave

9th Ave

11th Ave

Warren Dr

Clarendon

Dellbrook

Olympia Way

183

Lawton St

Moraga St

Noriega St

Ortega St

Laguna Honda Blvd

Panorama Dr

Portola Dr

48th Ave

40th Ave

39th Ave

37th Ave

35th Ave

33rd Ave

31st Ave

29th Ave

27th Ave

25th Ave

23rd Ave

21st Ave

19th Ave

17th Ave

Funston Ave

Pacheco St

444 445

Sunset Blvd

Great Highway

47th Ave

45th Ave

43rd Ave

41st Ave

Quintara St

Woodside Ave

207 211

185 184

West Sunset
Playground

Santiago St

14th Ave

Dewey Blvd

Vasquez Ave

Kensington Way

Claremont Blvd

Juanita Way

Marietta Dr

Teresita

Rockdale Dr

Myra

Del Sur

Omar

O'Shaughnessy

Ulloa St

206

Portola Dr

Mt Davidson
Park

204

Bella Vista Way

205

Wawona St

W Portal Ave

Lenox

Santa Clara Ave

Yerba Buena Ave

Los Palmos

Dr

Bosworth St

Lippard Ave

203

Pine Lake Park

35

Sloat Blvd

Sloat Blvd

Ocean Ave

Monterey Blvd

Gennessee St

Joost Ave

Flood Ave

Foerster St

Judson Ave

186 189

Ocean Ave

1

Phelan Ave

197 199

Balboa
Park

Lake

Merced

35

San Francisco
State University

477 479

190 196

Holloway Ave

Ocean Ave

480

481

San Francisco
City College

Balboa Park

280

1

81

Map by Eurydice Thomas

101

101

101

1

191 [COMPETITIVE AND RECREATIONAL SWIMMING], 1976
SFSU Physical Education,
Recreation and Leisure Studies, School of Health
San Francisco State University gymnasium, (pool),
19th Avenue and Holloway
24' x 28', Acrylic on concrete
Troy Dunham

192 *[UNTITLED], 1977
SFSU Pan African Student Office
San Francisco State University,
Pan African Student Office, B132 Student Union,
19th Avenue and Holloway
6' x 25', Acrylic on canvas
Suzanne de Sandies

193 COMMUNIVERSIDAD, 1977
SFSU Associated Students
San Francisco State University,
Student Union basement,
19th Avenue and Holloway
Two walls, 12' x 30' each,
Politec acrylic on concrete
La Raza Mural Workshop: Ray Patlan, Tony Triqueros,
    with Casper Montemayor, Arla d. Escontrias, Theresa
    L. Guitron, Paco Reyesfahad, Raul Martinez, Betty
    Jones, Virginia Milligan, Jorge Enrique Ocon, Yolanda
    Reyes Fayad, Delia Sanchez, Marciana, Brad Berlin,
    Bill O'Dea, Laura Moral, Tuti Rodriguez, Oswaldo
    Lopez, Carlos Gallardo, Tazaya C. Gonzalez, Angele
    Andino, Roberto Amaraz, Kevin Foutch, David Foutch,
    Patricio Lamorie, Oscar Aviles, Rupert Garcia,
    Angelina Lopez, Zala Nevel, Ivory Walker, and Juan
    Rodriguez

194 CASA BLANCA, 1988
Dr. August Coppola; SFSU School of Creative Arts
San Francisco State University,
School of Creative Arts Building hallway,
19th Avenue and Holloway
Four walls and hallway: 2 walls, 9' x 25',
3 walls, 9' x 17,
Politec acrylic on concrete/plaster
Emmanuel Montoya

195 [FLUTE PLAYER AND CRANES], 1988
SFSU Humanities Department
San Francisco State University,
Humanities Department, HLL 304,
10' x 30', Oil on concrete
Ji Chang-Xiang and Zhang Hong-bin

196 TREGANZA ANTHROPOLOGY MUSEUM, 1990
SFSU Anthropology and Museum Studies Departments
San Francisco State University,
Science Building, third floor (interior)
8' x 60', Acrylic on concrete
Eduardo Pineda

INGLESIDE-CITY COLLEGE OF SAN FRANCISCO

197 PAN-AMERICAN UNITY (MARRIAGE OF THE ARTISTIC
    EXPRESSION OF THE NORTH AND SOUTH OF THIS
    CONTINENT), 1940
Golden Gate International Exposition; Timothy Pflueger
City College of San Francisco, Little Theater lobby,
Ocean and Phelan Avenues
22' x 73', Fresco on movable steel frames
Diego Rivera

198 EDUCATION, 1940
WPA
City College of San Francisco,
Science Hall, north and south porticos,
Ocean and Phelan Avenues
Two panels, 50' x 45' each, Mosaic
Herman Volz

199 EDUCATION, 1940
WPA
City College of San Francisco,
Science Hall, main entrance,
Ocean and Phelan Avenues
Two panels, 12' x 8' each, Fresco
Fred Olmsted, Jr.

CAYUGA

200 IN GOD WE TRUST, 1982
OCD
Balboa High School,
1000 Cayuga Street at Onondaga
45' x 10', Politec acrylic on plaster
Pasto Medina

201 COMMUNITY SPIRIT, 1935
SERA
Alemany Day Treatment Center waiting room,
45 Onondaga Street at Alemany
Approx. 8 1/2' x 5', Fresco
Bernard Baruch Zakheim, Phyllis Wrightson, and Joseph
    Kelly (plasterer)

MISSION TERRACE

202 *A PORTRAIT OF THE SAN FRANCISCO ARTS
    FESTIVAL, 1981
American Express for the San Francisco Arts Festival
Excelsior branch, San Francisco Public Library
Conference room, 4440 Mission Street near Cotter
8' x 16', Politec acrylic on canvas
Precita Eyes Muralists: Susan Cervantes, Margo Bors,
    Tony Parrinello, Judy Jamerson, and Patricia Rose

GLEN PARK

203 THE BICENTENNIAL, 1976
Glen Park Association
Glen Park School, 151 Lippard Avenue
15' x 30', Cal-Western paints on concrete
Fran Valesco and school children

SHERWOOD HEIGHTS

204 [KINDERGARTEN, ALPHABET, AND LANDSCAPE],1980
CETA
Mira Loma School Parents Association
Mira Loma School, 175 Omar Way near Myra
One panel, 4' x 5', and two panels, 6' x 15',
Roy Anderson paint on two wood walls
and one concrete wall
Fran Valesco

205 [CHILDREN'S FANTASY ANIMALS IN A FANTASY
    LANDSCAPE], 1979
CETA
Mira Loma Park, Omar Way and Sequoia
12' x 50', Politec acrylic on concrete
Cynthia Grace

WEST PORTAL

206 [HISTORY OF WEST PORTAL], 1978
Greater West Portal Neighborhood Association; NIIP
West Portal branch, San Francisco Public Library,
190 Lenox Way at Ulloa
30' x 13', Politec acrylic on stucco
Nancy Thompson and residents

LAGUNA HONDA

207 UNTITLED, 1977
CETA
San Francisco Youth Guidance Center,
(cell doors in the maximum security section),
375 Woodside Avenue
8' x 4' each, Politec acrylic on metal
Miranda Bergman and detainees in Youth Guidance
    Center

208 *HISTORY OF SAN FRANCISCO, 1976
CETA; San Francisco Department of Electricity
Twin Peaks Communication Tower,
Twin Peaks Boulevard
Three panels, 15' x 30'; three panels, 15' x 4',
Politec acrylic on concrete
Fran Valesco, Jean Gindreau, Carol Nast, and Beatrice
    Spiegel

209 FIRE, EARTH, WATER, AIR [STEEL, FARMING,
    FISHING, FLIGHT], 1934
PWAP
Laguna Honda Hospital main lobby,
375 Laguna Honda Boulevard
8' x 6', Oil on canvas
Glen Wessels

210 [ECUMENICAL SPIRIT], 1976
CETA
Laguna Honda Hospital (interior),
375 Laguna Honda Boulevard
500 square feet,
Politec acrylic on plaster or stucco
Karen Ezekiel, Lee Hastings, and Jill Light

211 THE CITY'S MUSIC, 1990
Private funding
Laguna Honda Hospital, 8th floor east interior,
375 Laguna Honda Boulevard
Eight shaped panels, approx. 3' x 4' each,
Acrylic on plywood
Mike Mosher

212 [WILDLIFE AND INDIAN TRIBES OF THE SAN
    FRANCISCO PENINSULA], 1981
CETA; MRC
Josephine Randall Junior Museum lobby,
199 Museum Way
12' x 30', Politec acrylic on concrete
Mike Mosher

213 UNTITLED, 1983
CAC; Eureka Valley Trails and Art Network
Retaining wall, Market and 19th Street
Approx. 15'-20' x 254',
Politec acrylic on concrete
Betsie Miller-Kusz and 135 contributors

214 BEAVER MOUNTAIN, 1975
Private funding
Residence, 4550 18th Street,
Exterior of two-story house,
Politec acrylic on stucco and wood
Timothy Jencks

EUREKA VALLEY

215 EUREKA VALLEY RECREATION CENTER, 1977
CETA
Eureka Valley Recreation Center,
Collingwood between 18th and 19th Streets
Approx. 12' x 200', Politec acrylic on concrete
Cynthia Grace

NOE VALLEY

216 ALVARADO ELEMENTARY SCHOOL MURAL, 1972
Zellerbach Family Fund
Alvarado Elementary School schoolyard,
625 Douglass Street
2,770 square feet, Mosaic
Nancy Thompson

217 THE ALPHABET, 1975
Alvarado School Art Workshop; CETA
Alvarado Elementary School,
625 Douglass Street
3' x 117', Acrylic with sealer on concrete
Fran Valesco

218 *NOCHE VERACRUZANO, 1983
Private funding
Pablo's Restaurant (interior),
4166 24th Street between Castro and Diamond
8' x 25', Politec acrylic on stucco,
sealed with Danacolors plastic sealer
Juana Alicia

219 *LA OAXAQUENA, 1983
Private funding
Pablo's Restaurant (interior),
4166 24th Street between Castro and Diamond
8' x 25', Politec acrylic on stucco,
sealed with Danacolors plastic sealer
Juana Alicia

SOUTH OF MARKET

220 I.L.W.U. MURAL-SCULPTURE, 1986
I.L.W.U. and other unions; OCD
Free-standing sculpture, Mission and Steuart Streets
18' x 24', AwL Grip polyurethane epoxy
on 3/8" structural steel
M.E.T.A.L.
(Mural Environmentalists Together in Art Labor): Miranda
    Bergman, Tim Drescher, Nicole Emanuel, Lari Kilolani,
    James Morgan, Ray Patlan, Eduardo Pineda, James
    Prigoff, O'Brien Thiele, and Horace Washington

221 HISTORY OF·SAN FRANCISCO, 1948
Treasury Department Section of Painting
Rincon Center lobby, Spear and Mission Streets
Twenty-one panels totaling 8' x 460',
Casein paint on prepared walls
Anton Refregier

222 [LABOR HISTORY AND PRINTING TECHNOLOGY], 1983
Bay Area Typographical Union
Bay Area Typographical Union second floor,
433 Natoma Street
4' x 16', Acrylics and collage on masonite
Jenny McClure, Mike Mosher, Evelyn Nizberg, Lynette
    Neidhardt, and Fred Nizberg

223 [PHOENIX DINING ROOM], 1967
Standard Oil Company
Standard Oil Company building, 555 Market
12' x 110', Oil and acrylic tempera on canvas
Edith Hamlin

224 DANCE OF LIFE, 1978
Private funding
Storefront, 693 Mission Street
8' x 12', Politec acrylic on masonite
Claire Josephson

225 DESCENDANTS OF LAPU-LAPU/ANG LIPI NI LAPU-
    LAPU, 1984
OCD
Dimasalang House, 50 Rizal Street
90' x 25', Politec acrylic on concrete
Johanna Poethig, Vic Clemente, and Presco Tabios

226 UNCLE SAM, 1988
Chevrolet Automobiles
Wall, 660 3rd Street near Townsend
35' x 50', Oil on brick
Artist unknown

227 [RAINBOW], 1982
NIIP; OCD
Filipino Education Center,
824 Harrison Street near 4th Street
Approx. 20' x 65', Politec acrylic on concrete
Judy Jamerson

228 MY JOURNEY, 1986
AT&T; CAC; FSSA; Pacific Bell
Filipino Education Center,
824 Harrison Street near 4th Street
15' x 100', Politec acrylic on concrete
Johanna Poethig and Southeast Asian children

229 WONDERS OF THE WORLD, 1987
AT&T; CAC; Pacific Bell
Filipino Education Center,
824 Harrison Street
26' x 80', Acrylic on concrete
Johanna Poethig

230 [WORKERS AND TRACTORS], 1948
Private funding
Caterpillar Tractor Company
943 Harrison Street at Oak Grove
15' x 39', Oil on concrete
Don Clever

231 *CENTRAL CITY HEAD START, 1976
CETA
Storefront, 360 5th Street
9' x 15', Politec acrylic on plaster
Cynthia Grace

232 SUN MOSAIC, 1986
CAC; Ursula McGuire
Creatice Polite Apartments,
321 Clementina Street
5' x 5', Venetian glass mosaic
Johanna Poethig and Ursula McGuire

233 ELEMENTS OF INFINITY, 1982
OCD
St. Patrick's Day Care Center (side),
366 Clementina Street near Gallagher
32' x 80', Politec acrylic on concrete
Selma Brown, Johanna Poethig, and Claire Josephson

234 REFLECTIONS, 1984
Bank of America; OCD
Wall facing parking lot, 260 5th Street
30' x 100', Politec acrylic on concrete aggregate
John Wehrle, with Dan Fontes and Jim Petrillo

235 LAND AND FOODSCAPE, 1978
City and County of San Francisco
San Francisco Community College Downtown Center
Cafeteria, 4th and Mission Streets
6' x 60', Politec acrylic on canvas
Cynthia Grace

236 *SISTERSONGS OF LIBERATION, 1975
Rhine and Morgan
San Francisco Neighborhood Legal Assistance
Foundation, third floor, 109 Market Street
8' x 22', Politec acrylic on canvas
Jane Norling

237 PEOPLE'S PARK, 1979
CETA
Park, 6th Street between Mission Street and Minna
15' x 60', Acrylic on concrete
Bob Gayton and CCSF Center Crew

238 [ABSTRACT], 1976
NIIP
South of Market Health Center,
551 Minna Street
40' x 88', Colony acrylics on concrete
Jane P. Speiser assisted by B. Marchal

239 PHIL-AM FRIENDSHIP, 1983
OCD; Philippine-American Friendship Association
Building, Howard and Langton Streets
32' x 100', Politec acrylic on concrete
Peretti and Park

240 TWO HUNDRED YEARS OF CHILDREN'S TOYS AND
    GAMES, 1976
NEA; SFMMA
Bessie Carmichael Prekindergarten Center,
55 Sherman Street
8' x 20', Politec acrylic on masonite
Shoshana Dubiner and twenty-nine fourth grade children

241 *[JAIL/STREET SCENE], 1982
San Francisco Sheriff's Department
County Jail #2, seventh floor lobby,
850 Bryant Street
Two walls, 12' x 12' each,
Two walls, 12' x 24' each,
Politec acrylic on concrete
Mike Mosher

242 [UNTITLED], 1979
San Francisco Sheriff's Department
San Francisco Hall of Justice, sixth floor,
Women's section, 850 Bryant Street
3 1/2' x 35', Acrylic on concrete wall
Emmanuel Montoya

PACIFIC OCEAN

Golden Gate Bridge

Bay Bridge

GOLDEN GATE PARK

101

101

Lake Merced

Central Ave
Waller St
Duboce Ave

154

Buena Vista Park

Masonic Ave
Clayton St
Clifford Ter
Roosevelt Way
Corona Hts Playground
Henry St
States St

212

17th St
Corbett Ave
18th St

482
214

Market St

Hoffman Ave
Grand View Ave

216
217

484
483

485

Eureka St
Diamond St
Douglass St

Collingwood St
Castro St
Noe St
Sanchez St

Liberty St
Elizabeth St
Jersey St
Clipper St

487
309

Church St
Dolores St

Linda St

505

251
256

262

264
270

266
267
268

272
273
277
443
276
300
297

486

265

488

271

Portola Dr
Diamond Heights Blvd
Shaughnessy Blvd

Chenery St
Bosworth St
Laidley St
Armington St
Glen Park

Valley St
Day St
30th St
Army St
27th St
28th St
29th St

Randall St
Highland Park
Crescent

Chenery St

Golden Gate Bridge

Waller St
Dubose Ave

Market St

SEE INNER MISSION MAP

14th St
15th St
16th St
16th St Mission
17th St
18th St
19th St
20th St
21st St
22nd St
23rd St
24th St
25th St
26th St
Army St

Valencia St
Guerrero St
Dolores St
Capp St
Shotwell St
Mission St
S Van Ness Ave
Folsom St
Harrison St
Treat Ave
Bryant St
Florida St
York St
Hampshire St
Alabama St

249

499
498
244
245
248

Van Ness Ave
11th St
12th St

Mariposa St
18th St
19th St

24th St Mission

Precita Ave

395
399

Coso Ave
Fair Ave
San Jose Ave
Mission St
Coleridge St
Elsie St

Duncan St

411
570

431

576
578

430

432
437
432
438
139
579
581

Eugenia Ave
Cortland Ave

Bocana St
Andover St
Moultrie St
Ellsworth St
Nevada St
Folsom St
Putnam St

Peru Ave
Silliman St
Silliman St
Avalon Ave
Excelsior Ave
Brazil Ave
Russia Ave
Naples St
Athens St
Persia Ave
Edinburgh St
Paris St
Madrid St
France Ave
Italy Ave
Amazon Ave
Geneva Ave
Moscow St

Mission St

Ney St
Silver Ave
Pioche St
Yale St
Cambridge St
Oxford St
Harvard St

Alemany Blvd

280

Gaven St
Hale St
Silliman St
Felton St
Burrows St
Bacon St

101

575
435
433

Arleta Ave
Raymond Ave
Leland Ave
Visitacion Ave
Delta Ave
Cora Ave
Rutland St
Desmond Ave
Sunnydale Ave
Hahn St

434

Bayshore Blvd

101

Embarcadero

220
489
221

Steuart St
Main St
Spear St
Beale St
Fremont St

San Francisco-Oakland Bay Bridge

80

Montgomery

223

1st St
2nd St
3rd St

224

Market St
Powell

235
222
233
491
232
225
493
238
494
496
234
230
497
239
240
242

6th St
5th St
Mission St
Minna St
Natoma St
Howard St
7th St
8th St
Folsom St
Harrison St
9th St
10th St

227
229

492

226

Bryant St
Brannan St
Townsend St
King St
Berry St

Civic Center

80

243
244

Channel St
6th St
Owens St

280

Illinois St
3rd St

415

16th St

417
418

Rhode Island St
Kansas St
Vermont St
Utah St
Carolina St
Arkansas St
Connecticut St
Missouri St
Mississippi St
Tennessee St
Minnesota St
Indiana St

571

Potrero Hill Playground

374
379
562
564

419

Potrero Ave

563

382
384
385

22nd St
23rd St
24th St
25th St
26th St

Pennsylvania Ave

280

572

Army St
Napoleon St

Jerrold Ave
Toland St
Innes Ave

Custer St
Evans Ave
Cargo Way

McKinnon Ave
Oakdale Ave
Industrial St
Rankin St
Quint St

Jerrold Ave
Phelps St
Newhall St
Mendell St

Silver Ave
Topeka Ave
Egbert Ave
Ingalls St

425
423
424
574

LaSalle Ave
Newcomb Ave
Palou Ave
Revere Ave
Keith St
Lane St

422

Thornton Ave
Williams Ave

383
426
428
429

Newhall St
Van Dyke Ave
Thomas Ave
Hawes St
Griffith St

India Basin

Innes Ave
Jerrold Ave
Crisp Ave

Carroll Ave
Armstrong Ave

Gilman Ave

Griffith St
Fitch St

573

South Basin

85

Map by Eurydice Thomas

243 TRANSFORMATION AND HEALING, 1987
CAC; Private funding
Northeast Lodge
272 9th Street near Folsom
18' x 40', Acrylic on concrete
Johanna Poethig and clients of Northeast Lodge

244 LOST CITY, 1987
CAC; Private funding
Northeast Lodge
272 9th Street near Folsom
Several panels, Acrylics on walls and stairs
Johanna Poethig and clients of Northeast Lodge

245 UNTITLED, 1978
CETA; NAP; SFAC
South of Market Cultural Center, back of garden,
934 Brannan Street
Two portable panels painted on both sides,
4' x 8' each, Politec acrylic on plywood
Fran Valesco

246 SAN FRANCISCASTROLOGY, 1980
CETA; MRC
South of Market Cultural Center, back of garden,
934 Brannan Street
8' x 24', Politec acrylic on plywood
Mike Mosher, Leo Hennessey, and Laralyn Lambert

247 BUFFALO SKY, 1982
NIIP
South of Market Cultural Center,
934 Brannan Street
30' x 50', Politec acrylic on concrete
with Triangle Sealer
Fran Valesco, CETA Summer Youth, and volunteers from
   the Sunset Mural Workshop

248 ARTIFACT, 1990
FSSA; MRC; OCD
South of Market Cultural Center, west wall,
934 Brannan Street
40' x 80', Acrylic on concrete
Johanna Poethig

249 MANPOWER, 1977
CETA
Office building, interior, 1453 Mission Street
8' x 22', Politec acrylic on masonite
Cynthia Grace and Carol Nast

MISSION DISTRICT

250 *WHEN THE BUFFALO WERE ON THE MOUNTAINS,
   1976
CETA; SFAC
American Indian Center,
225 Valencia Street near Duboce
Two panels, 16' x 30' and 12' x 22',
Unknown paint on concrete
Gary McGill

251 [HOT AIR BALLOONS ABOVE BRYCE CANYON], 1975
CETA
Valencia Gardens,
Guerrero Street between 14th and 15th Streets
Approx. 20' x 10', Politec acrylic on concrete
Jack Frost

252 REDWOOD CREEK, 1979
CETA
Valencia Gardens,
Guerrero Street between 14th and 15th Streets
Dimensions unknown, Politec acrylic on concrete
R.D. James

253 GARDEN VEGETABLES, 1976
CETA
Valencia Gardens,
Guerrero Street between 14th and 15th Streets
Dimensions unknown, Politec acrylic on concrete
Shoshana Dubiner

254 [SILHOUETTE MANDALA], 1976
CETA
Valencia Gardens,
Guerrero Street between 14th and 15th Streets
Approx. 30' x 15', Politec acrylic on concrete
George Mead

255 [WORLDVIEW], 1976
CETA
Valencia Gardens,
Guerrero Street between 14th and 15th Streets
30' x 15', Politec acrylic on concrete
George Mead

256 PLANET EARTH, 1975
CETA
Valencia Gardens,
Guerrero Street between 14th and 15th Streets
Dimensions unknown, Acrylic on concrete
Guillermo Pulido

257 OUR PRESIDENT RICHARD NIXON AND DAUGHTERS
   JULIE AND TRICIA VISIT PAT NIXON IN THE
   HOSPITAL, 1978, 1988
Private funding
Storefront studio, 14th Street and Natoma
12' x 18', Latex on wood
Bill Wolf

258 LILLI ANN, 1986
OCD
Lilli Ann Building, 17th Street and Harrison
48' x 46', Oil on concrete
Chuy Campusano, Elias Rocha, Samuel Duenas, Roger
   Rocha, Carlos Anaya, and members of Signpainters
   Local 510

259 MISSION NEIGHBORHOOD HEALTH CENTER, 1976
CETA
Mission Neighborhood Health Center,
240 Shotwell Street near 16th Street
25' x 20', Politec acrylic on stucco or
plaster over concrete
Michael Rios

260 HUMANIDAD, 1976
CETA
Mission Neighborhood Health Center,
240 Shotwell Street near 16th Street
25' x 20', Politec acrylic on concrete
Graciela Carrillo

261 DREAMER'S GAZE, 1982
OCD
Victoria Theater,
2961 16th Street near Capp Street
45' x 90', Politec acrylic on brick
cleaned with water blaster
Claire Josephson and Monica Armstrong

278 *REAL ALTERNATIVES PROGRAM, 1981
RAP
Storefront, 16th and Mission Streets
Four panels, 4' x 8' each,
Politec acrylic on masonite
Chuy Campusano and RAP Youth

279 *[UNTITLED], 1981
RAP
Storefront, 16th and Mission Streets
8' x 32', Acrylics on plywood
Raul Martinez, Carlos Gonzalez, and area youth

280 EL FARO SAN FRANCISCO Y LA MISSION, 1987; 1988
Private funding
El Faro Restaurant, 20th Street and Folsom
12' x 90', Politec acrylic on wood
Michael Rios

281 NEW VISIONS BY DISABLED ARTISTS, 1986
Columbia Foundation; OCD; Zellerbach Family Fund
Apartment building, 20th Street and Folsom
24' x 37', Politec acrylic on plywood
Susan Greene, Jane Norling, Eduardo Pineda, Eddie
    Hippley, Vincent Jackson, Melody Lima, Michael
    Bernard Loggins, and Cam Quach

282 REFLECTIONS, 1982
OCD
Las Americas Children's Center,
3200 20th Street between Folsom and Harrison
8' x 16', Politec acrylic on plywood
Precita Eyes Muralists: Kit Davenport, Karin Schlesinger,
    and Judy Jamerson

283 CELESTIAL CYCLES, 1982
OCD
Las Americas Children's Center,
3200 20th Street between Folsom and Harrison
8' x 16', Politec acrylic on plywood
Precita Eyes Muralists: Luis Cervantes and Susan
    Cervantes

284 THE UNICORN'S DREAM, 1982
OCD
Las Americas Children's Center,
3200 20th Street between Folsom and Harrison
8' x 16', Politec acrylic on plywood
Precita Eyes Muralists: Patricia Rose, Beatrice Spiegel,
    Carlos del Valle, Margo Bors, and Luis Cervantes

285 EVERY CHILD IS BORN TO BE A FLOWER, 1979
OCD
Las Americas Children's Center,
3200 20th Street between Folsom and Harrison
8' x 16', Politec acrylic on plywood
Precita Eyes Muralists: Kit Davenport, Pat Stallings,
    Denise Mehan, Judy Jamerson, Susan Cervantes,
    Barbara Kosman, Greg Edwards, Thomas Gaviola, and
    Star Carroll-Smith

286 SUARO'S DREAM, 1979
OCD
Las Americas Children's Center
3200 20th Street between Folsom and Harrison
8' x 16', Politec acrylic on plywood
Precita Eyes Muralists: Tony Parrinello, Margo Bors, Basil
    Brummel, Jeanne Babette, Karin Schlesinger, Beatrice
    Spiegel, Luis Cervantes, and Joe Gomez

287 MASKS OF GOD/SOUL OF MAN, 1978
CETA
Las Americas Children's Center,
3200 20th Street between Folsom and Harrison
8' x 16', Politec acrylic on plywood
Precita Eyes Muralists: Susan Cervantes, Tony Parrinello,
    Judy Jamerson, Margo Bors, Karen Magnusen, Star
    Carroll-Smith, Thomas Gaviola, Beatrice Spiegel, Joe
    Gomez, Pete Anoa'i, and Denise Mehan

288 WONDER WELDERS, 1982
Private funding
John O'Connell School interior,
Harrison Street and 21st Street
9' x 20', Acrylic on plaster
Vicky Hamlin and students

289 PEOPLE'S RESTAURANT MURAL, 1977
Private funding
San Francisco Mime Troupe back lot,
855 Treat Street between 21st and 22nd Streets
4' x 30', Acrylic on plywood
Vicky Hamlin and Dan Macciarini

290 FOR THE ROSES/PA' LAS ROSAS, 1985
OCD; Pacific Bell
San Francisco Mime Troupe studio,
855 Treat Street between 21st and 22nd Streets
30' x 50', Politec acrylic,
Danacolors, and plastic sealer on concrete
Juana Alicia

442 UNTITLED, 1989
Parks and Recreation Department
Mission Recreation Center interior,
Treat Street between 20th and 21st Streets
Two walls totalling 12' x 30',
Acrylic on plaster
Betsie Miller-Kusz

291 BARRIO FOLSOM, 1982
OCD; Zellerbach Family Fund;
Youth Environment Study
Playground, 21st and Folsom Streets
5' x 200', Politec acrylic on concrete
Ray Patlan and playground youth

292 DESERT, 1982
NIIP
St. John's School,
1050 South Van Ness near 21st Street
11' x 86', Politec acrylic on concrete
Fran Valesco

447 [TROPICAL SCENE], 1983
Private funding
Cafeteria, Day Treatment Center, Mission Mental Health
    Center
365 South Van Ness
8' x 20', Politec on concrete
Patricia Rodriguez and clients

293 *[UNTITLED], 1976
Private funding
Building at 20th Street and South Van Ness
18' x 20', Acrylic on plaster
City Muralists

294 [HOMAGE TO SIQUEIROS], 1974
Bank of America Community Outreach
Bank of America, 22nd and Mission Streets
10' x 90', Liquitex on Japanese birchwood
Chuy Campusano

295 ALTO AL FUEGO/CEASEFIRE, 1988
Private funding
Cafe Nidal, 21st and Mission Streets
9' x 13', Politec and Novacolor acrylics on stucco
Juana Alicia

296 EVERYONE DESERVES A HOME, 1990
Private funding
Storefront, 21st and Mission Streets,
14' x 29', Acrylic on stucco and wood
Break the Silence Mural Project: Miranda Bergman,
    Susan Greene, and Marlene Tobias

297 UNTITLED, 1986
CAC; La Raza Graphics;
Walter and Elise Haas Foundation
La Raza Graphics Center,
938 Valencia Street at Liberty
Three panels, 40" x 60", Politec acrylic on wood
Sylvia Soriano

298 UNTITLED, 1986
CAC; La Raza Graphics;
Walter and Elise Haas Foundation
La Raza Graphics Center,
938 Valencia Street at Liberty
40" x 60", Politec acrylic on wood
Juana Alicia

299 UNTITLED, 1986
CAC; La Raza Graphics;
Walter and Elise Haas Foundation
La Raza Graphics Center,
938 Valencia Street at Liberty
40" x 60", Politec acrylic on wood
Juan Antonio Aviles

300 UNTITLED, 1986
CAC; La Raza Graphics;
Walter and Elise Haas Foundation
La Raza Graphics Center,
938 Valencia Street at Liberty
40" x 60", Politec acrylic on wood
Bob Thawley

301 INSPIRE TO ASPIRE: TRIBUTE TO CARLOS SANTANA,
    1987
OCD
Apartment house, 22nd Street and South Van Ness
35' x 95',
Novacolor, Politec, and Golden colors on wood
Michael Rios, Carlos Gonzalez, and Johnny Mayorga

302 EL LENGUAJE MUDO DEL ALMA/THE SILENT
    LANGUAGE OF THE SOUL, 1990
Columbia Foundation; LEF Foundation; OCD;
Zellerbach Family Fund
Hawthorne School,
Shotwell between 22nd and 23rd Streets
32' x 300', Acrylic on stucco
Juana Alicia and Susan Cervantes

303 IMAGINATION, 1986
San Francisco Educational Fund;
Parents Club; NYC
Hawthorne School, east wall,
Shotwell between 22nd and 23rd Streets
6' x 200', Acrylic on concrete
Scott Brown, Juana Alicia, Susan Cervantes, and Enrique
    Rodriguez

304 *HORIZONS UNLIMITED, 1972
NAP; STEP
Horizons office interior and exterior,
22nd and Folsom Streets
6' x 15' (exterior only),
Outdoor enamel on stucco
Bob Caff, Chuy Campusano, Ruben Guzman, and Spain

305 *MCO, 1972
Galeria de la Raza; STEP
Mission Coalition Organization legal office,
23rd Street and Folsom
15' x 80', Politec acrylic on wood
Michael Rios

306 PEOPLE WE KNEW, THE BEAUTY OF LIFE, and
    DREAMS AND FANTASIES, 1983
CAC
Mission Mental Health Center,
810 Capp at 23rd Street
8' x 20', Politec acrylic on plywood
Patricia Rodriguez and MHC clients

307 SOCIALIST BOOKSTORE, 1985
Private funding
Socialist Bookstore,
3284 23rd Street at Mission
15' x 30',
Politec and Liquitex acrylics on concrete
Susan Greene and Pedro Oliveri

308 THE SCARLATA MURAL, 1977
Private funding
Dr. Scarlata's dental office waiting room,
2639 Mission Street
12' x 45', Liquitex on birchwood
Chuy Campusano

309 [JAMESTOWN MURAL], 1973
STEP
Jamestown Community Center,
Second floor hallway,
180 Fair Oaks Street at 23rd Street
5' x 10', Indoor enamel on plaster
Patricia Rodriguez, Chuy Campusano, Ruben Guzman,
    Consuelo Mendez, Jerome Pasias, Elizabeth Raz, and
    Tom Rios

310 [AZTEC, EARLY CALIFORNIA, AND COSMIC HISTORY],
    1988
Private funding
Garage doors, Bartlett Street at 24th Street
7' x 25', Acrylic on wood
M. Paredes

311 UNTITLED, 1979
Private funding
Building, Bartlett Street and 24th Street
Approx. 12' x 30', Unknown paint on stucco
Anodea Judith

312 BART, 1975
CETA; NEH
BART Station,
Mission Street and 24th Street
Approx. 12' x 100', Politec acrylic on concrete
Michael Rios, Anthony Machado, and Richard Montez

313 *PARA EL MERCADO, 1974 (partially saved)
Mr. Bonilla
Paco's Tacos fence,
South Van Ness and 24th Streets
24' x 76',
Politec and Cal-Western acrylics on wood
Mujeres Muralistas: Graciela Carrillo, Consuelo Mendez,
Susan Cervantes, and Miriam Olivas

314 CARNAVAL, 1983
MRC
Apartment above House of Brakes,
South Van Ness and 24th Streets
24' x 76',
Primer, oil enamel, and plastic shield on wood
Daniel Galvez, with Dan Fontes, James Morgan, Jan
Shield, and Keith Sklar

315 *CASA SANDINO, 1979 (replaced by #316)
Private funding
Wall, 24th Street at Balmy Alley
9'-12' x 75', Oil enamel on wood
Brigada Orlando Letelier

316 *CULTURE OF NICARAGUA, 1983 (replaced by #352)
Casa Cultural Nicaraguense; UNE
Wall, 24th Street at Balmy Alley
9'-12' x 75', Acrylic on wood
Nicole Emanuel, Nicole George, and Patricia Rodriguez

BALMY ALLEY

Murals are listed beginning on the west side of the alley at 24th
Street and continuing toward 25th Street. Murals are located on
fences, walls, and garage doors. Dimensions of most murals are
approximately 6'-10' x 25'. Restoration of Balmy Alley murals
began in 1990.

317 *UNTITLED, 1973
Private funding
Balmy Alley between 24th and 25th Streets
Politec acrylic on wood
Susan Cervantes, Carlos Loarca and children

318 *REGENERATION/REGENERACION, 1984
PLACA
Balmy Alley between 24th and 25th Streets
Politec acrylic and spray can on wood
PLACA: Osha Neumann

319 [AZTEC MYTHOLOGY], 1990
PLACA
Balmy Alley between 24th and 25th Streets
Acrylic on wood
PLACA: Antonio Chavez and Guillermo Galicia

320 WOVEN MASKS/MASCARAS TEJIDAS, 1984
PLACA
Balmy Alley between 24th and 25th Streets
Politec acrylic on wood
PLACA: Susan Greene

321 YOUTH OF THE WORLD, LET'S CREATE A BETTER
WORLD/JUVENTUD DEL MUNDO VAMOS A CREER
UN MUNDO MEJOR, 1984
PLACA
Balmy Alley between 24th and 25th Streets
Politec acrylic on wood
PLACA: Crystal Nevel and Xochitl Nevel-Guerrero

322 UNITED IN THE STRUGGLE/UNIDOS EN LA LUCHA,
1984
PLACA
Balmy Alley between 24th and 25th Streets
Politec acrylic on wood
PLACA: Jose Mesa

323 GUERRA, INCORPORATED, 1984
PLACA
Balmy Alley between 24th and 25th Streets
Politec acrylic on wood
PLACA: Roberto Guerrero

324 *THE RESURRECTION OF THE CONQUEST/
LA RESURRECCION DE LA CONQUISTA, 1984
PLACA
Balmy Alley between 24th and 25th Streets
Politec acrylic on wood
PLACA: Patricia Rodriguez

325 GIRLS' FUTURE CAREERS, 1990
PLACA; YWCA
Balmy Alley between 24th and 25th Streets
Acrylic on wood
PLACA: Patricia Rodriguez, Sandra Fottin, Alicia Gomez,
Ruby Hernandez, Maribel Martinez, Sally Mendez,
Carolina Nunez, Laura Ordonez, and Karina Segura

326 *TO THREE NUNS AND A LAYPERSON/A UNA MUJER
SECULAR Y TRES MONJAS, 1984
PLACA
Balmy Alley between 24th and 25th Streets
Politec acrylic on wood
PLACA: Randall Bronner and Jim Lewis

327 *INDIGENOUS BEAUTY/BELLEZA INDIGENA, 1984
PLACA
Balmy Alley between 24th and 25th Streets
Politec acrylic on wood
PLACA: Nicole Emanuel

328 INDIGENOUS EYES, 1990
PLACA
Balmy Alley between 24th and 25th Streets
Politec and Novacolor acrylics on wood
PLACA: Susan Cervantes

329 ON THE WAY TO THE MARKET/CAMINO AL
MERCADO, 1984
PLACA
Balmy Alley between 24th and 25th Streets
Politec acrylic on wood
PLACA: Ray Patlan and Francisco Camplis

330 KEEPING THE PEACE (IN CENTRAL AMERICA)/
PRESERVANDO LA PAZ (EN CENTRO AMERICA),
1984
PLACA
Balmy Alley between 24th and 25th Streets
Politec acrylic on wood
PLACA: Carlos "Cookie" Gonzalez and Julian "Jueboy"
Torres

331 AFTER THE TRIUMPH/DESPUES DEL TRIUNFO, 1984
PLACA
Balmy Alley between 24th and 25th Streets
Politec acrylic on wood
PLACA: Herbert Siguenza

332 WAVES/ONDAS, 1984
PLACA
Balmy Alley between 24th and 25th Streets
Enamel on wood
PLACA: Kriska Boiral

Map by Eurydice Thomas

333 FOR CENTRAL AMERICA/PARA CENTRO AMERICA, 1984
PLACA
Balmy Alley between 24th and 25th Streets
Enamel on wood
PLACA: Keith Sklar

334 [UNTITLED], 1990
PLACA
Balmy Alley between 24th and 25th Streets
Acrylic on wood
PLACA: Codices

Murals on the east side of the alley are listed beginning at 25th Street and continuing toward 24th Street.

335 UNTITLED, 1973
Private funding
Above garage doors,
Balmy Alley between 24th and 25th Streets
Politec acrylic on wood
Irene Perez

336 MY CHILD HAS NEVER SEEN HIS FATHER/VOLAN LEJOS LOS SENTIMENTOS CUANDO LOS AMADOS HAN MUERTOS TODOS, 1984
PLACA
Balmy Alley between 24th and 25th Streets
Enamel on wood
PLACA: Brooke Fancher

337 *WE HEAR YOU GUATEMALA/TE OIMOS GUATEMALA, 1984
PLACA
Balmy Alley between 24th and 25th Streets
Politec acrylic on wood
PLACA: Juana Alicia

338 UNA LEY INMORAL, NADIE TIENE QUE CUMPLIRLA/NO ONE SHOULD COMPLY WITH AN IMMORAL LAW, 1990
PLACA
Balmy Alley between 24th and 25th Streets
Acrylic on wood
PLACA: Juana Alicia

339 *POWER PLAY/JUEGOS DE PODER, 1984
PLACA
Balmy Alley between 24th and 25th Streets
Politec acrylic on wood
PLACA: Eduardo Pineda

340 [UNTITLED], 1990
PLACA
Balmy Alley between 24th and 25th Streets
Acrylic on wood
PLACA: Edythe Boone, Bosmi Arens, Regina Davis, and Zigi Lowenberg

341 NEW UN-IMPROVED WASH 'N' WAR/NUEVECITO SIN MEJORAMIENTO LA ROPA DE GUERRA, 1984
PLACA
Balmy Alley between 24th and 25th Streets
Politec acrylic on wood
PLACA: Wendy Miller, Marsha Ercegovic, Michele Tavernite, and Janet Storm

342 A DREAM OF DEATH FALLING, SPIRIT RISING: PEACE TO CENTRAL AMERICA/UN SUENO DE LA MUERTE CALLENDO Y EL ESPIRITU LEVANTANDOSE: PAZ PARA CENTRO AMERICA, 1984
PLACA
Balmy Alley between 24th and 25th Streets
Politec acrylic on wood
PLACA: Susan Cervantes

343 THE VOICE OF MUSIC/LA VOZ DE LA MUSICA, 1984
PLACA
Balmy Alley between 24th and 25th Streets
Politec acrylic on wood
PLACA: Carl Araiza

344 THE CONTEST BETWEEN THE SUN AND THE WIND/ EL TORNEO ENTRE EL SOL Y EL VIENTO, 1984
PLACA
Balmy Alley between 24th and 25th Streets
Politec acrylic on wood
PLACA: Fran Valesco

345 UNTITLED, 1972
Private funding
Balmy Alley between 24th and 25th Streets
Politec acrylic on wood
Patricia Rodriguez and Graciela Carrillo

346 GIVE THEM ARMS AND ALSO TEACH THEM HOW TO READ/DARLES ARMAS Y TAMBIEN ENSENARLES A LEER, 1984
PLACA
Balmy Alley between 24th and 25th Streets
Politec acrylic on wood
PLACA: Jane Norling

347 CULTURE CONTAINS THE SEED OF RESISTANCE WHICH BLOSSOMS INTO THE FLOWER OF LIBERATION/ LA CULTURA CONTIENE LA SEMILLA DE LA RESISTENCIA QUE RETORNA EN LA FLOR DE LA LIBERACION, 1984
PLACA
Balmy Alley between 24th and 25th Streets
Politec acrylic on wood
PLACA: Miranda Bergman and O'Brien Thiele

348 UNTITLED, 1984
PLACA
Balmy Alley between 24th and 25th Streets
Politec acrylic on wood
PLACA: Terry Brackenbury, Gary Crittendon, and Marsha Poole

349 HONOR THE AMERICAN INDIANS/HONOR A TODOS LOS INDIOS DE AMERICA, 1984
PLACA
Balmy Alley between 24th and 25th Streets
Politec acrylic on wood
PLACA: Zala Nevel

350 TRIBUTE TO ARCHBISHOP OSCAR ROMERO/ HOMENAJE A ARZOBISPO OSCAR ROMERO, 1984
PLACA
Balmy Alley between 24th and 25th Streets
Politec acrylic on wood
PLACA: James Morgan and Karen Bennett (thanks to Mike Mosher)

351 TINY THUMB/EL PULGARCITO, 1984
PLACA
Balmy Alley between 24th and 25th Streets
Politec acrylic on wood
PLACA: Anne Fitzpatrick, Anthony Senna, Jose Antonio
   Ochoa, Jo Tucker, and Arch Williams

352 [INTERGENERATIONAL MURAL], 1990
Festival 2000
Balmy Alley at 24th Street
Acrylic and multimedia on plywood
PLACA: Susan Cervantes, Mia Gonzalez, and local
   residents

353 *UNTITLED, 1976; 1977; 1978
CETA
Mission Family Center,
3013 24th Street
Block long series of panels, windows, and doors,
Measuring 2' x 2' - 4' x 8',
Politec acrylic with varnish sealer on stucco and wood
Susan Cervantes

354 A BOUNTIFUL HARVEST, 1978
Private funding
China Books,
2929 24th Street between Florida and Alabama
Approx. 20' x 25', plus top area, 4' x 6',
Politec acrylic on stucco
Precita Eyes Muralists: Denise Mehan, Susan Cervantes,
   Tony Parrinello, Margo Bors, Jose Gomez. Assistants:
   Kathryn Brousse, Thomas Gaviola, S. McViker, Pete
   Anoa'i, and China Books staff

355 CLUB LATINO, 1981
Fuller O'Brien
St.Peter's School, Florida Street and 24th Street
8' x 29', Enamel on wood
Mike Mosher, Laura Parks, and members of the Club
   Latino (mostly eighth grade girls)

356 *VIETNAMESE, 1975
CETA
Punjab restaurant, 24th Street and Bryant
40' x 80', Politec acrylic on un-prepared wood
Michael Rios

MINIPARK

Murals were restored in 1990.

357 [QUETZALCOATL], 1974
CETA
Minipark, 24th Street near Bryant (east side)
8' x 32', Politec acrylic on wood
Michael Rios, Anthony Machado, and Richard Montez

358 [CHILDREN DANCE AROUND THE WORLD], 1982
CETA
Minipark, 24th Street near Bryant (east side)
15' x 30', Politec acrylic on wood
Michael Rios

359 UNTITLED, 1975
CETA
Minipark, 24th Street near Bryant
Approx. 15' x 20', Politec acrylic on wood
Michael Rios, Anthony Machado, and Richard Montez

360 *NO SOMOS HIPPOS PLASTICOS, 1975
Private funding
Minipark, 24th Street near Bryant
8' x 12', Acrylic paint on a wooden fence
Gerald Concha

361 UNTITLED, 1983 (partially destroyed in 1990)
OCD
Minipark,
24th Street near Bryant (back and west side)
20' x 20', Danacolor on wood
Emmanuel Montoya, Ben Morales, and Noel Santiago

362 HOMENAJE A RALPH MARADIAGA, 1990
OCD
Minipark, 24th Street near Bryant
10'-30' x 40', Acrylic on wood
Tirso Gonzalez and Ricardo Anguio

363 FANTASY WORLD FOR CHILDREN, 1975
CETA; NAP
Minipark, 24th Street near Bryant
40' x 20', Politec acrylic on wood
Mujeres Muralistas: Graciela Carrillo, Irene Perez, and
   Patricia Rodriguez

364 *PSYCHO-CYBERNETICS, 1975
(replaced in 1982 by #365)
CETA; NAP
Minipark, 24th Street near Bryant Street
40' x 20', Acrylic on wood
Domingo Rivera

365 ABC, 1982
OCD
Minipark, 24th Street near Bryant
40' x 20', Politec acrylic on wood
Michael Rios

366 UNTITLED, 1977
Private funding
Madero Realty, 24th Street at York
5' x 5', Acrylics on stucco
Graciela Carrillo

367 Y TU Y YO Y QUE, 1984
24th Street Merchants Association; OCD
Storefront, 24th Street and York
12' x 60', Politec acrylic on stucco
Ray Patlan and Carlos Gonzalez

368 THE WOMEN LETTUCE WORKERS/LAS
   LECHUGUERAS, 1985
OCD
Market, York and 24th Streets
30' x 50', Politec acrylic, Danacolors, and
plastic sealer on stucco and wood
Juana Alicia

369 EVERY CHILD IS A FLOWER, 1989
Precita Eyes Workshop,
Bryant School, 1050 York at 23rd Street
Eight sections, 9' x 27', Nova acrylic on concrete
Vicky Rega, Susan Greene, Margo Bors, Marta Estrella
   and Susan Cervantes

370 [FANTASY SCENE], date unknown
Funding unknown
Bryant School cafeteria,
1050 York Street
8' x 200', Politec acrylic on plasterboard
Peretti and Park, and students

371 *UNTITLED, 1970
NYC
Martin de Porres House, 23rd Street near Bryant
Approx. 15' x 50', Unknown paint on plaster
The Brothers of Martin de Porres and Neighborhood
   Youth Corps

372 *PRISM, 1983
Private funding
Fairway Produce, Bryant and 22nd Streets
16' x 80', Politec acrylic on stucco
Johanna Poethig and Charlie de Limur

373 THE CIRCUS, 1974
Private funding
Building, Bilbao Iron Works, 2509 Bryant Street
20' x 50', Housepaint on brick
No Moral Muralists

374 UNTITLED, 1974
Private funding
San Francisco General Hospital,
Mechanical Building courtyard,
1001 Potrero at 23rd Street
8' x 20', Mosaic
Gerald Concha

375 UNTITLED, 1974
Private funding
San Francisco General Hospital,
Mechanical Building courtyard,
1001 Potrero at 23rd Street
8' x 20', Mosaic
Carlos Loarca

376 UNTITLED, 1974
Private funding
San Francisco General Hospital,
Mechanical Building courtyard,
1001 Potrero at 23rd Street
8' x 20', Mosaic
Michael Rios

377 UNTITLED, 1974
Private funding
San Francisco General Hospital,
Mechanical Building courtyard,
1001 Potrero at 23rd Street
8' x 20', Mosaic
Manuel Villamor

378 CHILDREN'S MURAL, 1977
San Francisco Hotel Tax Fund
San Francisco General Hospital,
Sixth floor waiting room,
1001 Potrero at 23rd Street
4' x 10', Politec acrylic on plywood
Selma Brown and Ruby Newman

379 GARDENS OF HEALING, 1986
Volunteers of San Francisco General Hospital
San Francisco General Hospital,
Child and Adolescent Sexual Abuse Resource Center,
1001 Potrero at 23rd Street
8' x 18', Acrylic on canvas
Jo Tucker

380 A LETTER TO THE FUTURE/UNA CARTA AL FUTURO,
1986
CAC; La Raza Graphics;
Walter and Elise Haas Foundation
Good Samaritan Community Center interior,
1294 Potrero at 24th Street
Two panels, 9 1/2' x 18', and 9 1/2' x 9 1/2',
Politec acrylic on sheetrock
Juana Alicia, Mauricio Aviles, Corrano, Kathy D'Onofrio,
Carol Fadeff, Guillermo Galicia, Carmen Matthew,
Maria Theresa Ramos, Sylvia Soriano, and Bob
Thawley

381 *MY TIS OF THEE. . . , 1974
Funding unknown
San Francisco Department of Social Services,
Potrero at 24th Street
10' x 20', Enamel on brick
Tomas Belsky, Bob Primus, and others

382 OUR CHILDREN ARE OUR ONLY REINCARNATION,
1985
Precita Eyes Workshop; Susan Cervantes
The Farm,¬1499 Potrero at Army
8' x 8', Politec acrylic on exterior plywood
Susan Cervantes

383 HARVEST, 1985
Precita Eyes Workshop; Patricia Rose
The Farm, 1499 Potrero at Army
8' x 8', Politec acrylic on exterior plywood
Patricia Rose

384 UNTITLED, 1985
Precita Eyes Workshop; Henry Sultan
The Farm, 1499 Potrero at Army
8' x 8', Politec acrylic on exterior plywood
Henry Sultan

385 UNTITLED, 1985
Precita Eyes Workshop; Karl Lorenzin
The Farm, 1499 Potrero at Army
8' x 8', Politec acrylic on exterior plywood
Karl Lorenzin

386 UNTITLED, 1985
Precita Eyes Workshop; Michelle Irwin;
Rita Luisa Bairley
The Farm, 1499 Potrero at Army
8' x 8', Politec acrylic on exterior plywood
Michelle Irwin and Rita Luisa Bairley

387 RETABLO OF PARENTS/RETABLO DE LOS PADRES,
1988
OCD
Family Development Center,
25th Street and Bryant
28' x 60', Novacolor acrylic on concrete
Eduardo Pineda

388 *[CIA DIARY], 1975
CETA
Garfield Park Pool, north side,
Harrison and 25th Streets
Approx. 20' x 100', Politec acrylic on stucco
Domingo Rivera

389 [AZTEC SPACE SHIP], 1975
CETA
Garfield Park Pool, east side,
Harrison and 25th Streets
Approx. 12' x 36', Politec acrylic on stucco
Domingo Rivera

390 THE PRIMAL SEA, 1980; 1989
CAC; CETA; NYC; Parks and Recreation Department
Garfield Park Pool, Harrison and 25th Streets
Approx. 12' x 90', Politec acrylic on stucco
Precita Eyes Muralists: Susan Cervantes, Denise Mehan,
Pete Anoa'i, Star Carroll-Smith, Tony Parrinello, Nina
Eliasoph, and Joe Gomez

391 UNTITLED, 1976
CETA
Bernal Dwellings (facing Garfield Park),
Harrison and 26th Streets
29' x 36', Politec acrylic on stucco
Michael Rios, Graciela Carrillo, Sekio Fuapopo, Patricia
   Rodriguez, Fran Valesco, and the Neighborhood Youth
   Corps

392 UNTITLED, 1975
CETA
Bernal Dwellings (facing Garfield Park),
Harrison and 26th Streets
Approx. 29' x 36', Politec acrylic on concrete
Graciela Carrillo, Patricia Rodriguez, and the
   Neighborhood Youth Corps

393 KOOL BLUE, 1975
CETA
Bernal Dwellings,
Army Street near Harrison
29' x 36', Politec acrylic on concrete
Susan Cervantes, Patricia Rodriguez, Fran Valesco and
   the Neighborhood Youth Corps

394 *LULAC MURAL, 1975 (destroyed 1984)
Private funding
League for United Latin American Citizens
26th Street and Folsom
30' x 60', Unknown paint on concrete
Gilberto Ramirez

395 WE LEARN FROM EACH OTHER, 1989
OCD
Leonard R. Flynn Elementary School, east wall,
Army Street at Harrison
24' x 40', Novacolor acrylic on stucco
Ray Patlan, Eduardo Pineda, Mauricio Aviles, and
   Guillermo Galicia

396 TARGET, 1975
CETA; Alvarado School Arts Program
Leonard R. Flynn Elementary School handball court,
Precita Avenue at Harrison
12' x 30', Politec acrylic on concrete
Susan Cervantes and children

397 FAMILY LIFE and THE SPIRIT OF MANKIND, 1977
CETA; NIIP
Leonard R. Flynn Elementary School, south side,
Precita Avenue at Harrison
Two panels, 30' x 26', Politec acrylic on stucco
Susan Cervantes, Judy Jamerson, Tony Parrinello,
   Maurice Lacy, Robert Junti, and mural workshop
   volunteers

398 EARTH, FIRE, WATER, AIR, 1976
CETA; Alvarado School Arts Workshop
Leonard R. Flynn Elementary School,
Precita Avenue at Harrison
4'-12' x 120', Acrylic on concrete
Susan Cervantes and students

399 FOUR SEASONS OF LIFE, 1977
CETA; NIIP
Leonard R. Flynn Elementary School,
Precita Avenue at Harrison
12' x 7', Politec acrylic on stucco
Susan Cervantes, Judy Jamerson, and mural workshop
   volunteers

400 A DAY IN THE LIFE OF PRECITA VALLEY, 1974; 1984
NAP
Precita Valley Community Center
Precita Avenue
Two panels, 8' x 20', and 8' x 6',
Designers acrylics on plywood
Patricia Rodriguez, with Susan Cervantes, Ray Rios,
   Maria Brecker, Maria Juarequi, Dialo Seitu, Judy
   Jamerson, and Edith Jeffries

401 THE BEATLES, 1977; 1984
Private funding
Residence, 189 Precita Avenue
House facade, Enamel housepaint on stucco
Jane Weems

402 *LATINOAMERICA, 1974
Private funding
Mission Model Cities Building,
Mission Street between 25th and 26th Streets
20' x 76', Roy Anderson paints on concrete
Mujeres Muralistas: Patricia Rodriguez, Graciela Carrillo,
   Consuelo Mendez, Irene Perez, Tuti Rodriguez, Miriam
   Olivas, Esther Hernandez, and Xochitl Nevel-Guerrero

403 [TREE WITH ANIMALS], 1973
Mission Model Cities
Childcare Consortium interior,
Mission Street and 25th Streets
26' x 20',
Roy Anderson acrylic housepaint on concrete
Graciela Carrillo and Patricia Rodriguez

404 SIERRA QUEEN, 1983
Private funding
Retlaw Camera, Mission Street near 26th Street
Approx. 16' x 28', Politec acrylic on stucco
Susan Cervantes and the Precita Eyes Workshop

405 [NATIVE AMERICAN MEXICANS], 1982
CETA
Mission Cultural Center,
2868 Mission Street at 25th Street
30' x 160', Politec acrylic on concrete
Carlos Loarca, Manuel Villamor, and Betsie Miller-Kusz

406 THE STRUGGLE FOR LOW INCOME HOUSING, 1976
SFMMA
Mission Cultural Center,
2868 Mission Street at 25th Street
14' x 24', Acrylic on plywood
James Dong and Nancy Hom

407 HOMAGE TO WOMAN, 1978
CETA
Mission Cultural Center, second floor,
2868 Mission Street at 25th Street
12' x 36', Enamel on plaster
Carlos Loarca, Alvarado School Arts Program, Juanita
   Brand, Jaime Gomez, Jose Gutierrez, Maria Gomez,
   Dolores Miazzo, and Fernando Picazo

408 ESTA GRAN HUMANIDAD HA DICHO BASTA!/THIS
   GREAT PEOPLE HAS SAID ENOUGH!, 1976
SFMMA
Mission Cultural Center,
2868 Mission Street at 25th Street
8' x 12', Politec acrylic on masonite
Michael Rios and Anthony Machado

BERNAL HEIGHTS

409 TOOLS FOR PEACE, 1984
OCD
Building, Fair Street between Valencia and Mission
Approx. 15′ x 45′, Politec acrylic on cinderblock
Arch Williams, Jose Antonio Ochoa, Anne Fitzpatrick,
    Anthony Senna, and Jo Tucker

410 *PUERTO RICAN MURAL, 1977
CETA; Puerto Rican Club
Puerto Rican Center, north wall,
3249A Mission Street
36′ x 60′, Politec acrylic and sealer on wood
Fran Valesco, Theresa Baca, Gary Rees, Puerto Rican
    Club members, and volunteers

411 UNTITLED, 1982
OCD; Private funding
Bernal branch, San Francisco Public Library,
500 Cortland Avenue
1,100 square feet, Politec acrylic on stucco
Arch Williams, Carlos Alcala, Jo Tucker, and volunteers

412 *THE HOLLY COURTS HOUSING PROJECT, 1976
CETA; NIIP
Holly Courts Housing Project,
100 Appleton Street
30′ x 40′, Politec acrylic and sealer on concrete
Fran Valesco and tenants

413 *[MULTICOLORED FACES], 1980
OCD
Holly Courts Housing Project,
100 Appleton Street
Two panels, 6′ x 16′ and 8′ x 24′,
Acrylic on concrete
Mike Mosher

414 *UNTITLED, 1980
CETA; NIIP
Holly Courts Housing Project,
100 Appleton Street
Two panels, 8′ x 26′ and 28′ x 8′,
Acrylic on concrete and cinder block
Claire Josephson

POTRERO HILL

415 REFLECTIONS OF POTRERO HILL, 1987
Private funding; San Francisco Hotel Tax Fund;
New Lambda Foundation; OCD; Zellerbach Family Fund
Building, 1345 17th Street at Connecticut
20′ x 100′, Politec acrylic on concrete
Nicole Emanuel, Scott Branham, Brooke Fancher, Dan
    Fontes, Stormey Weber, and Luke McGlynn

416 *IRISES, 1979
Private funding
Mary Price Flowers, 1419 18th Street
10′ x 6′, Politec acrylic on plaster
Margo Bors

417 [FLYING CRANE], 1976
Private funding
Storefront,
247 Missouri Street near 18th Street
25′ x 30′, Politec acrylic and sealer on stucco
Karen Ezekiel and Lee Hastings

418 POTRERO HILL PAST AND PRESENT, 1982
Funding unknown
Potrero branch, San Francisco Public Library,
1616 20th Street
8′ x 8′, Politec acrylic on masonite
Margo Bors

419 [ATHLETES], 1977
Private funding
Potrero Hill Recreation Center,
Arkansas and Madera Streets
Approx. 8 1/2′ x 80′, Politec acrylic on stucco
Pamela Dickens

420 *BLACK HISTORY, 1976
CETA
Potrero Hill Legal Community Center,
Wisconsin and 23rd Streets
6′ x 100′, Politec acrylic and sealer on wooden fence
Graciela Carrillo, Patricia Rodriguez, and Fran Valesco

421 *MASTERS OF METAL, 1978
Private funding
Diamont Tool and Die Company, 1810 Army Street
8′ x 12′, Politec acrylic on masonite
Selma Brown

HUNTER'S POINT-BAYVIEW

422 SUNFLOWERS OF NATURE, 1985
OCD
Hunter's Point Housing, east wall,
1033 Oakdale
23′ x 23′, Acrylic on concrete
James Phillips, with Sara Williams and Todd Duncan

423 THE FIRE NEXT TIME I, 1977
CETA; NAP
Joseph P. Lee Recreation Center,
3rd and Oakdale Streets
35′ x 45′, Politec acrylic on concrete
Dewey Crumpler, assisted by Tim Drescher

424 THE FIRE NEXT TIME II, 1984
Dewey Crumpler's Uncle; OCD
Joseph P. Lee Recreation Center,
3rd and Newcomb Streets
5,500 square feet,
Politec acrylic on concrete
Dewey Crumpler

425 TUZURI WATU/WE ARE A BEAUTIFUL PEOPLE, 1987
OCD
Building, 4900 3rd Street at Palou
35′ x 60′, Liquitex on stucco
Brooke Fancher

426 FOOD FOR THE PEOPLE, 1989
S.H.A.R.E.; OCD;
SLUG (SF League of Urban Gardeners)
SLUG building, Newhall and Carroll Streets
21′ x 180′, Acrylic on concrete
Susan Cervantes

427 *EDUCATION IS TRUTH, 1971
SFMMA MIX Program
Hunter's Point II Elementary School,
Kiska Road
18′ x 35′, Latex acrylic housepaint on stucco
Dewey Crumpler

Diego Rivera. *The Making of a Fresco Showing the Building of a City*, 1931. Detail from a fresco painted in the San Francisco Art Institute. Photograph used by courtesy of the San Francisco Art Institute. (20)

Louie LaBrie. *San Francisco Rising*, 1976. Destroyed. Politec acrylic on concrete. (11)

Fran Valesco and others. (*Fish Swimming*), 1986. North Beach Swimming Pool. Detail. Acrylic on concrete. Photograph by James Prigoff. (31)

Arch Williams and others. *The Right of Education/The Seed of Freedom*, 1987. Francisco Middle School playground wall. Politec acrylic on concrete. Photograph by James Prigoff. (33)

Maxine Albro. *California*, 1934. Coit Tower, Telegraph Hill.
Fresco. Photograph used by courtesy of the San Francisco
Parks and Recreation Department. (46)

James Dong. *Fish Struggling Upstream*, 1983. Ping Yuen Housing Project. Various media
on asphalt playground. Photograph by James Dong. (65)

Victor Fan. (*Chinese-American History*), 1988. YMCA Playground. Acrylic on concrete. Photograph by James Prigoff.
(70)

James Dong and the Kearny Street Workshop. *International
Hotel Mural*, 1975. Destroyed. Acrylic on concrete, brick and
wood. Photograph by Fran Valesco. (73)

Ray Patlan. *Prime Time/No Time*, 1980. New College of
California Law School. One of two interior murals which face
each other. Politec acrylic on plaster. (104)

Keith Sklar. *Learning Wall*, 1988. San Francisco Unified
School District building. Acrylic on stucco. (107)

David Bradford. *WAPAC Mural*, 1975. Destroyed. Unknown
paints on wood. (112)

Peretti and Park. *The People's Game*, 1977. Raphael Weill Elementary School. Politec acrylic on concrete. (123)

Dewey Crumpler and others. *A Celebration of African and African-American Artists*, 1984. Western Addition Cultural Center. Politec acrylic on concrete. (135)

Johanna Poethig. *Harvey Milk Memorial Mural*, 1988.
Duboce Park. Acrylic on concrete. Photograph by James Prigoff. (146)

Kevin McCloskey. *Whale*, 1977. San Francisco Fire Department warehouse. Unknown paints on wood. (149)

Clarkston Peadee. (*Street Scene*), 1975. Church's Fried
Chicken. Acrylic on stucco. (150)

Haight-Ashbury Muralists. *Our History is No Mystery*, 1976.
Detail from a destroyed mural. Politec acrylic on concrete.
Educate to Liberate is now painted on this wall. (151)

Consuelo Mendez. *Untitled*, 1977. Haight-Ashbury Children's Center. Acrylic on concrete. (153)

Miranda Bergman and others. *Educate to Liberate*, 1988.
Wall at Hayes and Masonic Streets. Detail. Novacolor acrylic
on concrete. Photograph by James Prigoff. (152)

Haight-Ashbury Muralists. *Rainbow People*, 1974. Seeds of
Life Grocery. Politec acrylic on masonite. (156)

Victor Arnautoff. *Life of Washington*, 1935. George Washington High School. Fresco. (176)

Gordon Langdon. *Modern and Ancient Science*, 1936. George Washington High School. Fresco. (179)

Henry Sultan, the Sunset Mural Workshop and others. (*Kites, the Sunset Mandala, and Library Books*), 1982. Ortega branch, San Francisco Public Library. Politec acrylic on stucco. Photograph by James Prigoff. (184)

Ray Patlan and others. *Communiversidad*, 1977. SFSU Student Union basement. Politec acrylic on concrete. Photograph by Ray Patlan. (193)

M.E.T.A.L. *I.L.W.U. Mural-sculpture*, 1986. Side facing
south. Mission and Steuart Streets. Awl Grip polyurethane
epoxy on 3/8" structural steel. (220)

Anton Refregier. *History of San Francisco*, 1948. Rincon
Center. One of twenty-one panels. Casein paint on prepared
wall. (221)

John Wehrle and others. *Reflections*, 1984. Wall facing parking lot at 260 5th Street. Detail. Politec acrylic on concrete aggregate. Photograph by James Prigoff. (234)

Gary McGill. *When the Buffalo were on the Mountain*, 1976. One of two panels, both now destroyed. Unknown paints on concrete. (250)

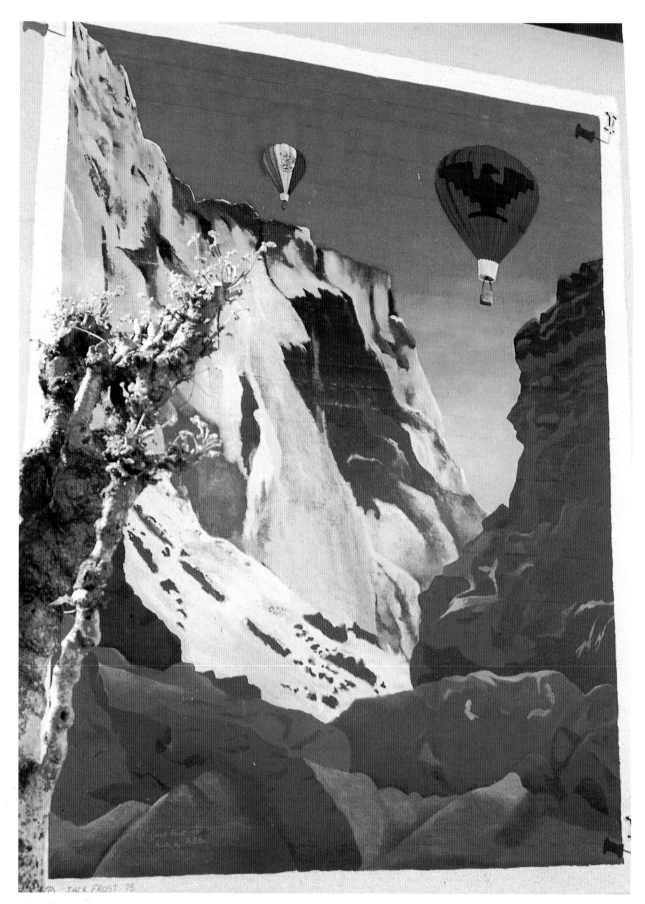

Jack Frost. (*Hot Air Balloons over Bryce Canyon*), 1975.
Valencia Gardens. Politec acrylic on concrete. (251)

Chuy Campusano and others. *Lilli Ann*, 1986. 17th Street and Harrison. Oil on concrete. (258)

Juana Alicia, Susan Cervantes and Raul Martinez. *New World Tree*, 1987. Mission Pool. Politec arylic and Novacolor on stucco. Photograph by James Prigoff. (277)

Susan Greene and others. *New Visions by Disabled Artists*,
1986. 20th Street and Folsom. Politec acrylic on plywood.
Photograph by James Prigoff. (281)

Graciela Carrillo. *Untitled*, 1980. Temporary painting for the
Galeria de la Raza billboard.

Derrik O'Keeffe. *Low 'n Slow*, 1975. Destroyed. Temporary
painting for Galeria de la Raza billboard.

Michael Rios. *Salsa Ahora*, 1975. Destroyed. Temporary
painting for Galeria de la Raza billboard.

Juana Alicia. *For the Roses/Pa' las Rosas*, 1985. San Francisco Mime Troupe studio. Politec acrylic, Danacolors and plastic sealer on concrete. Photograph by James Prigoff. (290)

Michael Rios. *MCO*, 1972. Detail from a destroyed mural. Politec acrylic on wood. (305)

Chuy Campusano. *Homage to Siqueiros*, 1974. Bank of
America. Liquitex on Japanese birchwood. (294)

Chuy Campusano and others. *Untitled*, 1973. Jamestown Community Center. Indoor enamel on plaster. (309)

Michael Rios, Anthony Machado, and Richard Montez. *BART*, 1975. BART Station at Mission and 24th Streets. Politec acrylic on concrete. (312)

Mujeres Muralistas. *Para el Mercado,* 1974. Detail from a destroyed mural. Primer, oil enamel and plastic shield on wood. (313)

Daniel Galvez and others. *Carnaval,* 1983. Apartment above House of Brakes. Primer, oil enamel and plastic shield on wood. (314)

Jose Mesa, PLACA. *United in the Struggle*, 1984. West side
of Balmy Alley. Politec acrylic on wood. (322)

Nicole Emanuel. *Indigenous Beauty*, 1984. Destroyed.
Balmy Alley. Politec acrylic on wood. (327)

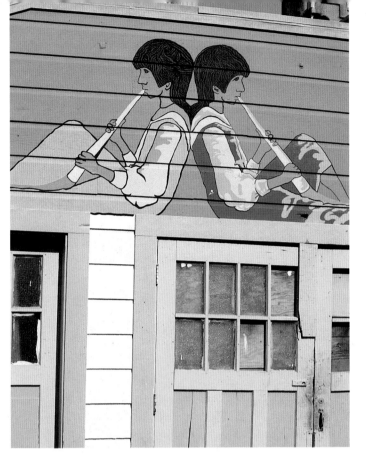

Irene Perez. *Untitled*, 1973. East side of Balmy Alley. Politec acrylic on wood. (335)

Miranda Bergman and O'Brien Thiele, PLACA. *Culture Contains the Seed of Resistance which Blossoms into the Flower of Liberation*, 1984. East side of Balmy Alley. Politec acrylic on wood. (347)

Domingo Rivera. *Psycho-Cybernetics*, 1975. Destroyed.
Minipark. Acrylic on wood. (364)

Juana Alicia. *The Women Lettuce Workers/Las Lechugueras*, 1985. Franklin market.
Politec acrylic, Danacolors, plastic sealer on stucco and wood. (368)

Michael Rios. *ABC*, 1982. Minipark. Politec acrylic on wood. (365)

Gilberto Ramirez. *LULAC Mural*, 1975. Destroyed. Unknown paints on concrete. (394)

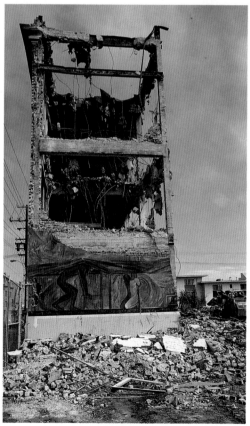

Gilberto Ramirez. *LULAC*, 1975. Destruction of the mural in 1984. Photograph by James Prigoff. (394)

Susan Cervantes, Judy Jamerson and others. *Family Life* and *The Spirit of Mankind*, 1977. Leonard R. Flynn Elementary School. Politec acrylic on stucco. Dedication of the murals. (397)

Mujeres Muralistas. *Latinoamerica*, 1974. Destroyed. Paint on concrete. (402)

Mike Mosher. [*Multicolored Faces*], 1980. Holly Courts. De-stroyed. Acrylic on concrete. Photograph by Mike Mosher. (413)

Dewey Crumpler with Tim Drescher. *The Fire Next Time I*, 1977. Joseph P. Lee Recreation Center. Politec acrylic on concrete. (423)

Nicole Emanuel and others. *Reflections of Potrero Hill*, 1987.
1345 17th Street. Politec acrylic on concrete. Photograph by
James Prigoff. (415)

Brooke Fancher. *Tuzuri Watu/We Are a Beautiful People*,
1987. Hunter's Point. Liquitex on stucco. (425)

Johanna Poethig and others. *Lakas Sambayanan/People's
Power*, 1986. Sun Valley Dairy. Acrylic on stucco. Photograph by James Prigoff. (431)

428 [AMERICAN BLACK HISTORY], 1984
OCD
Martin Luther King Jr. Swimming Pool,
3rd and Carroll Strets
Six panels, 6′ x 5′ each, Ceramic tiles
Painted with Roy Anderson and Liquitex acrylics
Horace Washington, Seitu Din, and Kate Singleton

429 UNTITLED, n.d.
Funding unknown
Martin Luther King, Jr. Swimming Pool,
3rd and Carroll Streets
8′ x 16′, Florentine glass mosaic
Anthony Stellon

UNIVERSITY MOUND

430 UNTITLED, 1956
Funding unknown
Hillcrest Elementary School library,
810 Silver Avenue
Seven panels, approx. 5′ x 3′ each, Mosaic
Emmy Lou Packard and Hillcrest School children

431 LAKAS SAMBAYANAN/PEOPLE'S POWER, 1986
OCD
Market,
300 Alemany Boulevard at Highway 101
35′ x 80′, Acrylic on stucco
Johanna Poethig, Vicente Clemente, and Presco Tabios

432 PROMISED LAND, 1939
Funding unknown
Jewish Home for the Aged, near main lobby,
302 Silver Avenue
10′ x 6′, Oil on canvas
Angelina Minultoli

433 SHARE OUR PAST, BUILD OUR FUTURE, 1988
CAC; OCD; San Francisco Conservation Corps
Visitacion Valley Recreation Center,
50 Raymond Street at Alpha
15′ x 200′, Acrylic on stucco
Jo Tucker and others

434 VALLEY VISION, 1987
OCD
Visitacion Valley branch,
San Francisco Public Library,
45 Leland Avenue at Desmond Street
25′ x 80′, Acrylic on stucco
Jo Tucker, Dick Fong, Terry Rayburn, and others

435 TREASURE OUR EARTH, 1989
CAC; OCD;
California Department of Conservation,
Division of Recycling
San Francisco Conservation Corps
325 Leland Street near Schwerin
Five walls, 2,000 square feet,
Acrylic on concrete and wood
Jo Tucker, Dick Fong, Maureen Kane, and others

SUNNYDALE

436 *SUNNYDALE COMMUNITY CENTER, 1975
NIIP
Sunnydale Community Center,
1654 Sunnydale Avenue
40′ x 30′, Acrylic on concrete
Bill Boseman and Ronnie Jacobson

EXCELSIOR

437 WAITING FOR THE 52, 1985
Excelsior Youth Club; Private funding
Storefront, Mission Street and Excelsior
25′ x 75′, Acrylic on stucco
Ron J. Mares, Jose Aguirre, Jr., Kim Hallinan (design),
and Pasto Medina, consultant

438 [DESIGNS], 1977
CETA; NAP
Excelsior Playground retaining wall,
Madrid Street at Russia
12′ x 180′, Acrylic on concrete
Sekio Fuapopo

439 *BARRIO GRANDE, EXCELSIOR, SAN PANCHO, 1980
Local Merchants; OCD
Excelsior Playground retaining wall,
Madrid Street at Russia
12′ x 180′, Acrylic on concrete
Excelsior Youth Club

NOTE: Eight recently added murals are listed in the correct geographic areas, but their numbers are not in chronological order. These murals are: #440 (listed after #105), #441 (listed after #150), #442 (listed after #290), #443 (listed after #277), #444 and #445 (listed after #185), #446 (listed after #73), and #447 (listed after #292).

The following additional murals, grouped by neighborhood, and listed on the appropriate maps, are provided in this expanded edition:

NORTH BEACH

450 REFLECTIONS, 1991
private
641–43 Bay Street, near Columbus
46′ x 30′, acrylic on wood and stucco
Bill Weber

451 MULTICULTURAL CABLE CAR, 1994 (replaces 28)
JAM
590 Francisco St. at Taylor
30′ x 12′, acrylic on concrete
Jason Leong, Dennis Taniguchi

452 [TELEGRAPH HILL NEIGHBORHOOD CENTER], 1975
NEA
500 Chestnut Street near Mason
30′ x 40′, acrylic on wood
Karen Ezekiel

CHINATOWN

453 THE SEEDS THAT WE PLANT NOW WILL GIVE OUR
CHILDREN SHADE, 1991
MOCD
Bartol Street off Broadway near Montgomery
6′-10′ x 97′, acrylic on concrete and plywood
Miranda Bergman, assisted by Selma Brown, Sylvia
Soriano, Suzie Rivo, Gayle Markow, Marlene
Tobias, mica Meri Furnari, Steve Lew, Rafael Chang

TENDERLOIN

454 ESCAPE INTO GRACE, 1992
509 Cultural Center, NBAGCF
Leavenworth at Ellis
18′-15′ x 100′, acrylic on brick and plywood
Johanna Poethig, Gia Hy Chung, Sokly Ny, Glades
Perreras, Pathara Chuop, and the Vietnamese
Youth Development Center

455 TEXTILE, 1993
509 Cultural Center
222 Leavenworth near Eddy
15′x 40′, acrylic on stone and plaster
Johanna Poethig with South East Asian youth through
Vietnamese Youth Development Center

POLK GULCH

456 LIVES, 1994
Tenderloin Development Coalition
Cohen Alley, bet. Ellis and Leavenworth
15′ x 50′, spray enamel on concrete
Brett Cook-Dizney

457 THE LEAP OF COMPASSION, 1992
Phoenix Hotel, Miss Pearl's Jam House
Eddy St. near Larkin
65′ x 100′, acrylic and enamel on concrete
Paul Scofield

458 MUSIC BREAKS DOWN BARRIERS. IT'S A
LANGUAGE WE CAN ALL UNDERSTAND, 1994
San Francisco University High School
Larkin Street at Eddy
1′-12′ x 70′, acrylic on concrete
Lydia Stone, Mercy Ringlemann, Alisa Alker, Sara
Pasquinelli, Emily Jan

459 LIFE AND NATURE, 1994
Sandoz Fern Alley, between Polk and Larkin
10′ x 40′, acrylic on concrete
Susan Evans and clients of St. Luke's Day Treatment
Center, and S.F. University High School students

460 QUILT MURAL, 1993
FSSA, MRC, OCD, Academy of Art Collage, Brownie's
Hardware, Createx Colors, Flax Art & Design,
Texicolor Corporation
1451 Jackson, bet. Hyde and Larkin
11′ x 50′, acrylic on plywood
Fran Valesco, assisted by Tonia Aminoff, children of
Spring Valley School, Chinatown Community Day
School, Karen Dobrony, Anatal Fawkes, Ulrike
Hoppner, Caleb Huynh, Eugene Ma, Izola Couther,
Terrill Couther, Angie Vasquez, Termeh
Yeghiazarian

CIVIC CENTER

461 *RHOMBOIDAL, 1974 (disassembled 1975, current
location unknown)
San Francisco Arts Festival
Civic Center
5 panels, approx. 7′x 7′, assembled as a rhomboid,
acrylic on canvas
Mujeres Muralistas (Patricia Rodriguez, Consuelo
Mendez, Irene Perez, Ester Hernandez, Miriam
Olivas, Tuti Rodriguez)

FILLMORE

462 WE COLOR THE WORLD, 1993
S. F. School District, NBAGCF
Raphael Weil School, 1501 O'Farrell St, near Webster
22′ x 29′, acrylic on stucco
Josh Sarantitis, Meera Desai, Kelley Kerslake

463 [TILES AND PLANTS], 1991
MRC, MOCD
Plaza East Housing Project, 1250 Eddy near Webster
15′ x 172′, ceramic tile and acrylic on concrete
Horace Washington, Ann Sherry

464 [UNTITLED], 1993
MOCD
Rosa Parks Senior Center, Webster at Golden Gate
8′ x 45′, spray can enamel on conglomerate and
stucco wall
Brett Cook-Dizney

UNION SQUARE

465 ALPINE MOTORCYCLE RALLY, 1994
S. F. City Earthquake Retrofit funds
parking lot interior on Ellis near O'Farrell
9′ x 35′, acrylic on concrete
Peter Collins, Catalina Gonzalez

HAYES VALLEY

466 THE WAVES OF AIDS, 1994
MOCD
California AIDS Intervention Training Center, 507
Divisadero at Fell Street
8′ x 12′, acrylic on masonite panels
Yvonne Littleton

467 CONVERGENCE, 1993
private
International School, Buchanan and Webster
10′ x 35′, acrylic on stucco
Claude Laurent

468 THE DREAM THEATER MURALS, 1991–1992
David Glass, owner of Little Hollywood launderette
Market at Laguna
12′ x 100′, acrylic on canvas, plaster, wood, and
concrete
Neil Levine

469 STAR ALLEY, 1993
private
Gough and Linden Alley
21′ diameter, Novacolor acrylic on plywood and
wooden siding
Neil Levine

GOLDEN GATE PARK

470 * TEOTIHUACAN, 1993
San Francisco Foundation
East wall of the M. H. de Young Memorial Museum
25′ x 20′, acrylic on stucco
Fresco (Ray Patlan and Eduardo Pineda), and students
from School of the Arts

HAIGHT-ASHBURY

584 TRIPTYCH, 1993
Frank's Liquors
Haight & Cole Sts.
12′ x 60′, spray enamel on plywood
Estria and EFX

471 (RE)MEMBERING AMERICAN ANARCHISM, 1886 TO
PRESENT, 1994
private
Bound Together Bookstore, 1369 Haight Street bet.
Masonic and Central
8′ x 16′, Novacolor acrylic on plywood
Susan Greene with Sarah Lewison

472 PEARLS OF WISDOM, WALL OF WORDS, 1991–1993
MOCD
DeAvila School, 1351 Haight Street, near Central
9′ x 180′, acrylic, ceramic tile, mosaic, clay on
concrete
Johanna Poethig and students

473 RESPECT IS THE ONLY THING WE HAVE, 1993
private
Haight and Central
8′ x 8′, spray enamel on plywood
Crayonne and TWS

474 ENVIRONMENT, 1993
private
Haight and Central
8′ x 30′, spray enamel on plywood
Crayonne and TWS

475 SAVIOUR PLANET, 1993
private
Haight and Central
8′ x 16′, spray enamel on plywood
Crayonne and TWS

OUTER RICHMOND

476 THE SALINAS VALLEY, 1986
private
Thom's Natural Foods
5843 Geary Blvd. and 23rd Avenue
10′ x 30′, Liquitex acrylic on plaster/drywall
Paul Scofield

SAN FRANCISCO STATE UNIVERSITY

477 CROSS OF QUETZALCOATL, 1991
Precita Eyes Muralists
Basement Cafeteria, SFSU Student Union
8′ x 12′, acrylic on plywood
Susan Cervantes, Luis Cervantes, Tony Parrinello,
Margo Bors, and others

478 MISSION STREET MANIFESTO, 1990
private
Basement Cafeteria, SFSU Student Union
12′ x 25′, acrylic on plywood
Juana Alicia

479 RAICES DE LIBERTAD/ROOTS OF FREEDOM, 1990
League of United Chicano Artists (LUCA), Taller de
Arte Publico
Basement Cafeteria, SFSU Student Union
10′ x 16′, acrylic on shaped plywood
Miranda Bergman, Raul Valdez, assisted by Ambray
Gonzalez

582 CESAR CHAVEZ, 1994
SFSU Student Union
Cesar Chavez Student Center
7′ x 9′, Novacolor acrylic on concrete
Carlos Gonzalez

585 * MALCOLM X, 1994
SFSU Student Union
Cesar Chavez Student Center
7′ x 9′, spray enamel on concrete
Senay

INGLESIDE

480 THE GREAT CLOUD OF WITNESSES, 1980–85
private
Ingleside Presbyterian Church and Community Center,
1345 Ocean Ave, at Granada (interior)
2 walls 15′ x 40′, 2 walls 15′ x 60′, collage on
plywood
Reverend Roland Gordon

481 THE GREAT CLOUD OF WITNESSES, 1992
MOCD
Ingleside Presbyterian Church and Community Center
1345 Ocean Ave at Granada
four walls, each 6′ x 60′, acrylic on sheetrock
Susan Cervantes with Selma Brown and Ronnie
Goodman

UPPER MARKET STREET

482 THE CHANT OF THE EARTH, THE VOICE OF THE
LAND, 1991 (replaces # 213)
NBAGCF
Retaining Wall, Market and 19th St.
15′-20′ x 254′, Novacolor acrylic on concrete
Betsie Miller-Kusz

EUREKA VALLEY - CASTRO DISTRICT

483 TIME AFTER TIME, 1993
Eureka Valley Trails and Art Network, NBAGCF, CAO's
Office
100 Collingwood St. nr. 19th St.
20′ x 60′, acrylic on concrete (also, 8′ x 30′ satellite
mural on nearby steps)
Betsie Miller-Kusz

484 THE TRANSFERENCE, 1987
Recreation and Parks Department
100 Collingwood nr. 19th St. (interior)
12′ x 20′, Politec acrylic on plaster
Betsie Miller-Kusz and 3 apprentices

485 HAHAH, 1990
private
Buffalo Natural Foods, 19th and Castro Streets
8′ x 20′, acrylic on concrete and plaster
Art Lick Gallery, Luiz daRosa, David Seibold

486 GOOD KARMA, 1977
private
18th Street at Dolores
12′ x 10′, acrylic on stucco
Apple Floating Cloud Productions

NOE VALLEY

487 CHURCH STREET RAINFOREST, 1993
private
1079 Church St., bet. 22nd and 23rd Streets
Housefront, 20′ x 20′, acrylic on stucco
Nicolai Larsen

488 RAINFOREST OF THE MIND, 1993
Precita Eyes Muralists
29th St. at Sanchez
8′ x 16′, acrylic on plywood panels
Henry Sultan

SOUTH OF MARKET

489 Five murals to be painted in spring 1994 on
construction fence at Mission and Steuart Streets at
the Embarcadero.
Artists: James Morgan, Senay, Rigo '94, Precita Eyes
Muralists, Brett Cook-Dizney, and TWS.

490 Five murals were painted in 1992 on construction fence
surrounding Yerba Buena Gardens. Current locations
unknown.
Muralists: Fresco (Ray Patlan and Eduardo Pineda),
Michael Rios, Johanna Poethig, TWIST, Brett Cook-
Dizney.

491 FROM THE MOUNTAINS, IN THE CLOUDS, 1994
MOCD
Woolf House, 801 Howard St. at 4th St.
2 plaques, each 2′ x 6′, ceramic, photo transfer and
handbuilt
Johanna Poethig and senior residents

492 TO CAUSE TO REMEMBER, 1992
MOCD
Welsh St., off 5th St. nr. Bryant
40′ x 80′, acrylic on concrete
Johanna Poethig

493 CONFUSED, FRUSTRATED, VANDALIZED,
MISGUIDED, ACTIVE, POOR, NEED LOVE, GATO,
DESOLATE, 1993
509 Cultural Center, TODCO
Howard Street, nr. 6th St.
8′ x 118′, spray enamel on plywood and paper
Brett Cook-Dizney

494 YOUR EYES EMBRACE MY WORLD, 1993
MOCD, NBAGCF
Minna St. at 6th Street
17′ x 88′, acrylic on cinderblock and artificial stone
Susan Cervantes with community people, assisted by
Precita Eyes Muralists

495 [PLANET EARTH], 1993
Precita Eyes Muralists
Minna Street at 6th Street
5½′ x 6′, acrylic on wood
Phil Morris

496 FAMILY, 1993
Precita Eyes Muralists
Minna Street at 6th Street
10′ x 5′, acrylic on plaster
Bob Gayton

497 ENDUP, 1993
private
995 Harrison at 6th Street
Two parts, 15′ x 30′ and 20′ x 45′, unknown paint on
wood and stucco
"Brett"

498 LOVE WILL COME YOUR WAY, 1992
McLaughlin, Piven & Vogel Securities, Inc., Dept. of
Social Services, New College of California
Children's Protective Services, 1440 Harrison nr.
10th St.
40 ft. squared, acrylic on wallboard
Susan Cervantes and students of the New College of
California arts and social change mural class.

499 (UNTITLED), 1994
private
96 Lafayette Street, off Howard between 11th and 12th
Streets
12′ x 36′, spray enamel on concrete and stucco
Benz

MISSION

500 EDUTAINMENT, 1991
Precita Eyes Apprentice Mural Program, MOCD, FSSA,
MRC
Marshall Elementary School, 15th and Capp Streets
12′ x 65′, acrylic on stucco
Susan Greene, with Meera Desai, Barry Hazzard,
Gabriela Halsey, and 8 others

501 UNIVERSAL LEARNING, 1992
MOCD, SFPD
Marshall Elementary School, 15th and Capp Streets
12′ x 65′, acrylic on plywood
Fresco (Ray Patlan and Eduardo Pineda)

502 GRACIAS A LA VIDA, 1992
MOCD
Centro Latino, 1656 15th St. near Mission
5′ x 15′, acrylic on canvas
Ester Hernandez

503 FRIDA, 1991 (replaces 257)
private
14th St. and Natoma
12′ x 18′, latex on wood
Bill Wolf

504 A BOOK IS YOUR KEY TO FREEDOM, 1993
private
Kirkpatrick Bakery
16th and Folsom
8′ x 35′, spray enamel on concrete
Dream

505 LA MADRE TONANTSIN, 1992
Coro Hispano
Sanchez at 16th Street
7′-8′ x 40′, acrylic on wooden fence
Colette Crutcher

CLARION ALLEY MURAL PROJECT (CAMP)

Murals are listed from the west (Valencia) on the south (right hand) side, then the opposite returning from Mission Street on the north side. Since additions are possible at virtually any time, be sure to check reality against this list. Funds are not dedicated to specific murals, but have come from private donations, Informal Nation Foundation, NBAGCF, local businesses, landlords, and The Zellerbach Foundation.

506 CAMP, 1993
(informational sign, in several languages)
8' x 12', acrylic on plaster

507 MISSION WILDLIFE HERITAGE, 1993
8' x 12', acrylic on plaster
Scott Williams

508 (UNTITLED), 1993
8' x 12', spray enamel on steel door
TWIST

509 OUR HEMISPHERE, 1993
8' x 12', acrylic on wood
Q. R. Hand

510 CHILDREN LEARN TOO, 1993
8' x 12', acrylic on plywood
Sebastiana with Casa de las Madres

511 VOICE OF THE GHETTO, 1993
12' x 10', spray enamel on steel door
Cuba

512 FEAR AND HOPE, 1994
Precita Eyes Muralists
11' x 22', acrylic on wood
Susan Cervantes, Marta Ayala, Constance Lombardo,
Kate Ruddle, Cynthia Rojos, and others

513 FAUX MISSION MAN, 1993
2½' x 6', pen and ink on plywood
Keith Knight

514 A HARD GOD(DESS) IS GOOD TO FIND, 1993–4
7' x 21', acrylic on wooden garage doors
Fresco (Ray Patlan and Eduardo Pineda)

515 (UNTITLED), 1993
7' x 10', acrylic on wood
Mario Joel

516 IF I COULD, 1993
acrylic on wood (a poem)
Al Rose

517 (UNTITLED), 1993
5' x 6', paper on wood and paper—collage
Mia Hoalberg

518 [ESCALATOR], 1993
10' x 12', acrylic on wood
Julie Murray

NORTH SIDE BEGINNING ON MISSION STREET

519 TRIBUTE TO FRANCIS BACON AND INDIGENOUS
MEXICAN THEMES, 1993
10' x 20', acrylic on plaster and plywood
Michael Roman

520 KEEP THE FAITH, 1993
7' x 10', acrylic on wood
Lily Rodriguez

521 [Collage of Women in Media], 1993
7' x 10', photographs on wood
Mari Kono

522 [door painted by children], 1993
7' x 3', acrylic on wood
The Alexis children

523 [Graffito], 1993
10' x 15', spray enamel on corrugated steel door
Krush

524 [UNTITLED), 1993
6' x 15', acrylic on brick
DX

525 [Collage], 1993
8' x 16', spray paint and pictures on plywood
Jesus Angel Perez

526 [UNTITLED], 1993
8' x 35', acrylic on wooden fence
Chuy Campusano

527 DON'T STOP THE FUNK, 1993
6' x 8', spray enamel on plywood
PEYA (Precita Eyes Youth Arts)

528 [Women's Building Mural], 1994
private donations, MOCD, Zellerbach Family Fund,
Astrae Foundation, Inc., Foundation for a
Compassionate Society
3543 18th Street at Lapidge
65' x 96', 65' x 96' (two sides of building), Novacolor
acrylic on stucco
Juana Alicia, Miranda Bergman, Edythe Boone, Susan
Kelk Cervantes, Meera Desai, Yvonne Littleton,
Irene Perez

586 [World Cup Soccer], 1994 (replaces 269)
Coca Cola U.S.A.
2300 Mission at 19th St.
10' x 80', acrylic on stucco
Fresco (Ray Patlan and Eduardo Pineda)

529 IS THIS THE END OR THE BEGINNING—THE LEAP,
1992
Precita Eyes Muralists
Las Americas Center, 20th St. at Harrison
8' x 12', acrylic on plywood
Luz Cervantes, Maria Chowentoska, Dierdre Weinberg

530 DEDICATED TO JOSE CORONADO, 1993
MOCD
Jose Coronado Park, Folsom at 21st Street
2½'-5' x 250', acrylic on concrete
Fresco (Ray Patlan and Eduardo Pineda)

531 MUSIC AND FLOWERS, 1991
Si Tashjian
21st Street at Mission
11' x 45', acrylic on stucco
Susan Greene and Barry Hazard, assisted by Meera
Desai

532 BUTTERFLIES, 1993
NBAGCF
Bartlett St. near 22nd Street
10' x 30', acrylic on stucco
Catalina Gonzalez and Precita Eyes Young Women's
Mural Workshop

533 WHATCHA WANNA DO?, 1994
Literary Arts Pilot Program of the SFAC
Bartlett Street near 22nd Street
12′ x 60′, spray enamel on stucco
Francisco Carrasco and PEYA

534 [UNTITLED, 1994
private
Valencia at 22nd Street
6′ x 15′, acrylic on plywood
P. van Lengen

535 MISSION, 1993
Kiel Company
New Mission Theater, Mission St. near 22nd St.
16′ x 28′, spray enamel on plywood barricade
Francisco Carrasco assisted by PEYA

536 VIVA LA HUELGA, 1993
NBAGCF, PEYA
Playground, Chavez School, Folsom, bet. 22nd
and 23rd Streets
5½′ x 70′, spray enamel on concrete
Francisco Carrasco assisted by PEYA

583 ROOTS AND FREQUENCIES BASIC TO OUR
        EDUCATION, 1994
MRC, NBAGCF
24th Street and Valencia
8′ x 20′, acrylic on plywood panels
Marta Ayala

537 EL UMBLIGO, 1994
MOCD
Capp Street near 24th St.
12′ x 125′, acrylic on wooden fence
Fresco (Ray Patlan and Eduardo Pineda)

538 FRIENDS DON'T LET FRIENDS DRINK AND DRIVE,
        1993
MCC, Kids' Workshop, RAP, MAS School, SFPD
Treat Street at 24th St.
12′ x 45′, acrylic on stucco
Ernesto Paul

539 MISSION FAMILY CENTER, 1992 (replaces 353)
MOCD
Mission Family Center, 24th St. at Balmy Alley
15′ x 80′, acrylic on stucco
Fresco (Ray Patlan and Eduardo Pineda)

BALMY ALLEY (west side)

540 [POEM], 1993
private
Balmy Alley (to the left of 317)
housepaint on wooden fence
anonymous

541 PODER ROSA, 1993
private
Balmy Alley (to the right of 318)
housepaint on wooden fence
anonymous

542 [UNTITLED], 1989 (replaces 318)
private
Balmy Alley
acrylic on wood
Carlos Gonzalez

543 INSTITUTIONS, 1990 (replaces 326)
Balmy Alley
spray can on door
Brett Cook-Dizney

544 LATINO PRIDE, 1993
PLACA
Balmy Alley (left of 329)
acrylic on wood
Francisco Carrasco and Garfield Park youth

BALMY ALLEY (east side)

545 HOY (VEY) COMO SIEMPRE, 1993 (replaces 339)
PLACA
Balmy Alley
acrylic on wooden door
Eduardo Pineda

546 COLORS, 1993 (replaces 341)
PLACA
Balmy Alley
acrylic on wooden fence
Rigo '93

547 CHANGES, 1990 (replaces 342)
PLACA
Balmy Alley
Spray can on plywood
Francisco Carrasco, and others

548 [UNTITLED], 1994 (replaces 343)
private
Balmy Alley
acrylic on wood
P. van Lengen

549 TOURIST PARODY, 1993
PLACA
Balmy Alley (to right of 350)
acrylic on wooden door
High School students at School of the Arts

550 [AZTEC WARRIOR], 1977
Dominguez Bakery
Alabama at 24th Street
5′ x 4′, unknown paint on painted brick
Gustavo

551 [AZTEC PRINCE AND MAIDEN], 1985
Dominguez Bakery
Alabama at 24th Street
2 panels, each 6′ x 6′, unknown paint on painted brick
K. Secrist, D. Jackson

552 AZTEC CALENDAR, 1991
Dominguez Bakery
Alabama at 24th Street
4′ x 3′, acrylic on painted brick
Ernesto Paul, Antonio Vasquez

553 EL INDIO FLECHADOR, 1990
Dominguez Bakery
Alabama at 24th Street
7′ x 6′, acrylic on stucco
Ernesto Paul, Carlos Gonzalez

554 VIRGEN DE GUADALUPE, 1990
Dominguez Bakery
Alabama at 24th Street
6′ x 14′, acrylic on stucco
Ernesto Paul

555 500 YEARS OF RESISTANCE, 1992–93
St. Peter's Church
24th Street at Florida Street
11′-25′ x 67′, acrylic on concrete and plaster
Isaias Mata

556 [UNTITLED], 1990
MOCD
Minipark, 24th and Bryant Streets
8′ x 20′, 10′ x 15′ panels, Novacolor acrylic on
    plywood
Betsie Miller-Kusz

557 HEROES, 1993–94 (replaces 367)
NBAGCF
York St. at 24th St.
12′ x 60′, acrylic on stucco
Cookie Gonzalez and RAP Youth

558 EVERY CHILD IS A FLOWER, 1989 (replaces 369)
MOCD
1050 Bryant, Bryant School bet. 22nd and 23rd Streets
12′ x 60′, acrylic on stucco
Vicki Rega, Susan Cervantes, Margo Bors, assisted by
    Precita Eyes Muralists

559 EL ARROYO, 1993
Reynaldo Serrano
Harrison at 23rd Street
15′ x 45′, acrylic on stucco
Ernesto Paul

560 CELEBRATING SUMMERS OF FUN, c. 1990
San Francisco Boys and Girls' Club
21st Street at Alabama
7′ x 45′, acrylic on plaster
anonymous, with children

561 OUR MISSION TO AZTLAN, 1993
MCC
York St at 21st Street
12′ x 36′, acrylic on stucco
Ernesto Paul

562 OCEAN FRONT, 1992
MOCD, private
Outpatient AIDS Ward 86, SFGH (interior)
7′ x 20′, Novacolor on oak panels
Arch Williams, Victor Fan, Antony Senna

563 FIESTA DE PAJAROS, 1994
MOCD, UCSF
SF General Hospital Dental School
9′ x 20′, acrylic on plywood
Carlos Loarca

564 [UNTITLED], 1992
Eikon Studios
7th floor Atrium, SFGH
10′ x 15′, unknown paint on concrete
Jessie Tapacio

565 PEACE IN THE BARRIOS, 1993
MOCD
Potrero del Sol Park, Potrero at 25th Street
15′ x 45′, acrylic on concrete
Fresco (Ray Patlan and Eduardo Pineda) and youth

587 VIVA EL SOL, 1991
The Plant, Inc.
Potrero del Sol Park, Potrero at 25th Street
16′ x 64′, acrylic on concrete
PEYA

566 [UNTITLED], 1994
NBAGCF
Osage Alley at 25th Street
10′ x 100′, acrylic on concrete
Isaias Mata and students

567 [UNTITLED], 1993
private
25th St. at Mission St.
15′ x 35′, acrylic on stucco
Ernesto Paul and Cruising Coyote Mural Workshop

568 OUR CULTURE, OUR ART/NUESTRA CULTURA,
    NUESTRA PINTURA, 1993
private
25th St. at Mission St.
15′ x 45′, acrylic on concrete and plywood
Ernesto Paul, students of M.A.S., and R.A.P.

BERNAL HEIGHTS

569 *[UNTITLED], 1975 (destroyed)
CETA
housing project, 100 Appleton Street
size unknown, acrylic on concrete
Patricia Rodriguez with high school youth

570 [UNTITLED], 1994
NBAGCF
Bernal Heights Playground, Andover nr. Cortland St.
12′ x 75′, acrylic on concrete
Lamont Gardner with youth

POTRERO HILL

571 NEW WORLDS, 1994
International Studies Academy
693 Vermont; 19th near Kansas
20′ x 100′, acrylic on concrete
Rigo '94 and students

572 WORTH SAVING, 1990
S. F. Conservation Corps, California Dept. of
    Conservation, Division of Recycling
Army Street at Indiana
25′ x 126′, acrylic on stucco
Jo Tucker, Dan Macchiarini and S. F. Conservation
    Corps

HUNTER'S POINT/BAYVIEW/CANDLESTICK

573 ALICE GRIFFITH MURAL, 1990
MOCD
2555 Griffith at Gilman St.
12′ x 60′, acrylic on plaster
Ray Patlan, Horace Washington

574 THE HISTORY OF BAYVIEW-HUNTER'S POINT
    MURAL PROJECT, 1994
Businesses of Hunter's Point Shipyard
3rd Street and Revere Street
8′-30′ x 114′, acrylic on stucco and concrete
Shipyard Artists: Heidi Hardin, Mary Southall, Peggy
    Huff, Wendy Robushi; and Hunter's Point
    neighborhood artists: Mary LaJackson, Peter Dent,
    Kathy Perry, Keith Lewis, Laboria Moore, Sister
    Lillian Briggs.

VISITACION VALLEY

575 LIFE UNDER WATER, 1992
MOCD
Coffman Pool, Visitacion and Hahn Streets
8′ x 72′, acrylic on stucco
Meera Desai, Barry Hazzard, Monica Henderson, Julia
Baier

UNIVERSITY MOUND

576 THIS IS OUR HOPE, THIS IS OUR FAITH, 1994
S. F. Housing Authority
Alemany Housing Project, Ellsworth bet. Crescent and
Alemany
20′ x 25′, acrylic on concrete and wood
Josh Sarantitis, assisted by Anthony Greene, David
Mason, Mico Zanders and members of the Alemany
Projects community

577 Two additional murals will be painted by the same
and group of artists at the Alemany Housing Project in
578 the summer and fall of 1994.

EXCELSIOR

579 KEEP OUR ANCIENT ROOTS ALIVE, 1993–1994
MOCD (first phase); LEF Foundation, McDonald's
Children's Charities, Zellerbach Fund (second
phase)
Cleveland School, Persia and Moscow Streets
Two panels, 40′ x 28′ each and nine recessed panels,
3½′ x 4′ each, Novacolor acrylic on stucco
Susan Kelk Cervantes, Alexandra Fomina, Nicolai
Bogomolov (Russia), Allen Cowan (London),
assisted by Precita Eyes Muralists

580 TRUST, 1993
PEYA, NBAGCF
Cleveland School bungalow, Persia and Moscow
Streets
20′ x 25′, spray enamel on wood
Christina Brown and Eduardo Ramos, and PEYA

581 RESPECT, 1993
PEYA, NBAGCF
Cleveland School bungalow, Persia and Moscow
Streets
20′ x 25′, spray enamel on wood
Eric Norberg (SPIE), assisted by PEYA

NOTE: Five recently added murals are listed in the correct
geographic areas, but their numbers are not in chronological
order. These murals are 584 (listed after 470), 582 (listed after
479), 585 (listed after 582), 586 (listed after 528), 583 (listed after
536), and 587 (listed after 565).

List of East Bay Murals

The information for each mural is presented in the following order:

Title [unofficial titles in brackets]. An asterisk indicates that the mural no longer exists.
Date completed
Funding source
Location
Size, medium and wall type [height precedes width. Sizes are often approximations]
Artist(s)

UNION CITY

EB 1 MAYAN MARKETPLACE, 1977
Alameda County Neighborhood Arts Program
Market, Alvarado Niles Road, Union City
9' x 20', Politec acrylic on plaster
Enrique Romero and NYC youth

EB 2 SI SE PUEDE, 1976
Private funding
Casados Market, 5th and 'E' Streets, Union City
15' x 25', Politec and sealer on stucco
Rogelio Cardenas, Enrique Romero, and youths

EB 3 DECOTO PLAZA MURAL, 1978
ACTEB/ACAP; C.U.R.A., Inc.; S.P.E.D.Y.; Searles
    School; The City of Union City; Y.C.C.I.P.
Decoto Plaza
6th and 'E' Streets, Union City,
5 1/2' x 60', Acrylic on particle board
Calvin Barajas, Danny Sanchez, Maria De Araujo,
    Vicente Sanchez, Art Aguilar, Esperanza Lopez,
    and Gyeong Yoon

EB 4 [UNTITLED], 1978
Alameda County Neighborhood Arts Program
Our Lady of the Rosary Church,
6th and 'C' Street, Union City
8' x 18', Acrylic on wood slats
Enrique Romero

EB 5 RAZA, EARTH, WIND, AND FIRE, 1976
Alameda County Youth Employment
Tiburcio Vasquez Medical Clinic,
9th Street, Union City
12' x 16', Politec acrylic on plywood and wood
Rogelio Cardenas, Enrique Romero, and Jose Luis
    Ramirez

EB 6 THE C.U.R.A. MURAL, 1978
ACTEB/ACAP; C.U.R.A., Inc.; S.P.E.D.Y.;
Searles School; The City of Union City;
Y.C.C.I.P.
33923 10th Street, Union City
12' x 25', Politec acrylic and latex on redwood
Circulo Anahuac

EB 7 [UNTITLED], 1976
The City of Union City
Union City Youth Program,
33623 Mission Blvd., Union City
Panels, 20' x 20'; 1 panel, 20' x 35',
Politec acrylic on stucco
Zala Nevel and Larry Orozco

EB 8 OICW MURAL, 1976
Neighborhood Youth Corps; OICW
OICW office interior,
Whipple Road, Union City
8' x 20', Politec acrylic on stucco
Enrique Romero

HAYWARD

EB 9 IN RECOGNITION OF 'LA MUJER', WE DEDICATE
THIS MURAL TO CELIA DE LA RIVA WHO
REPRESENTS THE ENERGY AND THE LOVE
FOR OUR RAZA. WE ALSO ACKNOWLEDGE OUR
YOUTH—YOU ARE THE FUTURE AND OUR
SURVIVAL, 1978
ACNAP; NYC
Market, 'A' Street and Princeton, Hayward
20' x 90', Acrylic on stucco
Rogelio Cardenas, Carmen Cesena, and Brocha de
    Hayward

EB 10 RURAL LANDSCAPE, 1938
TRAP
Hayward Post Office, 'C' Street, Hayward
5' x 10', Oil on canvas
Tom E. Lewis

EB 10a HIJOS DEL SOL, 1981
Hijos del Sol Youth Program,
La Familia Counseling Service
Tennyson center, Pompano Avenue, South Hayward
1900 square feet, Acrylic on stucco
Enrique Romero and local youth

OAKLAND

EB 11 DOLLAROCRACY, 1966
I.L.W.U. Local 6
Union Hall,
Hegenberger Road and Pardee Drive, Oakland
8' x 22', Mosaic tile
Beniamino Bufano

EB 12   THE CASTLEERS, 1989
         Jim's Liquors; The Castleers
         Jim's Liquors,
         MacArthur Blvd., and 83rd Street, Oakland
         9' x 20', Enamel on stucco
         Dewey Crumpler

EB 13   PRIDE OF THE PAST, FAITH IN THE FUTURE, 1989
         Oakland Arts Council; OCD
         Castlemont High School,
         8601 MacArthur Blvd., Oakland
         8' x 40', Danacolor on stucco
         Nzinga Kianga, Joel Freeman, and JPTA youth

EB 14   STUDENT LIFE, 1990
         Merritt College Mural Course
         Merritt College, Building R,
         12500 Campus Drive, Oakland
         8' x 22', Novacolor acrylics on concrete
         James Morgan and Merritt College Mural Students

EB 14a   REDWOODS, 1981
         Private funding
         Highway 13 underpass at Aliso Avenue
         and Carson Street, Oakland
         21'-24' x 35', Politec acrylic on concrete
         with graffiti sealer
         Dan Fontes

EB 15   [UNTITLED], 1978
         Oakland Neighborhood Arts Program
         I-580 underpass,
         MacArthur Blvd. and High Streets, Oakland
         20' x 170',
         Politec acrylic, sealer, and varnish on concrete
         Tony Machado and Richard Montez

EB 16   STRENGTH AND WISDOM, 1978
         Oakland Neighborhood Arts Council
         Spanish-Speaking Unity Council Building courtyard,
         1900 Fruitvale, Oakland
         12' x 40', Politec acrylic, primer, and varnish
         Tony Machado and Richard Montez

EB 17   *[SHADOW MURAL], 1977
         California Arts Council Grant
         Head Start Building, 65th Avenue, East Oakland
         27' x 20',
         Politec acrylic, sealer and varnish on stucco
         George Mead and CCAC students

EB 18   MELROSE '79, 1979
         Bilingual Arts Residency Program; CAC
         Melrose School,
         52nd and East 14th Street, Oakland
         15' x 30',
         Politec acrylic, primer, sealer, and varnish on wood
         Ester Hernandez and students

EB 19   WALL OF FRIENDSHIP, 1979
         Bilingual Arts Residency Program; CAC
         Wall, 53rd and East 14th Street, Oakland
         26' x 20',
         Politec acrylic primer and sealer on plaster
         Ester Hernandez, Pauline Hom, and Maria Pabeyta

EB 20   *MURAL DE LA RAZA, 1977
         Funding unknown
         Building, East 14th and 43rd Street, Oakland
         20' x 40',
         Latex, Politec acrylic and sealer on stucco
         Ray Patlan, Zala Nevel, and Xochitl Nevel-Guerrero

EB 20a   SPIRIT OF CHILDHOOD, 1983
         OCD
         Franklin Recreation Center,
         1010 East 15th Street, Oakland
         10' x 30', Acrylic on concrete
         Gary Graham and Vista College mural students

EB 21   [UNTITLED], 1977
         Clinica de la Raza
         Clinica de la Raza,
         Fruitvale near East 14th Avenue, Oakland
         12' x 52', Politec acrylic and sealer on plaster
         Xochitl Nevel-Guerrero, Zala Nevel, and Consuelo
             Nevel

EB 22   NEIGHBORHOOD PRIDE, 1988
         CAC; Oakland Cultural Arts Division;
         Oakland Graffiti Abatement; OCD;
         Parks and Recreation; Spanish Speaking
         Citizens Foundation
         Sanborn Park Clubhouse,
         East 16th Street and Fruitvale, Oakland
         10' x 45', Acrylic on wood
         Xochitl Nevel-Guerrero, Victor Acosta, and Crystal
             Nevel-Kaiser

EB 23   *CENTRO LEGAL, 1975
         Alameda County Neighborhood Arts Program
         Storefront office,
         East 14th and Fruitvale, Oakland
         8' x 60' (plywood panels), Politec acrylic and primer
         Irene Perez

EB 24   *EAST OAKLAND YMCA, 1986; 1987
         Funding unknown
         East Oakland YMCA, Oakland
         30' x 40', Latex on concrete
         Malaquias Montoya and CCAC students

EB 25   *[UNTITLED], 1970
         Latin American Library;
         Oakland Public Library Funds
         East Oakland Latin American Library,
         Miller and East 14th Street, Oakland
         Five murals in skylight- 4' x 17' (x4 sides),
         Liquitex acrylic on masonite
         Malaquias Montoya, Manuel Hernandez, Andreas
             Cisnero, Domingo Rivera and CCAC students

EB 26   *[UNTITLED], 1973
         Funding unknown
         Lazear School, 824 29th Avenue, Oakland
         16' x 80', Liquitex acrylic on masonite
         Manuel Hernandez

EB 27   *[UNTITLED], 1972; 1973
         Funding unknown
         Lazear School, 824 29th Avenue, Oakland
         8' x 24', Liquitex on masonite and concrete
         Malaquias Montoya and CCAC students

EB 28   *[UNTITLED], 1969
         Funding unknown
         Fruitvale Development Center,
         East 14th Street and Fruitvale, Oakland
         3' x 24', Liquitex on canvas
         Manuel Hernandez

EB 29 *[UNTITLED], 1970
Private funding
Emiliano Zapata Street Academy,
East 14th Street and Fruitvale, Oakland
Dimensions and materials unknown
Malaquias Montoya, Sergio Arroyo, Albert Amesquita,
    Richard Apodaca, Teresa Mendoza, Frank Garcia,
    and CCAC students

EB 30 OAKLAND IS PROUD, 1989
Private funding
St. Joseph's Professional Care Center,
East 12th and East 27th Streets, Oakland
8' x 350', Spraycan on brick
Joel (Phresh) Freeman

EB 31 [UNTITLED], 1976
SFMMA Bicentennial Funds
Centro Infantil,
3rd Avenue and East 11th Street, Oakland
8' x 15', Politec acrylic paint and sealer on wood
    panels
Graciela Carrillo and Irene Perez

EB 32 NUESTRA HISTORIA, 1983
CCAC Mural Class
Centro Infantil,
3rd Avenue and East 11th Street, Oakland
13' x 40', Latex enamel on wood
Malaquias Montoya and CCAC students

EB 33 NO HAY ROSAS SIN ESPINAS, 1985
CCAC Mural Class
Centro Infantil,
3rd Avenue and East 11th Street, Oakland
13' x 40', Latex on wood
Malaquias Montoya and CCAC students

EB 34 [UNTITLED], 1986
CCAC Mural Class
Centro Infantil,
3rd Avenue and East 11th Street, Oakland
10' x 60', Latex on concrete
Malaquias Montoya and CCAC students

EB 35 [UNTITLED], 1988
CCAC Mural Class
Centro Infantil,
3rd Avenue and East 11th Street, Oakland
8' x 64', Latex on plywood
Malaquias Montoya and CCAC students

EB 36 EN EL LIBRO TU LIBERTAD/IN KNOWLEDGE THERE
    IS LIBERATION, 1979; 1980
CCAC Mural Class; Oakland Arts Commission; OCD
Clinton Park School,
6th Avenue and 12th Street, Oakland
13' x 24', Latex on wood siding
Malaquias Montoya and CCAC students

EB 37 THE LIMITS OF TYRANTS, 1980
CCAC Mural Class
Supporting Future Growth Child Development Center,
1825 San Pablo Avenue, Oakland
15' x 35', Latex enamel and primer on stucco
Malaquias Montoya and CCAC students

EB 38 *[UNTITLED], 1975
Laney College
Laney College cafeteria, 900 Fallon Street, Oakland
7' x 15', Politec acrylic on stucco
Lou Silva

EB 39 *OPPRESSION VERSUS RESISTANCE, 1976
Laney College
Laney College campus, 900 Fallon Street, Oakland
15' x 45', Politec acrylic
and plastic sealer on concrete
Gary Graham, Saul Hopi Means, Terry Phillips, Paula
    Simon, and Third World Artists' Caucus

EB 40 ORCA FAMILY, 1989
California Pacific Designs
Whales and Friends Office,
550 2nd Avenue, Oakland
15' x 50', Novacolor on sheetrock
Dan Fontes

EB 41 MANY BOOKS, ONE WORLD, 1988
Alameda County Arts Commission
Oakland Public Library,
12th Street and Madison, Oakland
25' x 72', Golden colors acrylic on concrete
Brooke Fancher and Kriska

EB 42 OAKLAND ARTS EXPLOSION, 1986; 1987; 1988;
    1989
Alameda County Arts Commission;
Oakland Festival of the Arts
Hyatt Regency Hotel lobby,
10th Street and Broadway, Oakland
8' x 48', Enamel on canvas
Dan Fontes

EB 43 MITZVAH: THE JEWISH CULTURAL EXPERIENCE,
    1985
CAC; Hebrew Free Loan Association;
Jewish Community Relations Council;
Koret Foundation; L and D Scaffolding;
Office of Economic Development
Office building,
1404 Franklin near 14th Street, Oakland
105' x 100', Danacolor enamel on stucco
Keith Sklar, Brooke Fancher, and Dan Fontes

EB 44 MARCH OF EXCELLENCE, 1986
City of Oakland; East Bay Community Foundation
Peralta Village, Poplar Street between 12th and
10th Streets, Oakland
Six walls totaling 8' x 112', Acrylic on concrete
WALLSPEAK!: Dewey Crumpler, Edythe Boone and
    Kim Anno

EB 45 UNITY, 1989
City of Oakland; East Bay Community Foundation;
Oakland JPTA; Oakland OCD; Private Donations;
Ruth Mott Fund; World Council of Churches
Peralta Village,
10th Street between Cypress and Union, Oakland
25' x 30', Acrylic on concrete
WALLSPEAK!: Nzinga Kianga, Edythe Boone, Kim
    Anno, Karen Bennett, Miranda Bergman, and local
    youth

EB 46 KNOWLEDGE, 1988
City of Oakland; East Bay Community Foundation;
Oakland JPTA; Oakland OCD; Private Donations;
Ruth Mott Fund; World Council of Churches
Peralta Village,
10th Street between Cypress and Union, Oakland
25' x 30', Acrylic on concrete
WALLSPEAK!: Dewey Crumpler

EB 47   AND STILL WE SPEAK OF PEACE, FREEDOM AND
        DIGNITY, 1988
        City of Oakland; East Bay Community Foundation;
        Oakland JPTA; Oakland OCD; Private Donations;
        Ruth Mott Fund; World Council of Churches
        Peralta Village, 12th Street at Kirkham, Oakland
        25' x 30', Novacolor acrylic on concrete
        WALLSPEAK!: Jimi Evins

EB 48   BLACK AMERICAN, 1988
        City of Oakland; East Bay Community Foundation;
        Oakland JPTA; Oakland OCD; Private Donations;
        Ruth Mott Fund; World Council of Churches
        Peralta Village, 12th Street at Kirkham, Oakland
        25' x 30', Spraycan on concrete
        WALLSPEAK!: Joel (Phresh) Freeman

EB 49   *ACORN MURAL, 1976
        NEA; National Paint and Coatings Association
        Cathedral Building,
        Broadway and Telegraph Avenue, Oakland
        100' x 30', Danacolor, primer and sealer on stucco
        George Mead, Mike Hardeman, Claire Freitas,
        and Ivor Heskett

EB 50   HEARTS AND HANDS, 1989
        City of Oakland Streetworks
        Smith Street Building, 15th and Broadway, Oakland
        8' x 12', Acrylic on stucco
        James Morgan and Edythe Boone

EB 51   *OAKLAND'S PORTRAIT, 1981
        Pro Arts; ACAC; OCD; Liberty House; A Central Place;
        L.J. and Mary Skaggs Foundation
        Kahn's Alley, 15th Street between Telegraph
        and San Pablo, Oakland
        23' x 185', Enamel on stucco
        Daniel Galvez, Keith Sklar, Juan Cannon-Karlos

EB 52   STREET TATTOO, 1982
        CAC; OCD
        I-580 underpass at San Pablo Avenue and
        West Grand Street, Oakland
        15' x 220', Oil enamel on concrete
        Daniel Galvez, James Morgan, Dan Fontes, Keith
          Sklar, O'Brien Thiele and others

EB 53   GRAND PERFORMANCE, 1984
        CAC; East Bay Community Foundation;
        Zellerbach Family Fund; Kaiser Cement
        I-580 underpass at Grand Street, Oakland
        23' x 145', Oil enamel on concrete
        Keith Sklar, Daniel Galvez, Brooke Fancher, Dan
          Fontes, and Karen Sjoholm

EB 54   GIRAPHICS, 1984
        Oakland OCD
        I-580 underpass at Harrison Street, Oakland
        Seven giraffes: 32' x 6' to 16' x 5',
        Oil on concrete
        Dan Fontes

EB 55   ANIMURALS, 1985
        Oakland OCD
        I-580 underpass at Broadway, Oakland
        Six zebras: 16' x 18' to 12' x 6',
        Oil on concrete
        Dan Fontes

EB 56   LAKE MERRITT MURAL PROJECT, 1988
        Alameda County Arts Commission;
        Oakland Redevelopment Agency; Supervisor's Fund
        Auto dealership, 27th Street and Broadway, Oakland
        28'-21' x 89', Oil on concrete
        Dan Fontes

EB 57   [AGAINST IMPERIALISM], 1979
        Private funding
        Oakland Technical High School,
        4351 Broadway at 42nd Street, Oakland
        8' x 24', Acrylic on masonite panels
        Brigada Orlando Letelier

EB 58   CHILDREN'S MURAL OF THE NORTH OAKLAND
        WELFARE DEPARTMENT OFFICE, 1975
        North Oakland Welfare Department
        4501 Broadway, Oakland
        10' x 29', Politec acrylic on interior plasterboard
        Osha Neumann and Janet Kranzberg

EB 59   *CCAC MURAL, 1981
        CCAC Mural Class
        California College of Arts and Crafts,
        Broadway at College, Oakland
        25' x 16', Latex enamel and oil primer on plywood
        Malaquias Montoya and CCAC Mural Class students

EB 60   *[WOMEN'S LIBERATION], 1984
        CCAC Mural Class
        California College of Arts and Crafts,
        Broadway at College, Oakland
        25' x 16', Latex on plywood
        Malaquias Montoya and CCAC Mural Class students

EB 61   *[UNTITLED], 1988
        CCAC Mural Class
        California College of Arts and Crafts,
        Broadway at College, Oakland
        25' x 16', Latex on plywood
        Malaquias Motoya and CCAC Mural Class students

EB 62   *CENTRAL AMERICA, 1988
        CCAC Mural Class
        California College of Arts and Crafts,
        Broadway at College, Oakland
        25' x 16', Latex on plywood
        Malaquias Montoya and CCAC Mural Class students

EB 63   THE OTHER SIDE OF CENSORSHIP IS SELF-
        DETERMINATION, 1989
        CCAC Mural Class
        California College of Arts and Crafts,
        Broadway at College, Oakland
        25' x 16', Latex on plywood
        Malaquias Montoya and CCAC Mural Class students

EB 63a FRONTIERS OF SPACE, 1980
        Caltrans; OCD
        Rockridge BART station,
        College Avenue and Grove-Shafter Freeway, Oakland
        20' x 120', Acrylic on concrete
        Gary Graham, Charles Lobdell, Jack Greene, and
          Vista College Mural Class students

EB 64   *STAR WARS MURAL, 1978
        CAC; Oakland Housing Authority
        449 49th Street, Oakland
        12' x 16', Politec acrylic and varnish
        George Mead and area children

EB 65 *LAKE TEMESCAL, 1978
Private funding
L.J. Kruse Plumbing and Heating Company,
6247 College Avenue, Oakland
9' x 12', Acrylic and latex paint and varnish on stucco
Stefen

EB 66 BUTLER'S FARM, 1978
Private funding
Butler's Natural Foods, 2944 College Avenue, Oakland
2,000 square feet,
Acrylic and varnish on interior wall
Stefen and Anodea Judith

EB 67 *BEGGAR'S BANQUET, 1977
Berkeley Art Services; CETA
University Lutheran Chapel, Emergency Food Project
2425 College at Haste, Oakland
8' x 50', Politec primer, acrylics,
and sealer on plasterboard
Osha Neumann and O'Brien Thiele with others

EB 68 OCEANUS, 1978
Caltrans; Laney College; Vista College
Underpass,
Claremont Boulevard near Highway 24, Oakland
20' x 150', Politec acrylic
and plastic sealer on concrete
Gary Graham, Lou Silva, Ed Monroe and mural
    workshop participants

EB 69 NDEBELE ARTISTS, 1987
Private funding
The Urban Village,
4401 Telegraph Avenue at 44th Street, Oakland,
6' x 25', Danacolors on masonite
Nzinga Kianga

EB 70 [UNTITLED], 1975
Recycling Center Summer Program
Recycling Center,
Telegraph Avenue and 54th Street, Oakland,
15' x 30', Politec acrylic on wood
Osha Neumann

EB 71 GEOMETRIC SPIRAL, 1979
OCD
Highway 24 ramp,
Telegraph Avenue and 51st Street, Oakland
20' x 25', Acrylic on concrete
Lois Mann Fischer and Vista College Mural Class
    students

EB 72 *SELF DETERMINATION, 1983
CCAC Mural Class
Magnetic Imaging affiliate
of the Alta Breast Center,
5730 Telegraph Avenue at 58th Street, Oakland
25' x 100', Latex on stucco
Malaquias Montoya and CCAC Mural Class students

EB 73 [UNTITLED], 1985
Funding unknown
Magnetic Imaging affiliate
of the Alta Breast Center,
5730 Telegraph Avenue at 58th Street, Oakland,
20' x 100', Unknown paint on stucco
Gary Graham, Charles Lobdell, Matt Courtway, and Ed
    Monroe

BERKELEY

EB 74 [UNTITLED], 1987
CCAC Mural class
Willard Junior High School, 2425 Stuart at
Telegraph Avenue, Berkeley
8'-15' x 135', Latex enamel on concrete
Malaquias Montoya, CCAC students and students from
    Willard Junior High School

EB 75 INTERSECTIONS, 1980
CAC
Willard Junior High School gymnasium,
Telegraph Avenue at Ward, Berkeley
45' x 67', Acrylic on stucco
Osha Neumann and Daniel Galvez

EB 76 *TAKE CONTROL, 1978
Berkeley Women's Health Collective Raffle
The Berkeley Women's Health Collective,
2942 Ellsworth near Howe, Berkeley
8' x 16', Politec acrylic and varnish on plywood
Deborah Greene and Ariella Seidenberg

EB 77 BLOOMING, 1974
Private funding
Center for Independent Living,
2539 Telegraph Avenue, Berkeley,
12' x 80', Acrylics on stucco
Gary Graham and Joan Briscoe

EB 78 [UNTITLED], 1977
Center for Independent Living; Laney College
Center for Independent Living,
2539 Telegraph Avenue, Berkeley,
8' x 75', Paints and primer on concrete
Gary Graham

EB 79 A PEOPLE'S HISTORY OF TELEGRAPH AVENUE,
    1976
(At least two other murals were painted on this wall.
One was done c.1969 and the other in the early
    1970s.)
Private donations
Wall, Telegraph Avenue and Haste, Berkeley
20' x 88', Politec acrylic, oil primer, and
epoxy varnish on stucco
Osha Neumann, Daniel Galvez, Janet Kranzberg, and
    O'Brien Thiele

EB 80 *SERVE THE PEOPLE, 1976
Chicano Studies Department
Villa Hermosa Restaurant (interior),
Telegraph Avenue and Haste, Berkeley
12' x 30', Latex and Politec acrylics and sealer
on plaster
Ray Patlan and Patricia Rodriguez

EB 81 *STORY OF THE RAINBOW, 1978
Private funding
Sunset Gold Store, 2911 Telegraph Avenue, Berkeley
6,000 square feet (interior walls and ceiling),
Gibson latex on plaster
Anodea Judith, Roxanne Hanna, and Stefen

EB 82 *RAINBOW BRIDGE, 1978
Private funding
Rasputin's Records (north interior wall),
2379 Telegraph Avenue, Berkeley
12' x 50', Politec, liquitex, and Gibson paints
Stefen and Anodea Judith

EB 83   LARRY BLAKE'S RATHSKELLER-RESTAURANT,
               1974
         Private funding
         Larry Blake's Rathskeller-Restaurant,
         2367 Telegraph Avenue, Berkeley
         Two walls, 8' x 9' each, and the ceiling,
         Oil base primer, latex and acrylic on plywood
         Stefen

EB 84   STILL LIFE AND BLOSSOMING ALMOND TREES,
               1931
         Sigmund Stern Family
         Stern Hall (foyer), Gayley Road near Hearst Avenue,
         University of California campus, Berkeley
         5' x 8 1/2', Fresco
         Diego Rivera

EB 85   [UNTITLED], 1977
         Chicano Studies Mural Class
         Wurster Hall (5th floor), University of California,
         Berkeley
         10' x 20', Politec acrylic on concrete and wood
         Ray Patlan and Patricia Rodriguez

EB 86   [UNTITLED], 1979
         Lucas Bookstore
         University Press Bookstore, 2430 Bancroft Way,
         Berkeley
         18'-28' x 128', Latex primer, Politec and latex
         paints on stucco
         Lou Silva

EB 87   [UNTITLED], 1978
         Private funding
         YWCA Daycare Center, Allston Street at Oxford,
         Berkeley
         6' x 80', Politec gesso on plaster and brick
         Ariella, Bonita, Buffy, Burl, Carolyn, Deborah Greene,
               Osha Neumann, and Victor

EB 88   INCIDENTS IN CALIFORNIA HISTORY, 1937
         TRAP
         Berkeley Main Post Office,
         Milvia and Allston Streets, Berkeley
         8' x 16', Tempera and oil on canvas
         Suzanne Scheuer

EB 89   [UNTITLED], 1976
         Berkeley Art Services
         Berkeley High School, 2246 Milvia, Berkeley
         Three panels, 7' x 15', Politec acrylic,
         gesso and sealer on concrete
         Waldo Nilo and Irene Perez

EB 90   *YMCA ENTRANCE, 1975
         Berkeley Art Services; CETA
         Berkeley YMCA, 2001 Allston, Berkeley
         Two panels 11' x 11' and 8' x 4',
         Politec primer and acrylic on concrete
         Irene Perez

EB 91   *[UNTITLED], 1975 (destroyed 1990)
         Berkeley High School
         Berkeley Community Theater,
         Allston near Martin Luther King, Jr. Way, Berkeley
         6'-15' x 100', Acrylic on concrete
         Victor Ichioka, Barbara Scales, and students

EB 92   BERKELEY, ITS CITY AND ITS PEOPLE, 1973
         City of Berkeley; NEA; Civic Arts Commission;
         Zellerbach Family Fund
         Berkeley Unified School District Building,
         (2nd floor council room), Berkeley
         11' x 15 1/2', Mixed media on panels
         Romare Bearden

EB 93   [BERKWOOD-HEDGE MURALS], 1980 (partially
               destroyed 1989)
         Private funding
         Berkwood-Hedge School,
         1809 Bancroft Way at McKinley Avenue, Berkeley
         Three panels, 10' x 60' total, but only one remains,
         Acrylic on stucco and cinderblock
         Brigada Orlando Letelier and students

EB 94   MANY ROADS TO HEALTH, 1977
         Berkeley Arts Services; CETA; Herrick Hospital
         Herrick Hospital Emergency Room,
         2001 Dwight Way near Milvia Street, Berkeley
         10' x 12', Politec acrylic, primer, and
         sealer on framed masonite panels
         Osha Neumann and O'Brien Thiele

EB 95   [UNTITLED], 1981
         Herrick Hospital Mural Fund and private donations
         Herrick Hospital Operating Room,
         2001 Dwight Way near Milvia Street, Berkeley
         8' x 20', Acrylic on plaster
         Margo Bors

EB 96   RECYCLING CENTER, 1978
         Private funding
         Recycling Center,
         Dwight and Martin Luther King, Jr. Way, Berkeley
         6' x 25', Politec primer and sealer,
         wax sealer on plywood
         Osha Neumann

EB 97   MALCOLM X SCHOOL, 1976
         Berkeley Arts Services
         Malcolm X School, Ellis and Ashby Streets, Berkeley
         20' x 70', Politec acrylic, gesso, and varnish
         on concrete
         Waldo Nilo and Irene Perez

EB 98   STARRY PLOUGH, 1979
         Private funding; Vista College
         Starry Plough Pub,
         3101 Shattuck and Prince Streets, Berkeley
         13' x 10', Politec primer and acrylic on stucco
         Osha Neumann and the VISTA College Mural
               Workshop

EB 99   SONG OF UNITY, 1978; repainted 1986
         Commonarts, Private funding, BCD, ACAC
         La Pena Cultural Center, 3105 Shattuck Avenue,
               Berkeley
         75' x 40', Politec sealer and acrylic
         on papier-mache and masonite
         Commonarts: Ray Patlan, Osha Neumann, O'Brien
               Thiele,and Anna de Leon

EB 100   *ALCATRAZ LIQUORS, 1977; 1978
         Private funding, Commonarts
         Alcatraz Liquors, Alcatraz and Sacramento Streets,
         Berkeley
         4' x 30', Latex and Politec acrylic on aluminum
         Commonarts: Ray Patlan and O'Brien Thiele

EB 101 *[GROVE STREET MURALS: BLACK, LATINO,
        PUERTO RICAN STRUGGLES], 1969
        Private funding
        Grove Street College, Martin Luther King, Jr. Way
        and 58th Street, Berkeley
        Three panels, approx. 10' x 50' each, Oil on wood
        Wilma Bonnett, Joan X, Shirley Triest, David Bradford,
            Manuel Hernandez, Malaquias Montoya and David
            Salgado

EB 102 *[UNTITLED], 1978
        Alameda County NAP; CETA; Private donations
        Warehouse, 61st-62nd Street and Doyle, Emeryville
        30' x 110', Latex and primer on wood, metal and
            concrete
        Anna Horvath and Foad (Floyd) Satterfield

EB 103 VIVA LA RAZA, 1977
        CETA
        Goodwill, 1512 Adeline Street, Berkeley
        15' x 70', Masonry primer/sealer, latex primer,
        enamel, oil, varnish on brick
        Daniel Galvez, Osha Neumann, O'Brien Thiele, and
            Stephanie Barrett

EB 104 *SOME OF OUR BEST FRIENDS, 1978, 1979
        Private funding
        Berkeley Humane Society Adoption Center,
        8th Street and Carlton, Berkeley
        12' x 30', Politec, MPC base and sealer on stucco
        Ariella Seidenberg and Deborah Greene

EB 105 THE FIFTH STAR, 1987
        Private funding
        Outback, 2517 Sacramento Street at Blake, Berkeley
        20' x 100', Latex ultracolor on brick
        Rick Molina

EB 106 *[UNTITLED], 1979
        CETA; Commonarts
        East Bay Skills Center, San Pablo and 67th Avenue,
            Berkeley
        10' x 15', Politec on interior wallboard and plaster
        Commonarts: Osha Neumann, Ray Patlan, and O'Brien
            Thiele

EB 107 [ABSTRACT], 1990
        Private funding
        Berkeley Potter's Studio, San Pablo and Channing,
            Berkeley
        20' x 60', Enamel on stucco
        Kai

EB 108 [UNTITLED], 1978
        Private funding
        Berkeley Youth Organization, Allston and Bonar,
            Berkeley
        5' x 30', Acrylic on stucco
        Ray Patlan and the Berkeley Youth Organization

EB 109 THE TREE OF LIFE, 1981
        Berkeley Parks Design Department
        Columbus School, Allston Way at 7th Street, Berkeley
        25' x 20', Acrylic on concrete
        Eduardo Pineda and Linda Wolfe

EB 110 BASKET FULL OF FUN, 1987
        Berkeley Arts Fund Special Projects
        Columbus School, Allston Way at 7th Street, Berkeley
        8' x 28', Acrylic on concrete
        Eduardo Pineda and Linda Wolfe

EB 111 *ADELANTE, 1979
        California Arts Council
        Adelante, Inc., Allston Way and 6th Street, Berkeley
        14' x 25', Politec acrylic, sealer,
        and latex primer on stucco
        Ray Patlan

EB 112 *LA FAMILIA, DENTAL ENTRANCE, SANDPAINTING,
            AFRICAN, 1976
        Berkeley Arts Services
        Berkeley Health Clinic, 7th and University, Berkeley
        Four panels: 6' x 12', 4' x 6', 3' x 6', 2' x 15',
        Politec acrylic, gesso and varnish on concrete
        Irene Perez

EB 113 BERKELEY READS, 1988
        Berkeley Reads (Literacy Program)
        West Berkeley Library, 1125 University Avenue,
            Berkeley
        Two panels, 12' x 14' and 13' x 9', Acrylic on stucco
        Ray Patlan, Eduardo Pineda, and Jim Valdez

EB 114 WINDS OF CHANGE, 1977 (partially obscured)
        Co-Op Credit Union
        Andronico's Park and Shop, University Avenue,
            Berkeley
        16' x 135', Politec primer and acrylic on stucco
        Commonarts: Osha Neumann, O'Brien Thiele, Daniel
            Galvez

EB 115 *THE SAN FRANCISCO BAY AS SEEN FROM
            BERKELEY (THE DUTCH BOY MURAL), 1974
            (destroyed 1977)
        Dutch Boy Paints and Stefen
        James' Painting and Decorating Company,
        2000 University Avenue, Berkeley
        25' x 100', Latex acrylic on stucco
        Stefen, with Gary Graham

EB 116 [UNTITLED], 1986
        CCAC Mural Class
        Assemblyman Tom Bates' office, Berkeley-Richmond
        Jewish Community Center, 1414 Walnut, Berkeley,
        8' x 24', Latex on plaster
        Malaquias Montoya and CCAC Mural Class students

EB 117 AN CISCO, 1979
        Brother's Bagel Factory; Private donations
        Toot-Sweets Bakery, 1277 Gilman Street, Berkeley
        13' x 62', Acrylic primer, oil paints
        and varnish on stucco
        John Wehrle

EL CERRITO

EB 118 [AZTEC MOTHER], 1989
        CAC; Richmond Arts Center
        El Cerrito High School, Ashbury and Central, El Cerrito
        10' x 20', Acrylics on fiberboard
        Johanna Poethig and Latino Student Union

EB 119 REFLECTIONS, 1990
        CAC; Richmond Arts Center
        El Cerrito High School, Ashbury and Central, El Cerrito
        10' x 40', Acrylics on fiberboard
        Johanna Poethig and Black Student Union

RICHMOND

EB 120   PAST PERFECT, 1990
Richmond Arts Center
I-80 underpass at MacDonald Street, Richmond
16 1/2' x 150', Unknown paints on concrete
John Wehrle

EB 121   FAMILIAS UNIDAS, 1987
Funding unknown
Clinic, 205 39th Street, Richmond
Dimensions unknown, Roy Anderson paints and
Politec on stucco
Eduardo Pineda, Laurali Patneaud, Dina Moreno,
    Andrea Davis, Dedtra Williams, Marcell Arcea,
    Michelle Nath, Bakeeba Waters, and Eric
    Whittington

EB 122   RICHMOND LIBERTY FERRY, 1989
City of Richmond
BART underpass, Barrett and Marina Way, Richmond
4'-20' x 200', Bott's Dots Highway Markers on
    concrete
Rigo, assisted by Dina Diniz

EB 123   MURAL CITY (unfinished), 1986
Contra Costa College Mural Class
Storefront, 141 Harbor Way near Chancellor,
    Richmond
15' x 35', Acrylic on concrete
Eduardo Pineda and CCC students

EB 124   GETAWAY, 1986
Contra Costa College Mural Class
St. Mark's Church, 131 Harbor Way near Chancellor,
    Richmond
12' x 35', Acrylic on stucco
Eduardo Pineda and CCC students

EB 125   STAND TOGETHER, 1986
Private funding
St. Mark's Church, 131 Harbor Way near Chancellor,
    Richmond
40' x 12', Politec acrylic on concrete
Eduardo Pineda and St. Mark's Leadership students

The following additional murals, grouped by community, are provided in this expanded edition:

HAYWARD

EB 126   CENTENNIAL HALL, 1979
NEA, Mervyn's
Centennial Hall, Hayward Civic Center, 22292 Foothill
    Rd.
3 panels, each 8' x 14', pencil and acrylic on stretched
    canvas
William T. Wiley

EB 127   RANCHO SAN LORENZO, 1800, NEAR HAYWARD,
    1987
private
Mission and D Streets
8' x 30', acrylic and varnish sealer on stucco
Ricardo

SAN LEANDRO

EB 128   WOMEN IN ART MAKE A DIFFERENCE, 1994
private
Harlan St. off San Leandro Blvd.
15' x 120', acrylic on stucco
Alice Campbell and 65 women

OAKLAND

EB 129   HARLEM RENAISSANCE, c.1986
Castlemont High School
Castlemont High School, 8601 Macarthur Blvd.
15' x 45', acrylic on stucco
Sharon Davis, Frederick Gums, Anthony Wright,
    Wanda Scott Alex—Supervising Teacher

EB 130   [RAINFOREST], 1992
Castlemont High School
Castlemont High School, 8601 Macarthur Blvd.
18' x 120', acrylic on stucco
Violet Chew MacLean (teacher) and students

EB 131   [UNTITLED], 1994
Calif. Department of Conservation, Division of
    Recycling,
Oakland Society for Prevention of Cruelty to Animals
8323 Baldwin at Hegenberger Road
13 medallions, 24' diameter each, acrylic on plywood
Caryl Henry, Colette Crutcher, Debra Disma, Nestor
    Gonzalez, and members of Project YES (Youth
    Engaged in Service) from Carter, Claremont, Frick,
    Roosevelt and Westlake middle and junior high
    schools

EB 132   ABE SOUZA, 1991
Oakland Coliseum and Oakland Athletics
Oakland Coliseum, interior behind home plate (one in
    a series)
10' x 10', enamel on concrete
Daniel Galvez, Jos Sances

EB 133   CHARLIE SANTANA, 1992
Oakland Coliseum and Oakland Athletics
Oakland Coliseum, interior behind home plate (one in
    a series)
10' x 10', enamel on concrete
Daniel Galvez, Jos Sances

EB 134   SYLVESTER JACKSON, 1993
Oakland Coliseum and Oakland Athletics
Oakland Coliseum, interior behind home plate (one in
    a series)
10' x 10', enamel on concrete
Daniel Galvez, Jos Sances

EB 135   AS LONG AS THE MIND IS ENSLAVED, THE BODY
    WILL NEVER BE FREE, 1993
East Bay Regional Park District's Martin Luther King,
    Jr.
Grant Program and Calif. Dept. of Conservation, Project YES
Lockwood School, 6701 East 14th St. at 67th Ave.
10' x 33', acrylic on stucco
Caryl Henry

EB 136 NEL, 1993
Public Art Program, Cultural Arts Division, City of
Oakland; Narcotics Education League
Fruitvale Plaza, 35th Ave and E. 14th Street
25′ x 62′, Novacolor on brick
Fresco (Ray Patlan and Eduardo Pineda)

EB 137 [UNTITLED], 1993
private
1470 Fruitvale Ave. near E. 14th Street
20′ x 60′, acrylic on stucco
Jose Meza-Velasquez, Xochitl Nevel-Guerrero

EB 138 HOMAGE TO AMERICA, 1991
Calif. Dept. of Conservation, Division of Recycling,
Project Y.E.S.
34th Ave. at Farnam
10′ x 60′, acrylic on stucco
Jose Meza-Velasquez, numerous foreign artists, and
youth from Carter, Claremont, Frick, Roosevelt and
Westlake middle and junior high schools.

EB 139 I HAVE A DREAM, 1993
East Bay Regional Park District's Rev. Martin Luther
King, Jr. Grant Program, and the Calif. Dept. of
Conservation, Division of Recycling, Project Y.E.S.
Warehouse at 2834 Ford Street at 29th Avenue
8′ x 50′, Novacolor on stucco
Emmanuel Montoya and students

EB 140 UNTITLED, 1993
Local 28, Hotel and Restaurant Employees Union
548 20th Street near Telegraph
15′ x 45′, acrylic on mosaic
Jose Meza-Velasquez, Jose Hernandez Delgadillo

EB 141 DON'T LET OUR PEOPLE GO UP IN SMOKE, 1993
Calif. Dept. of Health Services, Prop.99, The Tobacco
Tax Initiative, Asian Health Services, East Bay
Asian Youth Center
Roosevelt Junior High School, 19th Ave. at E. 20th St.
12′ x 15′, acrylic on stucco
Healthy Neighborhood '93 (27 students)

EB 142 NO JUSTICE, NO PEACE, 1993
private
Roosevelt Junior High School, 20th Ave. and E. 19th
Street
9′ x 65′, spray enamel on stucco
anonymous

EB 143 JURASTIC PARK, 1992
private
E. 14th St. at 15th Ave.
12′ x 75′, spray enamel on concrete cinderblock
Phresh with Krash

EB 144 ARE WE QUESTIONING OUR FREEDOM? 1990
private
E. 14th St. at 15th Ave.
12′ x 18′, spray enamel on concrete cinderblock
Phresh

EB 145 MYSTICAL, 1992
private
E. 14th St. at 15th Ave.
12′ x 18′, spray enamel on concrete cinderblock
Phresh

EB 146 MARILYN, 1990
private
15th Ave. at E. 14th St.
12′ x 40′, spray enamel on concrete cinderblock
Phresh

EB 147 MARBEI THE DO NOTHING COMIC, 1993
private
15th Ave. at E. 14th St.
15′ x 14′, spray enamel on concrete cinderblock
Phresh

EB 148 HOLLYWOOD MOVIE MONSTERS, 1992
private
15th Ave. at E. 14th St.
15′ x 40′, spray enamel on concrete cinderblock
Krash, Phresh, Poem

EB 149 INDIGENOUS ANIMALS OF CALIFORNIA, 1992
Project YES, EBCC
Bella Vista School, 11th St. between E. 24th and E.
28th St.
16′-4′ x 193′, Liquitex on concrete
Brett Cook-Dizney, assisted by Emmanuel Montoya
and students

EB 150 EXPLORATION—SETTLING IN CALIFORNIA, 1937
FAP
Alameda County Courthouse lobby, 1225 Fallon
2 panels, each 15′ x 7′, marble tile
Marion Simpson

EB 151 HOW CHINESE HELPED BUILD CALIFORNIA
WATERWAYS, 1992
EBMUD
EBMUD Headquarters, 11th St. at Franklin (interior)
5′ x 32′, acrylic on wallboard
Nancy Hom with Selma Brown

EB 161 [STAINED GLASS MOTIF], 1994
Department of Public Works, Oakland
13th and Clay Sts.
8′ x 500′, acrylic on plywood
Dan Fontes

EB 152 PASSAGES, 1992
Public Art Program, Cultural Arts Division, City of
Oakland
Oakland Convention Center, Broadway at 10th St.
8′ x 16′, mixed media on wood
Marie Johnson Calloway, April Watkins, Heather
Watkins

EB 153 OAKLAND CITY LIFE, 1992
MOCHA, St. Elizabeth Youth Employment
Broadway at 14th Street (construction fence)
8′ x 81′, acrylic on plywood
Edythe Boone, Susan Greene, and Summer Youth
Program members

EB 154 CHOICES, 1992
Project YES, EBCC
Broadway at 14th Street (construction fence)
8′ x 66′, acrylic on plywood
Brett Cook-Dizney and youths

EB 155 THE DOWNTOWN OAKLAND BLACK HISTORY
MURAL PROJECT, 1992
Calif. Dept. of Conservation, Division of Recycling, and
City of Oakland, Office of Economic Development &
Employment, Project YES (Youth Engaged in Ser-
vice) of the East Bay Conservation Corps
Broadway, Telegraph and San Pablo at 15th Street
4 large entrances, each approx. 12′ x 10′, acrylic on
plywood
Ivan Watkins with Project YES Clubmembers from
Carter, Claremont, Frick, Roosevelt and Westlake
middle and junior high schools

EB 156 TWIST OF FATE, 1993
Public Art Program, Cultural Arts Division, City of
Oakland
City Hall Plaza (construction fence)
8′ x 180′, acrylic on plywood
Daniel Galvez

EB 157 PARAMOUNT THEATER, 1929 (restored, 1972)
Miller and Pflueger
Paramount Theater, 2025 Broadway
2 panels, each 50′ x 15′, mosaic
Gerald Fitzgerald

EB 158 I HAVE A DREAM, 1993
East Bay Regional Park District's Rev. Martin Luther
King, Jr. Grant Program and Calif. Dept. of
Conservation, Project Y.E.S.
Martin Luther King, Jr. School, 960 10th St. near
Market St.
12′ x 48′, acrylic on stucco
Sana Makhoul

EB 159 [UNTITLED], 1987
Thomas A. Short Company
billboard nr. Wood and 34th St., visible from
eastbound I-580 billboard
Mr. Frazier

EB 160 POOL, 1993
Public Arts Program, Cultural Arts Division, city of
Oakland
de Fremery Park Swimming Pool, Poplar and 18th St.
2 panels, each approx. 20′ x 4½′, monochrome tile
Mike Mandel and Larry Sultan

EB 164 through EB 168 reserved for future use.

EB 169 KNOWLEDGE IS POWER, 1993
CAC, MOCHA
Ralph Bunche School, 18th St. and Poplar
16′ x 36′, Novacolor acrylic on plywood
Susan Greene and school students

EB 170 THE NINETIES MURAL, 1990
private
West St. and San Pablo Avenue
15′ x 45′, airbrush exterior housepaint with verathane
coating on brick
Darien Hamilton

EB 171 FREEDOM IS NEVER VOLUNTARILY GIVEN BY THE
OPPRESSOR; IT MUST BE DEMANDED BY THE
OPPRESSED, 1993
East Bay Regional Park District's Rev. Martin Luther
King, Jr. Grant Program and Calif. Dept. of
Conservation, Project Y.E.S.
Marcus Book Store, 3900 Martin Luther King, Jr. Way
at 39th St.
10′ x 12′, acrylic on plywood
Jimi Evins

EB 172 NO SMOKE SCREENS/NO COLOR LINES, 1993
Lowell Street Mural Project, Summer Youth Training
Program, City of Oakland Office of Housing and
Neighborhood Development, East Bay Community
Foundation, LEF Foundation
Golden Gate Recreation Center, 1075 62nd St. at
Herzog
15′ x 45′, Novacolor on concrete
Rigo '93 and 9 youths

EB 173 OUT OF MANY ONE, 1991
private
4927 Shattuck Ave., at 51st Street
15′ x 45′, acrylic on stucco
J. J. Jackson

EB 174 HOPE IS ALIVE, 1994
private, The Center
Shattuck Ave. at 59th Street
18′ x 47′, acrylic on stucco
O'Brien Thiele, Sharon Siskin, and people living with
HIV and their friends, including Kerrie L. Campbell,
John Nielson, Marlon Kera, Ron Coleman, Ed
Seidel, Richard "RC" Comstock, Lowell Brook, and
others

EB 175 SURREAL BEACH AND DECO FOUNTAIN AND
MOON, 1989
private
apartment house at 5915 Telegraph Ave., near 59th St.
20′ x 12′, 2 panels 20′ x 10′, acrylic on stucco
Ray Regan

EB 176 JUNGLE MURAL, 1989
private
Campanile Veterinary Clinic, 5666 Telegraph Ave at
59th St.
20′ x 18′, acrylic on stucco
Ray Regan

EB 177 PROJECT YES, 1990–1992
Project Y.E.S. (Youth Engaged in Service) and EBCC
Telegraph Ave under Highway 24 overcrossing, nr.
Aileen
10′ x 60′, acrylic on concrete
anonymous

EB 178 HISTORY OF COFFEE, 1993
private
6021 College Ave at Claremont Ave (interior)
10′ x 30′, acrylic on sheetrock
Josh Sarantitis with Roberto Guerrero

EB 179 FREE WINDS BLOW. . . , 1966
funding unknown
Lake Temescal Park underpass, south end off
Broadway Terrace
5′ x 60′, 2 panels, paint unknown on concrete
(sprayed?)
Anthony, OP and Timothy, OP

EB 180 ONE BLIND MOUSE, 1992
CCAC
CCAC, Broadway at College
25′ x 16′, acrylic on plywood
Juana Alicia and CCAC students

EB 181 CALIFORNIA HISTORY, 1927
Graduating classes
Oakland Technical High School
30′ x 68′, above proscenium in theater (believed de-
stroyed, but may be in storage)
Maynard Dixon

EB 182 PAY EQUITY, 1991
SEIU
SEIU local 790, 522 Grand Ave. at Perkins (interior)
8′ x 16′, Novacolor on masonite
Fresco (Ray Patlan and Eduardo Pineda)

EB 162 GIRAFFICS PARK, 1994
CalTrans
Harrison St. at I-580
32′ - 35′ high pillars, Danacolor on steel
Dan Fontes

EB 183 TO IGNORE EVIL IS TO BECOME AN ACCOMPLICE
        TO IT, 1993
Project Y.E.S., EBCC, Calif. Dept. of Conservation,
        EBRPD, MLK Jr. Grant
Lake Park Ave and Lake Shore Ave (under I-580
        overpass)
13′ x 30′, Novacolor on concrete
Susan Greene, Meera Desai

EB 184 INVISIBLE COLORS, 1992
Public Art Program, Cultural Arts Division, City of
        Oakland
Park Blvd. and Highway I-580 underpass
8′ x 150′, outdoor white paint with glass "highway
        beads"
Seyed Alavi and 16 high school students

EB 185 INFORM(N)ATION, 1992
Public Art Program, Cultural Arts Division, City of
        Oakland
Fruitvale Ave. and Highway I-580 underpass
8′ x 160′, outdoor white paint with glass "highway
        beads"
Seyed Alavi and 16 high school students

EB 186 eRACISM, 1992
Public Art Program, Cultural Arts Division, City of
        Oakland
High St. and Highway I-580 underpass
8′ x 80′, outdoor white paint with glass "highway
        beads"
Seyed Alavi and 16 high school students

EB 187 D FFERENCE, 1992
Public Art Program, Cultural Arts Division, City of
        Oakland
Buell St. and Highway I-580 underpass
15′ x 140′, outdoor white paint with glass "highway
        beads"
Seyed Alavi and 16 high school students

PIEDMONT

EB 188 POPPIES, 1934
FAP
Piedmont High School, 800 Magnolia St. (interior)
6′8″ x 14′2″, fresco
Claire von Falkenstein

EB 189 SCHOOL LIFE, 1937/1973 (copy)
Piedmont High School
Piedmont High School, 800 Magnolia St. (interior)
6′ x 6′, fresco
Hideo Noda

EB 190 EDUCATION: ANCIENT AND MODERN, 1937
FAP
Piedmont High School, 800 Magnolia St. (interior)
2 panels, 12′ x 8′ each, mosaic
Edgar Taylor

EB 191 JUNIPERO SERRA, 1937
PWAP
Piedmont High School, 800 Magnolia St. (interior)
12′ x 8′, tempera
Joseph Sheridan

EB 163 THE MONTCLAIR DUCK POND MURAL, 1994
Department of Public Works, Oakland
Montclair Recreation Center
Moraga Ave. at Hy. 13
10′ x 27′, acrylic on cinderblock
Dan Fontes

BERKELEY

EB 192 [PEOPLE'S PARK BATHROOM MURALS], 1989–1994
private
Bathroom at People's Park, Haste Street east of
        Telegraph
8′ x 80′, acrylic and spray enamel on cinder block
anonymous

EB 193 [UNTITLED], 1936–37
WPA
U.C. campus office supplies bldg. (formerly Old
        Powerhouse), a brick building just east of Sather
        Gate, along Strawberry Creek.
2 panels 18′ x 10′, mosaic tile
Helen Bruton

EB 194 BEAR MURAL, 1993
University of California
south wall, Edwards Stadium, Bancroft and Oxford
        Streets
7′ x 14′, acrylic on concrete
Dale Bogaski

EB 195 WALL FOR PEACE, 1989
Alameda County (John George), Women for Peace,
        Clinton A. White, City of Berkeley, private
Rev. Martin Luther King Jr. Park, MLK Jr Way at
        Allston
10 panels 21″ x 111″, 10 panels 33″ x 111″, 2 panels
        39″ x 111″, fired ceramic tiles
Carolyn Marks and "5000 people who painted tiles—
        including Archbishop Desmond Tutu, the Reverend
        Jesse Jackson, Congressman Ronald V. Dellums."

EB 196 LEARNING TO FLY, 1993
private
Berkwood Hedge School, Bancroft Way at McKinley
        Ave.
12′ x 16′, Novacolor acrylic on painted concrete brick
Jane Norling, Tim Drescher

EB 197 GARDEN OF HOPE, 1990
Berkeley Unified School District, Zellerbach Foundation
Berkeley Adult High School, University Ave. at Curtis
8′ x 44′, Novacolor acrylic on plywood
Susan Greene and members of the Creative Living
        Center

EB 198 BY THE BAY, 1992
East Bay Conservation Corps, California Department of
Conservation: Division of Recycling, Bank of America,
        Stuttgart Foundation
Ecology Center, 2530 San Pablo Avenue at Parker
15′ x 50′, Novacolor on concrete
Jo Tucker with Dan Macchiarini, Terry Rayburn,
        Stephanie Fiske

EB 199 PINBALL FLOOR MURAL, 1992
For Private Amusement Only
1010 Grayson St. off 7th St.
17′ x 17′, enamel on hardwood floor
Dan Fontes

EB 200   [UNTITLED], 1994 (replaces 117)
         private
         Toot Sweets Bakery, 1277 Gilman
         13′ x 62′, Keim silicate on stucco
         John Wehrle

RICHMOND

EB 201   REVISIONIST HISTORY OF SAN PABLO AVENUE,
            1993/94
         Richmond Art Commission
         San Pablo Avenue at I-80 overpass
         21′ x 220′, silicate on concrete
         John Wehrle

EB 202   CITY OF RICHMOND, 1949
         City of Richmond
         Richmond City Hall, Supervisors' Chamber, City Hall
            Plaza, Nevin and 27th St.
         7′ x 12′, enamel on shaped metal relief panel
         Sargent Johnson

EB 203   RICHMOND TEEN MURAL PROJECT, 1993
         Chevron Harbour Way and Macdonald Ave
         8 panels, 8′ x 8′ each, Novacolor on plywood
         Fresco (Ray Patlan and Eduardo Pineda), Herschel
            West, Elizabeth Medrano and students

EB 204   SAY NO TO DOPE, 1990
         Neighborhood House of North Richmond
         305 Chelsey at 3rd St.
         10′ x 60′, Novacolor on cinderblock
         Fresco (Ray Patlan and Eduardo Pineda)

NOTE: Three recently added murals are listed in the correct geographic areas, but their numbers are not in chronological order. These murals are: EB 161 (listed after EB 151), EB 162 (listed after EB 182), and EB 163 (listed after EB 191).

Some Additions and Corrections to the Mural Lists

In a mural listing of this complexity, it is inevitable that mistakes have occurred. The following are some additions and corrections to the San Francisco Murals and East Bay Lists.

The Underwater Scene (91) was restored by Lou Silva, Joanne Wittenbrook and Juan Carlos in 1990.

Forest Scene (92) was painted by Lou Silva and the following artists: Joanne Wittenbrook, Mark Clark, Juan Carlos and Ed Monroe.

The City's Music (211) had eight shaped panels: 4 approx. 4′ x 4′, and 4 approx. 4′ x 16′. Funding was provided by Laguna Honda Hospital Volunteers, Inc.

Jail/Street Scene (241) should include one wall 6′ x 10′ which was painted in the weight room.

The Mission Reds at Woodward's Gardens (263) was painted out in February 1987, some seven years after the Holly Courts murals were destroyed.

The correct title for the Intergenerational Mural in Balmy Alley (352) is *The Five Sacred Colors of Corn*. It was funded by Grants for the Arts.

The correct title of the Holly Courts mural (413) was *Unified Diversity*. It was painted with Politec acrylics on concrete, and the photograph was taken by Claire Josephson. For murals 413 and 414 the correct information is one wall 22′ x 24′, 2 walls 8′ x 24′, one garbage structure, and 2 walls 6′ x 8′. The murals were painted out only five months after their creation!

The correct title for the untitled mural (442) is *El Encantimiento del Tiempo*.

One mural, finally, marked as destroyed, still exists. The information about this Oakland mural (EB 24) should read:

EB 24   *Youth Arrested,* 1986
         CCAC
         1612 45th Avenue near Bancroft
         25′ x 60′, acrylic on concrete
         Malaquias Montoya and CCAC students.

Index of Artists, Groups and Murals

Index and Abbreviations Used

ABBREVIATIONS

CAC	California Arts Council	NIIP	Neighborhood Initiative Improvement Program	SFAC	San Francisco Arts Commission
CETA	Comprehensive Employment and Training Act	NYC	Neighborhood Youth Corps	SFHA	San Francisco Housing Authority
FSSA	Friends of Support Services for the Arts	OCD	Office of Community Development (sometimes M [for Mayor's] OCD)	SFMMA	San Francisco Museum of Modern Art
MRC	Mural Resource Center	OHA	Oakland Housing Authority	WPA	Works Progress Adminstration's Federal Art Program.
NAP	Neighborhood Art Program	PWAP	Public Works of Art Project		
NEA	National Endowment for the Arts	RAP	Real Alternatives Project		
NEH	National Endowment for the Humanities	SERA	State Emergency Relief Administration		

Selected Bibliography

Cave Paintings:

Leroi-Gourhan, Andre. *The Dawn of European Art: An Introduction to Paleolithic Cave Painting.* Cambridge and other cities: Cambridge University Press, 1982. An excellent introduction to cave painting.

Raphael, Max. *Prehistoric Cave Paintings.* Washington, D.C. The Bollingen Series IV: Pantheon Books, 1945. Extremely difficult to find, but a brilliant essay.

Sieveking, Ann. *The Cave Artists.* London: Thames and Hudson, 1979. An excellent introduction to Paleolithic cave art.

Mexican Murals:

Hurlburt, Laurance P. *The Mexican Muralists in the United States.* Albuquerque: The University of New Mexico Press, 1989. An excellent book covering all the work done by Los Tres Grandes in the U.S.

Orozco, Jose Clemente. *Jose Clemente Orozco, An Autobiography.* Austin, University of Texas Press, 1962. A basic work on Orozco, but one wishes for a modern edition with better color.

Rochfort, Desmond. *Mexican Muralists: Orozco, Rivera, Siqueiros.* New York: Universe, 1993. Rochfort, a muralist himself, has put together the best introductory text on these important artists. His analysis of individual murals is especially good.

Siqueiros, David A. *Art & Revolution.* London: Lawrence and Wishart, 1975. A selection of writings from the most theoretical and political of the Tres Grandes.

Wolfe, Bertram D. *The Fabulous Life of Diego Rivera.* New York: Stein and Day, 1963. The standard biography of a fascinating life.

——. *Diego Rivera: A Retrospective.* New York and London: Founders Society of Detroit Institute of Art in association with W. W. Norton & Company, 1986. A fundamental work, with fourteen essays, an index of Rivera's works, bibliography, and excellent color plates. An exhibition catalogue.

New Deal Murals:

Jewett, Masha Zakheim. *Coit Tower: Its History and Art.* San Francisco: Volcano Press, 1983. A gem of a book with full discussion of the famous Coit Tower murals and excellent, complete color photographs.

McKinzie, Richard D. *The New Deal for Artists.* Princeton: Princeton University Press, 1973. An excellent survey of the whole spectrum of New Deal art programs.

Marling, Karal Ann. *Wall-to-Wall America: A Cultural History of Post-Office Murals in the Great Depression.* Minneapolis: University of Minnesota Press, 1982. Well illustrated and filled with anecdotes and information about New Deal post office murals.

O'Connor, Francis V. *Art for the Millions.* Boston: New York Graphic Society, 1973. Essays about the WPA written by artists and administrators of the program.

Park, Marlene, and Markowitz, Gerald D. *Democratic Vistas: Post Office and Public Art in the New Deal.* Philadelphia: Temple University Press, 1984. Another excellent survey of New Deal murals, also well illustrated.

Contemporary Community Murals:

Barnett, Alan W. *Community Murals: The People's Art.* Philadelphia: The Art Alliance Press, and New York and London: Cornwall Press, 1984. A large book, with much information and many photographs.

Cockcroft, Eva, John Weber and James Cockcroft. *Toward A People's Art. The Contemporary Mural Movement.* New York: E. P. Dutton & Co., Inc., 1977. An excellent book on the contemporary mural movement in the U.S. Written by muralists.

Cockcroft, Eva Sperling and Holly Barnett-Sanchez, Editors. *Signs From the Heart: California Chicano Murals.* Venice, California: Social and Public Art Resource Center, 1990. Two of five essays relate directly to San Francisco Chicano murals.

Dunitz, Robin. *Street Gallery: Guide to L.A.'s Murals.* Los Angeles: RJD Enterprises, 1993. This book offers accurate information, detailed maps and brief descriptions of a thousand Los Angeles murals, along with thorough indexes and small but useful photographs.

Rogovin, Mark, Marie Burton and Holly Highfill. *Mural Manual: How to Paint Murals for the Classroom, Community Center and Street Corner.* Boston: Beacon Press, 1975. The only how-to book about painting Community murals, with complete information and numerous illustrations. Out of print.

——. *Community Murals Magazine,* 1978–1987. Back sets/copies are available in some libraries. Contains articles and photographs of murals throughout the world.

Rolston, Bill. *Politics and Painting: Murals and Conflicts in Northern Ireland.* London and Toronto: Associated University Presses, 1991. This is an excellent (albeit somewhat scholarly) discussion of the often confusing politics of Northern Ireland and murals' role as a part of that conflict. Rolston's more accessible volume, *Drawing Support: Murals in the North of Ireland,* was published by Beyond the Pale Publications in 1992.

Spray Can Art:

A number of books and magazines have dealt with spray can art, both worldwide and in California. The most important are:

Castleman, Craig. *Getting Up: Subway Graffiti in New York.* Cambridge: M.I.T. Press, 1982.

Chalfant, Henry, and James Prigoff. *Spraycan Art.* London: Thames and Hudson, 1987. A superb photographic survey of the most sophisticated spray can work from the United States and Europe.

Cooper, Martha, and Henry Chalfant. *Subway Art.* New York: Holt, Rinehart and Winston, 1984. The standard work on New York's subway graffiti, with an astonishing collection of beautifully photographed trains in full color.